Counselling Suicidal Clients

Counselling in Practice

Series editor: Windy Dryden
Associate editor: E. Thomas Dowd

Counselling in Practice is a series of books developed especially for counsellors and students of counselling, which provides practical, accessible guidelines for dealing with clients with specific, but very common, problems. Books in this series have become recognized as classic texts in their field, and include:

Counselling for Grief and Bereavement, Second Edition
Geraldine M. Humphrey and David G. Zimpfer

Counselling and Psychotherapy for Depression, Third Edition
Paul Gilbert

Counselling for Post-Traumatic Stress Disorder, Third Edition
Michael J. Scott and Stephen G. Stradling

Counselling Survivors of Childhood Sexual Abuse, Third Edition
Claire Burke Draucker and Donna Martsolf

Career Counselling, Second Edition
Robert Nathan and Linda Hill

Counselling for Eating Disorders, Second Edition
Sara Gilbert

Counselling for Anxiety Problems, Second Edition
Diana Sanders and Frank Wills

Counselling for Alcohol Problems, Second Edition
Richard Velleman

Counselling for Stress Problems
Stephen Palmer and Windy Dryden

Counselling Suicidal Clients

Andrew Reeves

Los Angeles | London | New Delhi
Singapore | Washington DC

© Andrew Reeves 2010

First published 2010

Apart from any fair dealing for the purposes of research or private study, or criticism or review, as permitted under the Copyright, Designs and Patents Act, 1988, this publication may be reproduced, stored or transmitted in any form, or by any means, only with the prior permission in writing of the publishers, or in the case of reprographic reproduction, in accordance with the terms of licences issued by the Copyright Licensing Agency. Enquiries concerning reproduction outside those terms should be sent to the publishers.

SAGE Publications Ltd
1 Oliver's Yard
55 City Road
London EC1Y 1SP

SAGE Publications Inc.
2455 Teller Road
Thousand Oaks, California 91320

SAGE Publications India Pvt Ltd
B 1/I 1 Mohan Cooperative Industrial Area
Mathura Road, New Delhi 110 044

SAGE Publications Asia-Pacific Pte Ltd
3 Church Street
#10-04 Samsung Hub
Singapore 049483

Library of Congress Control Number: 2009928292

British Library Cataloguing in Publication data

A catalogue record for this book is available from the British Library

ISBN 978-1-4129-4635-3
ISBN 978-1-4129-4636-0 (pbk)

Typeset by C&M Digitals (P) Ltd, Chennai, India
Printed and bound by CPI Group (UK) Ltd, Croydon, CR0 4YY
Printed on paper from sustainable resources

Contents

List of Figures and Tables	vii
Praise for the Book	viii
Preface	ix
Acknowledgements	xiii

Part I Contextual Aspects of Working with Suicide Risk — 1

1. Suicide and Counselling: An Introduction — 3
2. Historical Perspectives on Suicide and the Emergence of the Medical Model — 15
3. Suicide Trends and Statistics — 21

Part II The Prediction-Prevention Model, Policy and Ethics — 29

4. Suicide Risk Factors and Assessment — 31
5. The Influence of Policy and the Prediction–Prevention Culture — 44
6. The Ethical Imperative of Suicide — 53
7. Confidentiality, Capacity and Consent — 60

Part III Organizations — 73

8. Counselling Suicidal Clients in Organizational Settings — 75
9. Developing Procedures and Guidance — 83

Part IV The Client Process — 89

10. Understanding Suicide — 91
11. The Use of Language in Counselling Suicidal Clients — 99
12. From Self-Murder to Self-Support — 108
13. Suicide and Self-Injury: Annihilation and Survival — 115

vi   Counselling Suicidal Clients

Part V   The Counsellor Process   **125**

14   The Counsellor and Suicide Risk: Personal Perspectives
     and Professional Actions   127

15   Potential Dangers and Difficulties   134

Part VI   Key Aspects of Counselling with Suicidal Clients   **141**

16   Tightropes and Safety Nets: Supporting Practice   143

17   Good Practice for Self-Support   150

18   Training Implications for Counselling   156

Part VII   Conclusions   **163**

19   Concluding Thoughts   165

References   170
Index   179

List of figures and tables

Figures

3.1	Suicide rates by age and gender, UK, 1991–2006	23
3.2	Rates of suicides and open verdicts for men in England and Wales, 1968–2007	25
3.3	Numbers of suicides and open verdicts for women in England and Wales, 1968–2007	25
3.4	Evolution of global suicide rates, 1950–2000	26
3.5	Distribution of global suicide rates by gender and age, 2000	26
3.6	Changes in the age distribution of global cases of suicide, 1950–2000	27
7.1	Release of information form	68

Tables

3.1	Age-standardized suicide rates for men by age group, UK, 1991–2006	24
3.2	Age-standardized suicide rates for women by age group, UK, 1991–2006	24
4.1	Factors associated with higher suicide risk	33
4.2	Suicide risk factors with illustrative research	34
4.3	Outline structure for assessment at the beginning of counselling	40
9.1	Sample guidance document for working with suicidal clients in organizational settings	86
10.1	Suicide as a means of ending existential crisis: an example from a transcript	94
10.2	Suicide as a means of removing a sense of being 'stuck' with the negotiations and manoeuvrings of life: an example from a transcript	95
10.3	Suicide as a means of ending apathy and fatigue generated by the burdensome nature of life: an example from a transcript	97
11.1	Ways in which clients talk about suicide	102
11.2	Predominant counsellor responses to client expressions of suicide	104
11.3	Counsellor deflection and retreat: an example from a transcript	105
11.4	An exploration of suicide potential: an example from a transcript	106
15.1	The difficulty of naming suicide: an example from a transcript	139
16.1	Breaking Josh's confidentiality	147
16.2	Maintaining confidentiality with Josh	148
18.1	Counsellor competencies for working with suicide risk	159

Praise for the Book

'Counselling suicidal clients is one of the most difficult tasks that we face, and Andrew Reeves approaches this subject with openness and integrity, writing about this difficult topic with warmth and empathy for the experiences of both counsellors and clients. There are no absolute, universally applicable answers to the complex issues that surround suicidality. This aspect of therapeutic work requires ethical awareness, a sound knowledge base and calm objectivity in assessing situations and at the same time, giving the very best we can each provide in therapeutic counselling skills. This book reflects these therapeutic requirements, as the author brings together his experience as a social worker, counsellor and academic, to create a very valuable resource for reflective practice.'
Barbara Mitchels, Solicitor and Director of Watershed Counselling Service, Devon.

'A uniquely accessible, comprehensive and practical guide. Essential reading for counsellors and psychotherapists and all helping professionals who work with clients at risk of suicide.'
Mick Cooper, Professor of Counselling, University of Strathclyde

'A "must read" for counsellors of all experience levels, offering sound practical strategies alongside thought-provoking case studies and discussion points. Reeves addresses this difficult topic with depth, breadth and integrity, questioning the over-simplifications of the "prediction-prevention" culture and challenging counsellors to develop context aware practices as well as personal position awareness. Excellent.'
Denise Meyer, C.Psychol & MBACP (Snr Accred), developer and lead author of award-winning website www.studentdepression.org

Preface

In my early career I would not have considered spending nearly 20 years of my life thinking, learning, talking and writing about suicide. For the most part I had not been touched by suicide, and it had remained almost entirely an intellectual consideration for debate and discussion, like politics or the economy. There had been quiet talk in my family of my cousin, living abroad, who had tried to 'top herself' – generally hushed and secretive discussions that I was excluded from as a child. Her 'activities' were not appropriate for my ears and as such suicide remained a distant knowledge, untouched by any sense of personal reality. My first real experience of death had been through early employment as a care assistant in a home for older people with severe and enduring mental health problems. This was the first time I had seen a dead person, and had come into personal contact with the process of living and dying. During the two years of this work I became familiar with the process of dying and cared for many dying and dead people. However, death had been as a consequence of age or disease, and as such had represented something of the natural progression of life.

Suicide began to impinge more closely on my life during my training and early work as a social worker. During training we had discussed the philosophical and legal implications of suicide, and had meandered through several enlightening and well-meaning debates about what were the 'rights' and 'wrongs' of the choice to take life. A social work placement in a hospice and oncology ward began to illustrate in a far more significant way the human realities and existential crises that contribute to an individual considering ending their own life. Many patients, diagnosed with terminal cancer, were torn between following the natural process of their disease, and reclaiming control over their dying.

The next transition, from the confinement of suicide to the safety of a textbook and classroom debate into my own experience, occurred in my contact with a 32-year-old man I was assigned to work with in my early social work career. Following a devastating diagnosis of a progressive condition, he quickly lost independence and autonomy over his life. We talked extensively about his wish to be dead, and his longing to act quickly while he could still complete suicide by his own hands.

With his permission I had talked to his counsellor with whom he also shared his suicidal desires. She was concerned for his safety, but felt that maintaining his confidentiality and not triggering an evaluation of his mental health state was the last dignity she could offer him. Due to a change in my working location I had to finish seeing him as his social worker. Four months later I heard of his death through an overdose. I battled with an internal debate about the nature of the dignity his counsellor's confidentiality had provided him – his right to choose set against an institution's capacity to prevent him from acting in such a way. I know that his choice and subsequent actions were informed and ultimately inevitable.

However, the ethical questions were not easy to resolve, and many years on, this remains the case.

Suicide had grown much closer to my experience in the same way that our own mortality creeps into all of our awareness as time passes. Then, during my training as a counsellor I wrote the following, an extract taken from a case study:

> 'I'm sorry to have to tell you that Isobel was found dead last night – she had taken an overdose.' This phone call abruptly and violently brought to an end six months of counselling which had touched on many painful and distressing life events, and had also shone light on Isobel's humanity and sensitivity which she so rarely felt able to recognize. Her fragile and painful grasp on life finally ended, leaving behind all that had brought her misery and despair. She left me with a cocktail of emotions and traumas – my own grief and anger at her actions, my own personal losses and bereavements and my overwhelming feeling of incompetence and failure as a counsellor.
>
> Our last session together had obvious signs of danger and imminent annihilation – Isobel was so positive and had a new energy, saying that she felt good – 'very, very good' – as she left the counselling room. I recall my own sense of lightness, exchanging a smile as the session finished, and feeling a completeness with a sense of some healing for her: that her pain today was not so great as it had been and that perhaps I had played some part in enabling that to happen.
>
> Possibly with a similar sense of lightness Isobel that night placed into her mouth large quantities of tablets which she washed down with a bottle of vodka and fell into sleep, and then death: perhaps for the first and final time feeling good – very, very good.
>
> I felt the tidal wave of her process the following morning. As I heard the news I felt a sense of sickness, almost like wanting to throw up something bad that I had swallowed. My stomach and throat creased into a tight knot and I felt a sense of separateness from what was happening around me – that I was spectating from a distance not quite making the connection. Someone asked me if I was okay, and I replied 'fine' as I left the room feeling devastated.

My relationship with suicidality had taken another, dramatic step forward. Isobel had been a client with whom I was working when based within a community mental health team (CMHT) and mental health crisis response service. Her death had personal and professional repercussions for me, and began a process of enquiry into suicide that I might never have otherwise anticipated.

Supervision, personal therapy and support from family and friends were invaluable in enabling me to consider the implications of Isobel's suicide in my personal and professional life, and regain the confidence to continue with counsellor training and in my work as an approved social worker (ASW) under mental health legislation. I was aware that my capacity to support myself with my anxieties and fears with regard to subsequent potential suicides was diminished. As I read about suicide, I became increasingly aware of the power of it in the life and work of professionals. This power was evident not only in the devastating experience for anyone working with someone who ends their life, but in my experience of building and maintaining a relationship with someone contemplating suicide.

As part of a masters degree, I embarked on a qualitative study to explore the experiences of counsellors who worked with suicidal clients. With a mixture of reassurance, identification and astonishment, I heard counsellors telling me that when a client talked about or alluded to their suicidal thoughts, they experienced a range of responses including fear, incompetence, impotence, anger, anxiety, sleeplessness, nightmares, intrusive thoughts and anticipated grief (Reeves and Mintz, 2001).

I had experienced a range of difficult feelings as a consequence of suicide, as had the counsellors in my masters study. It seemed likely that other counsellors might also experience similar things and if they did, how might that influence their ability to work with suicidal clients? How did counsellor training help them in this process – for my own counsellor training had not attended to suicide in any explicit way? A review of the available research indicated that the results found in my own masters degree study had been found elsewhere (Panove, 1994; B. Richards, 2000). Several important factors were emerging as my own questioning continued:

- My own experience of working with suicidal clients seemed closely related to that of other counsellors in their work with suicidal clients.
- Suicidality in counselling often initiated powerful and difficult emotional responses in therapists.
- My own experience of counsellor training was of little time spent exploring the implications of suicide in a counselling relationship, or acquiring and developing the necessary skills and knowledge to enable me to work effectively with suicidal clients.
- Other counsellors felt ill equipped by their counselling training experiences to work with suicidal clients.
- Given that most counsellors work within a contract of confidentiality that would require them to refer if their client was thought to present a 'harm to self or others', little research existed that explored how counsellors respond to suicidal clients within sessions or how decisions about 'harm' were made.
- While post-qualification risk assessment training programmes existed, they appeared to be either targeted at health care professionals, or generic in their target audience. Through an investigation of the literature and the professional journals, there was little evidence to suggest that resources existed specifically for counsellors to help them consider suicidality from a therapeutic perspective.

As will be discussed in later chapters, the plethora of resources and literature that attend to suicide predominantly do so from a risk-factor-based approach. That is, how can we predict suicide potential by applying generic risk factors (gender, age, employment status, etc.) to an individual? How can we incorporate those risk factors into questionnaires and assessment tools that will enable us to know who is more likely to kill themselves than others? To some extent these resources are invaluable in helping to create a broad understanding of an individual's distress. Yet, I would argue that for all the research and enquiry, there is only one way by which true understanding of suicidality can be reached, and that is by talking to the suicidal person about their experience.

That is not to say that this is an easy process. For a start, it is likely that the suicidal client will not necessarily understand their distress in an articulate way; some intrapersonal phenomena are extremely difficult to put into words. Additionally, it is possible that that 'helper' – counsellor, social worker, psychologist and psychiatrist, for example – will be inhibited by their own responses to suicidal potential to feel sufficiently confident to articulate their concerns. As we have seen, such responses can include fear, anxiety, anger, impotence and a sense of professional incompetence. These are difficult feelings to 'allow', and often the helper is caught in a process of denying their own responses, but still acting them out in the assessment encounter.

I am therefore interested in several areas, and hope that this book will provide the practitioner with sufficient provocation to facilitate a self-engagement in their journey into the world of the suicidal client. It is important that we are able to recognize our responses when thinking about suicide; are able to acknowledge those parts of ourselves that are fearful, judging or angry; are willing to ask the difficult questions; and know how to respond to the answers we might hear.

I am a registered social worker, and have for many years worked in multi-professional settings. I have worn my counsellor 'hat' while writing this book. However, it is important to stress that almost all of the factors that I discuss and explore about working with suicidal clients can be applied to most settings and helping professionals. I have tried to outline what we all do well, and areas that we can pay attention to. I hope that, whatever your professional background or working context, there is something in these pages that speaks to you.

There is no 'right' and 'wrong' position to take regarding suicide – just our own position. Throughout this book I will endeavour to draw out some of the difficulties and dilemmas faced by counsellors when working with suicide potential. These will, inevitably, be defined by context, amongst other factors. I will try to articulate my own position: however, that is not to say that other perspectives are less valid. I hope that in reading this book you will be encouraged or facilitated to engage with your own views, for ultimately it is those that you will take into your work with suicidal clients.

Andrew Reeves
Liverpool, UK

Acknowledgements

I am grateful to a number of people and organizations for their help in writing this book. To Rita Mintz, Sue Wheeler and Ric Bowl, who guided me through a personal and professional journey in my research. To Peter Jenkins and Barbara Mitchels, who kindly provided feedback on the first draft of Chapter 7, 'Confidentiality, Capacity and Consent'. To the team at Sage, and in particular Susannah Trefgarne and Alice Oven, for their support in preparing the manuscript. To BACP, for kind permission in allowing me to base Chapter 6 'The Ethical Imperative of Suicide', on an article I had previously published in *CPJ*[1]. To the World Health Organization, the Oxford Centre for Suicide Research, and the Office of Public Sector Information for permission to reproduce statistical information. To Taylor and Francis who provided permission for me to use material previously published in the following three articles:

Reeves, A., Bowl, R., Wheeler, S. and Guthrie, E. (2004). The hardest words: exploring the dialogue of suicide in the counselling process – a discourse analysis. *Counselling and Psychotherapy Research* 4(1), 62–71. www.informaworld.com.
Reeves, A. and Mintz, R. (2001). The experiences of counsellors who work with suicidal clients: an explorative study. *Counselling and Psychotherapy Research* 2, 37–42. www.informaworld.com.
Reeves, A., Wheeler, S. and Bowl, R. (2004). Confrontation or avoidance: what is taught on counsellor training courses. *British Journal of Guidance and Counselling* 32(2), 235–247. www.informaworld.com.

To the thousands of counsellors I have talked to over the years about their experiences of working with suicidal clients, and therefore for their huge contribution to the writing of this book. Finally, to Diane, Adam, Katie and Emily for putting up with the familiar sight of me sitting at the computer … again.

---

[1] Reeves, A. (2004). Suicide risk assessment and the ethical framework. *CPJ* May, 25–28.

Part I

Contextual Aspects of Working With Suicide Risk

1 Suicide and Counselling: An Introduction

> **Chapter overview**
>
> This chapter provides an overview for the rest of the book by discussing the role of counsellors with clients who are suicidal. It challenges the idea that counselling is generally not a helpful option for suicidal clients, or that counsellors generally should not see clients who are suicidal. It raises the dilemmas that counsellors face in managing and responding to suicide potential in their work. The overall structure of the book is outlined.

I can recall many years ago, when still early on in my research journey, looking at counselling and suicide risk. I had attended a conference (not about suicide) and was offered a lift home by a consultant psychiatrist psychotherapist. As the journey progressed the conversation moved to my research, and she asked more about it. I explained that I was interested in how counsellors work with clients who are suicidal; that is to say, how they use current information to inform their assessment of risk, whether they formally assess risk at all, how the counselling discourse was altered as a consequence of the disclosure of suicidal ideation, what the implications were of this influence, and so on. My listener was attentive and interested, but also confused. She eventually interrupted me with her statement, 'But counsellors would never see clients who are suicidal, they would be referred immediately to someone with greater competency.'

This made me reflect on my past and current client caseload. In secondary care nearly all of my clients had attempted suicide, and most were currently still actively suicidal. Since leaving secondary care and moving into higher education, a significant number of my current caseload (at the time of writing) had disclosed some degree of suicidal ideation, and a significant number had made attempts on their life. I didn't have any reason to assume that my caseload was particularly different to most other counsellors working in a variety of settings: primary care, secondary care, social services, mental health services, further education, higher education, bereavement services, voluntary services, independent practice, and so on. Indeed, if we relate counselling agencies to suicide risk factors – bereavement, relationship breakdown, psychopathology, physical health problems, etc. – it seemed a fair bet that virtually all counsellors would have some profile of suicide potential in their past or current caseload. I returned to the statement made by my listener, and wondered how quiet my caseload would in reality be if I referred everyone who presented with some degree of suicidal thought/intent to 'someone with greater competency'. I concluded, rightly or wrongly, that despite my listener's own competency and experience, she seemed to understand little about the nature of counselling.

It is difficult to make a definite statement about how many counsellors will have actively suicidal clients on their caseload, or how many counsellors will have seen actively suicidal clients in their professional lifetime, as I am not aware of any research that provides us with this information. My own study (Reeves and Mintz, 2001) indicated that most counsellors will have experience of supporting a suicidal client, although this was small scale and any wider conclusions are based only on estimations and extrapolated figures. Seber (2000) found, by analysing GP and practice nurse referrals for counselling in primary care, that such referrals often included clients with a previous history of suicide attempts. I developed a one-day training programme for counsellors to help them work more effectively with suicidal clients. During the development of this programme, and subsequent delivery, I have met with in excess of 3000 counsellors to specifically talk about suicide potential. Barely any, whether they be post-qualified, experienced counsellors or counsellors in training, did not have some experience of working with suicide potential, and too many had experienced the trauma of client suicide.

It might be helpful therefore to consider my listener's assertion in more detail.

Counsellors should not work with suicidal clients

Some might believe that the person who stated that counsellors should not work with suicide potential had a point. There are some interesting arguments that might contradict the accepted knowledge that counsellors are sufficiently competent to work with suicide risk. These might be summarized around four primary tenets: training around risk; knowledge of psychopathology; research awareness; and knowledge of relevant policy.

Training

> I just feel quite sad that it is an issue that does not come up more in training. It wasn't in ours but it is such an important thing that we should address. – Counsellor

Whether counsellors receive sufficient training to enable them to work effectively with suicide risk remains uncertain. Anecdotally, many counsellors will report that they did not feel sufficiently prepared by their core training to work with suicide potential. I undertook a questionnaire survey of all British Association for Counselling and Psychotherapy (BACP) accredited training programmes at that time to try to obtain a profile of risk competency development for counsellors (Reeves et al., 2004a), given that training courses have the task of preparing their trainees to become qualified and competent counsellors in a demanding and complex arena of helping.

There are many important and difficult areas to cover in training. Increasingly, as has been identified through the developments in mental health, risk assessment is one of these important areas (Department of Health, 1999b). No counsellor can ever accurately predict the behaviour or intent of their client, but counsellors must make use of their assessment knowledge and skills to maintain psychological contact with their clients as they explore these difficult areas of human experience.

The completed questionnaires returned by the respondents provided insight into trends and ideas informing counsellor training, as well as trainers'/counsellors' perceptions of the profession's response to risk.

The courses accredited at the time of my questionnaire study represented several primary theoretical models of practice: person centred, psychodynamic, psychosynthesis and gestalt, with several courses defining their model as integrative or eclectic. Person centred courses were the single largest group (which parallels the trend in BACP membership, with some estimating that 50% of the membership work within a person centred orientation: Thorne, 2004), followed by psychodynamic, integrative/eclectic programmes, psychosynthesis and gestalt.

There was no apparent difference for non-response between the core theoretical models of the courses. This is worth noting, given that a person centred approach is less likely to embrace the concept of risk 'assessment' than other models. Merry writes that 'issues concerning psychological assessment and "diagnosis" are complex, but the person centred approach tends to view these activities as unnecessary and even harmful to the development of a counselling relationship' (2002: 75). In written feedback received, those involved in person centred courses commented on the nature and meaning of risk assessment more than those running other courses. For example, comments included the belief that risk assessment 'pathologized' groups of people, and that the presence of the three core conditions as stated by Rogers (1997) – empathy, congruence and unconditional positive regard in work with clients at risk – was more important than the development of 'skills'. This philosophical difficulty with the questionnaire was further reflected by other comments stating that the questionnaire did not reflect the 'style' of training being offered.

Throughout the questionnaire the term 'assessment' was used frequently, chosen to reflect the language that is used in policy documents and mental health guidance, as well as within many medical and psychotherapeutic settings. However, it is important to acknowledge the potential philosophical difficulties that the term 'assessment' might have presented to some of the questionnaire respondents, and how that might in turn have influenced both the return rate and the nature of responses received. It might be the case that some courses or individual respondents did not see 'assessment' as having a relevant place within the philosophical context of a person centred training course. If this was an influencing factor, then other responses might have been received if different terms had been used, such as 'evaluation', 'exploration' or 'consideration' rather than 'assessment', for example.

Psychodynamic and integrative course respondents however were more likely to offer comments about the structure or design of the questionnaire. One respondent could not entirely understand the purpose of the questionnaire given that risk assessment was integral to their training and could 'never understand how colleagues work without it'. Other courses valued the structure and purpose of the questionnaire and believed the research question to be of significant value.

The returned questionnaires in general terms acknowledged the importance of understanding risk in the counselling process, and the need for trainees to be provided with appropriate opportunities to acquire knowledge and develop skills. However, there was less evidence that the acquisition of knowledge and development of skills were located within the core curriculum of training. Instead, many respondents stated that supervision was the primary source of risk-based teaching and development.

Competency of supervisors in working with risk

There are important questions about how supervisors develop their own specialist knowledge and skills in risk assessment. Many counselling supervisors begin their work in supervision through a process of evolution from counsellor to counsellor supervisor without additional training. At the time of writing there is currently no legislative requirement for counsellors to be registered, and there is no requirement for counsellor supervisors to have training in either counselling or supervision. Through the work of professional organizations such as BACP, and the development of the supervisor accreditation scheme, 'benchmarks' for supervision have begun to emerge. As a consequence there is an increasing number of supervisor training courses, although such courses are not yet able to apply for 'accreditation' in their own right.

The competency of supervisors to work with trainees around the complexities of risk assessment in their clinical work, including the development and enhancement of skills, is uncertain. That is to say not that supervisors are not competent, but that we just don't know. Due to the confidential nature of the supervisory relationship, the quality and standard of how risk is managed within supervision are also likely to be uncertain to the tutors on the training programme. In this context there is an argument to locate teaching about risk assessment and risk management more explicitly within the core curriculum. Supervision should build and develop knowledge and skills in working with clients at risk, rather than being the primary source of those qualities.

Importance of 'risk competency'

Neimeyer et al. (2001) stress the importance of training counsellors in risk assessment skills. This view is reiterated by other studies that note the importance of counsellors across a range of disciplines, including counselling, psychology, nursing and teaching, having the opportunity to develop skills in risk assessment (Appleby et al., 2001; Morriss et al., 1999; K.A. Richards, 2000; Werth, 2002). In this context it is important to note that while 95.8% of respondents believed that a specific consideration of risk was an essential component of a counsellor training curriculum, 47.8% did not include or had not considered including in their generic skills development work any opportunities for trainees to develop and practise skills for working with risk.

This result suggests that a number of training courses do not provide their trainees with opportunities to develop and practise risk assessment skills in their core teaching curriculum. This reflects comments received from some respondents that skills acquisition is less important than the presence of the 'core conditions' in the therapeutic relationship, for example. Competency development in this area instead is often located in external supervision contracts outside the immediate remit of the training course.

With the increasing likelihood of counsellors being based within a variety of working settings, including multi-disciplinary teams, it is worth noting that a majority of respondents stated that they considered different approaches to the assessment of risk of suicide within the teaching programme. This diversity might reflect the variation in clinical practice between different professional groups in the assessment and management of risk. It is interesting to note that some respondents did not believe their students were competent to work with suicide risk on completing the diploma programme. This is a surprising result, and begs the question as to how they believed competency was to be developed.

Learning is an ongoing process, and the diploma in counselling structure is increasingly seen as a basic level training from which counsellors should seek to further develop (Dryden and Thorne, 1991). Within the structure of BACP individual counsellor accreditation, applicants need to provide evidence of continuing professional development. However, whether competency in working with risk in counselling is required at a basic level or could be acquired later is an interesting consideration. Within their work, counsellors have the potential to work with clients at risk from the beginning of their training placement as well as from qualification.

While regular supervision is a BACP requirement for ethical practice, it could be argued that counsellors need to be competent in responding to clients at risk not only when they are no longer working within the context of a training placement but also at the beginning of such a placement. If this is true then perhaps all heads of training courses should ensure that their qualifying trainees are competent to work with clients at risk.

Given the complexities and unpredictable nature of client work, there is little time to adequately cover all important practice areas within the limited structure of counselling training. In the light of this, course leaders possibly believe that core training cannot provide trainees with all that they need for working with clients at risk, and that instead this is an ongoing developmental area. Alternatively or additionally, course leaders may consider that the acquisition and development of skills in working with risk are best located in clinical supervision, as has already been discussed.

This might reinforce the idea that risk is best included in the core curriculum given that trainee counsellors might need time to consider how they manage such demands on a personal and professional level. In practice terms, when working with a client at risk, it is helpful for counsellors to understand their own responses to the presenting risk and formulate a rationale for responses to their clients. In working within our own competence there are occasions where a client's level of risk requires the involvement of more specialist agencies. Training arguably has a role to play in helping counsellors to understand when this might be needed, and how it might be achieved. These findings perhaps leave questions unanswered as to whether current training benchmarks are sufficient to equip counsellors to work effectively with suicidal potential. Given the demands placed on counsellors when working with suicide potential, training needs to ensure that they are equipped with basic competencies. The training need of counsellors when working with risk of suicide is explored in more detail in Chapter 18, 'Training Implications for Counselling'.

Psychopathology and mental health systems

In my questionnaire study of BACP accredited training programmes, I was also interested in whether counsellors were given an opportunity to develop an understanding of theories of psychopathological and diagnostic structures, as well as mental health 'systems'. The majority of course leaders agreed that their trainees were provided with opportunities to understand the working of mental health 'systems'. Additionally, the majority of course leaders agreed that they spent course time considering how a diagnosis of mental illness was reached and the implications on a personal and societal level of such a diagnosis on an individual.

There was also general agreement that different 'models' of 'mental health' were considered. Within the context of broad agreement, there was disagreement by leaders of a small number of courses, all of whom were person centred in their theoretical approach. In disagreeing with these statements, the course leaders were perhaps again reiterating their view that the therapeutic process with an individual is more about the client/counsellor relationship, and the presence of the 'core conditions', than the context in which the relationship was located. Whether such a focus is sustainable in the longer term, given that person centred counsellors are employed to work in a variety of organizations, is uncertain. Some organizations and practice settings, such as in health care, as well as policy and legislative developments, may demand that counsellors are both competent and willing to practise with a broad and relevant mental health knowledge, which would include working with clients at risk and in multi-disciplinary settings.

However, it remains unclear whether counsellors fully integrated diagnostic thinking into their work. It is important to stress that in terms of this discussion, 'counsellors' is probably too generic a term, and that the extent to which psychopathology is seen as relevant or not is more likely to be determined by the core model of training. For example, cognitive behavioural or psychodynamic counsellors might see diagnostic terms as more pertinent to their core philosophy, whereas for person centred counsellors the principle of diagnosis would be contradictory to their core principles: 'Psychiatric diagnosis is of no issue in client-centred theory and therapy' (Sommerbeck, 2003: 33).

There are some useful discussions to be had around the relevance of diagnosis for counsellors. It is true to say that counsellors are not diagnosticians, so the expectation would never be that they would diagnose their clients. However, some might argue that diagnostic structures in themselves, as outlined in manuals such as the *Diagnostic and Statistical Manual of Mental Disorders* (DSM-IV: American Psychiatric Association, 1994), offer counsellors much insight into personality types. Certainly for working with suicidal clients, diagnoses can offer a useful structure of thinking that counsellors could use to help them order an approach. Additionally, given that higher suicide risk is correlated across pretty much all psychopathological diagnostic categories, a basic understanding of diagnosis is useful in helping counsellors to understand any increased suicide risk.

Sommerbeck (2003) discusses the importance of counsellors at least having an awareness of diagnostic structures, even if they are not actively implemented in their work:

- Counsellors will often receive questions from clients about diagnoses they have been given: 'It is important that the therapist is able to accommodate such a request for information in a qualified way when he deems it appropriate' (p. 33).
- In psychiatric and medical settings, diagnosis is the dominant language, 'and the client centred therapist must be able to communicate in the language with other staff and professionals when working in this culture' (p. 33).

- Counsellors need to be aware of the range of treatments that might be offered clients, and 'the client centred therapist will quickly experience the necessity of psychiatric diagnostics for many treatment modalities, especially for the psychopharmacological treatments that help many clients, in combination with psychotherapy, or without psychotherapy' (p. 34).
- Diagnosis is often central when considering the liberty of a client under mental health legislation, and a counsellor needs sufficient awareness of this to contribute usefully to that discussion, particularly in relation to client suicide potential.

As is the case with training competency, counsellors arguably need to interact more actively with basic concepts around psychopathology and diagnosis, congruent to their model of practice, to support their work with suicidal clients.

Research awareness

The context of working with suicide risk has been so profoundly informed by research that it is essential that counsellors have some awareness of the relationship between their practice and what the research says. As will be highlighted in other chapters, research has been pivotal in the development of an understanding of risk factors, and as a consequence in the development of the plethora of risk assessment tools, questionnaires, inventories, scales, and so on. Counsellors are traditionally not research aware, as for many decades training has tended to focus on skills development rather than research competency. As counselling training has increasingly moved into further and higher education settings, in addition to the many training programmes that are independent, research awareness has begun to change as trainees have been required to complete small scale research studies as part of their programme of study.

The work of organizations such as BACP in trying to make links between practice and research has resulted in research more and more appearing on the agenda of the counsellor. The push towards evidence-based practice, and the publication by the Department of Health in the UK of *Treatment Choice in Psychological Therapies and Counselling: Evidence-Based Clinical Practice Guideline* (2001), a document that identified preferred interventions based on research evidence, made research awareness a greater imperative.

However, many counsellors remain wary of and intimidated by research, believing it to have little relevance for their practice. Cooper, however, argues that 'research findings can be like good friends: something that can encourage, advise, stimulate and help us, but also something that we are not afraid to challenge and argue against' (2008: 1). This is certainly true for the research evidence in relation to suicidal potential. Understanding the evidence can certainly 'encourage, advise, stimulate and help us' when we are trying to make sense of another's suicidal experience, and the likelihood of them acting on their thoughts, but neither should it be a given that we feel unable to 'challenge and argue against' it. As stated elsewhere, there is a tendency to presume that risk factors in themselves are the panacea when working with suicide risk, whereas in truth they are but a starting point, a context, within which much more information and detail need to be gathered and interpreted.

Knowledge of relevant policy

The need for counsellors to be aware of policy that informs practice is essential across all aspects of professional work. Specifically in relation to suicide risk, there are a number of important documents that inform and shape the expectations of counsellors and other mental health practitioners. These are discussed more fully in Part II, 'The Prediction-Prevention Model, Policy and Ethics'. I am not aware of research that tells us whether social policy is adequately addressed within counsellor training. It is likely that counsellors will have awareness of policy directly relevant to their working context, but whether knowledge and understanding are achieved in a transferable way is less clear, e.g. a counsellor working in higher education understanding the practice implications of the *Suicide Prevention Strategy for England* (Department of Health, 2002). The need for counsellors to understand how practice is shaped and informed by policy is an important skill, given that intervention decisions are likely to be benchmarked against policy and good practice parameters at some stage.

My questionnaire survey asked course leaders to comment on whether they believed professional organizations adequately supported their members in acquiring knowledge of key policy documents, and their implications for counselling. The majority of respondents did not feel that professional organizations adequately met the information needs of counsellors in such important areas. Such initiatives can be essential in informing members about key practice and contextual changes across a range of topics. If such organizations are not providing information at a time of change in mental health legislation and policy development, they are potentially failing their members. However, it might be that such information is made available but that counsellors do not read or access it.

At the time of the study, the Department of Health (1999a; 1999b) had published important policy documents that created imperatives in mental health policy development and professional responses to risk. Guidance issued by professional organizations might not be reaching all the membership or might not be perceived by the membership as relevant for their practice. A proportion of respondents did not express confidence that appropriate or sufficient information was being provided by professional organizations in these areas. The nature of information that counsellors might see as relevant to their practice and the means of dissemination warrant further enquiry.

This is not a 'sexy' area for many counsellors. For other professional groups, such as social workers and nurses, social policy is an integral component of their core training curricula. This arguably allows for a greater critical awareness of the development of social policy, and a greater understanding of the implications of policy for the professional tasks in which they are being trained. However, social policy does not appear to be generally incorporated into counsellor training. During the workshop I developed for supporting counsellors in their work with suicidal clients, policy was the point at which many participants became 'glassy eyed' and were clearly switching off!

One explanation for this might be that as counsellors are not trained to think in policy terms, or to integrate policy information into their practice, they therefore do not value it as highly as interpersonal information, in which they receive extensive training. The consequences of this, however, are that many counsellors effectively practise in the dark – unaware of policy initiative and how practice is subsequently shaped by it. Alternatively, many counsellors do not appreciate the importance of using a political/policy process to support practice. This is the case in working with suicide potential: many counsellors will be expected to use risk assessment tools (developed through research and integrated into policy), and will feel that they influence their practice negatively. However, the more aware counsellors are of the context of such tools, the more they are able to use that information to support what they do, rather than let it change it, as is discussed in other chapters of this book.

Counsellors should work with suicidal clients

Why should counsellors continue to work with suicidal clients, particularly in the light of the potential difficulties around training, knowledge of psychopathology, lack of research awareness and lack of training about social policy? Essentially, because we are very, very good at it; and also because counselling offers suicidal clients a choice that goes far beyond traditional psychopharmacological or psychiatric interventions.

So why do I believe that 'we are good at it'? Primarily because the focus of the work of counsellors is relatively uncorrupted by extraneous factors, such as context. In many ways this is a difficult statement to make. I believe that it is essential that all counsellors think systemically in ways they currently don't. It is arguably impossible to help the whole person if they are continually viewed outside of their cultural, social or demographic context, for example. It is difficult for a client to really feel better about who they are if they live in squalid, uncaring surroundings. It is impossible to understand a client's suicidality if it is not viewed in the context of relationships, physical health or abuse, for example. So, I am not arguing here that counsellors should not think systemically, or encourage their clients to do so. However, by 'uncorrupted by extraneous factors', I mean that counsellors are perhaps in an almost unique position by comparison to many other mental health professionals to focus entirely on the 'self' of the client, using communication skills effectively and in a facilitative way to enable the person of the client to really explore who they are and how they feel.

Our theories and working models, regardless of orientation, are arguably designed to specifically facilitate the narrative of the client *for its own sake*, as opposed to then fit it into another box we might have waiting for it. However we construct personality, counselling is ultimately about giving voice to the client so that they can begin to make change through awareness, or perhaps remain unchanged but in awareness. This is particularly important when working with suicidality – enabling another person to begin to articulate their most difficult, painful thoughts in a way that ultimately aims to use those same thoughts as a means to moving on. Almost paradoxically, we are helping clients to use the awareness of their suicidal potential to begin to move away from it.

Having worked in secondary care for many years, I have met too many clients who have been treated by psychiatric or medical models for decades, without having had the opportunity to really talk about their problems. Isobel, whose suicide I described in the preface, said to me early on in our relationship, 'I've never really talked about this y'know. I've been in and out of hospital countless times, but have never really been asked about how I really feel.' That is not to say that the choice of counselling is necessarily an easy one: for Isobel it was perhaps the hardest (or most liberating?) thing she ever did. Also, the choice of counselling does not have to be one that excludes other interventions. For example, few might deny the benefits of counselling in conjunction with medication for depression, for example.

This is essentially why I passionately believe that counsellors should continue their work with suicidal clients: because it can be a lifeline when no others seem to exist. The other things – training, knowledge and research – we can change (and arguably are changing through the development of core competencies, for example). It is also because I believe counselling to be such an invaluable resource for people contemplating ending their own life that we need to do it as 'right' as we can.

The structure of this book

This book is structured across seven parts, each dealing with an aspect of working with suicide risk pertinent to practitioners. Part I, 'Contextual Aspects of Working with Suicide Risk', considers suicide in context. For example, it looks at how the emergence of the medical model and psychiatry has influenced not only the way in which suicide is understood, but how it might be responded to. This is pivotally important for counsellors, given that we don't work in a vacuum. The emphasis in many counsellor training programmes is on the understanding of the individual, the 'self', with less emphasis placed on 'self' in context. This is understandable and, in many ways, important. It is vital that new counsellors can fully understand a number of theories of psychotherapy and personality in order to be able to work effectively with people in a therapeutic relationship. However, if we can incorporate into our thinking and understanding the 'self' in relation to relevant historical developments, other forms of helping and understanding, and the ongoing evolution of counselling as a professional activity, we can begin to understand the distressed 'self', and indeed the suicidal 'self', in a three-dimensional way.

Part II, 'The Prediction–Prevention Model, Policy and Ethics', builds on Part I by exploring how these different aspects come together to inform intervention choices. More specifically, it looks at how the work of suicidologists has considerably informed and shaped our response to risk, through the development of risk assessment tools, questionnaires and inventories based on suicide risk factors. What I will call the 'prediction-prevention' culture of working with suicide risk is a direct consequence of a factor-based approach to understanding suicidality. While it is important to acknowledge the value of integrating an understanding of risk factors into our work, I will argue that for many counsellors a dialogic approach (as opposed to one based on questionnaire or statistical analysis) is not only much more congruent with how we work, but also probably more likely to help us and our clients understand suicidality in a much deeper way, gaining a better idea of the risk of suicidal thoughts being acted on. Finally, in this part I will provide a brief consideration of some of the factors that counsellors cite as problematic for them in working ethically and appropriately, such as managing confidentiality with suicidal clients, and understanding the implications of terms such as *capacity* and *consent*.

In Part III, 'Organizations', I will consider how organizations influence and shape counselling generally, and more specifically in work with suicidal clients. This is particularly important given the numbers of counsellors now working in statutory and non-statutory agencies, where practice is often directed by a risk policy or procedure. We will consider how counsellors can negotiate working within a policy that might contradict personally held views on suicide. Additionally, we will look at what factors might be usefully considered when developing a suicide risk policy, or when reviewing an existing policy.

Part IV, 'The Client Process', will consider in some depth the ways in which clients might explore their suicidal thoughts in sessions, or indeed might consciously or unconsciously avoid them. This is, of course, vitally important to counsellors given that we rely on the ways in which our clients are able to articulate their narrative, and how we can facilitate a greater understanding of it through therapeutic 'talk'. It could be argued that *how* clients talk (or don't talk) about their suicidal thoughts has direct implications for the nature of the therapeutic discourse. In the context of these implications, we will consider what skills and relational factors counsellors might keep in mind to help maintain and sustain therapeutic contact in the face of potential client self-annihilation.

Part V, 'The Counsellor Process' is perhaps of greatest importance for any counsellor who works with suicide risk. Over many years of research and reading into working with suicide risk, I have found that the practitioner process is consistently overlooked in favour of statistical trends, risk factors and other more generalized aspects of the work. Yet, and particularly in the context of a dialogic approach to suicide risk assessment, the *understanding* of what we hear from suicidal clients will be profoundly shaped by our own subjective position. Our own experiences of having been suicidal or of suicide within our family, our spiritual or religious beliefs, our responses to the particular client in question, for example, will all shape what we allow ourselves to hear, and then how we subsequently respond. Telling ourselves that, despite our personally held views, we will always be able to reach objective conclusions about a client's level of risk is at best a professional arrogance and at worst a disregard of the complexities of suicidality that might leave our clients at great risk at a time when they needed our intervention the most. For example, how easy is it to really hear what is being said and what is not being spoken from a place of our own fear and terror?

Part VI, 'Key Aspects of Counselling with Suicidal Clients', will attempt to draw these factors together and provide a consideration of what we should do when a client talks of feeling suicidal. This includes self-care, and ensuring that our practice and practice decisions are grounded in a secure knowledge base as well as an ethical context. Part VII offers my concluding thoughts and makes suggestions for future development.

I hope that you find this book helpful in supporting you in your work. Ultimately, the aim here is not to provide a book of answers, because in working with suicide risk there aren't concrete ones to be had. Instead, the hope is that you will find many aspects in this book that will facilitate further thinking, and provoke you into personal and professional reflection. The book is deliberately written in a non-model-specific way. My belief is that it is not the model or training orientation of the counsellor that will best lend themselves to be able to work effectively with people who are suicidal, but their willingness to listen, to question, to explore, to go to unknown and often difficult places, and ultimately to be able to sit with their not knowing.

My personal experience is that I have encountered most problems when searching for something concrete, realizing that in the absence of it I am left with my anxiety and fear. It is these feelings that I find I take into the counselling relationship (even though I am convinced that I don't!). As soon as this occurs, I cease to be of value to the client who is in a suicidal place because I parallel their chaos or struggle in the absence of my own 'grounding'.

My own view

I think it will be helpful here to be transparent about my own position in relation to suicide – though it must be said that this is inevitably a dynamic and changing one (as I suspect will be the case for you in reading this book). The chances that my perspective will have changed by the time this book appears in print, or by the time you read it, are extremely high.

Essentially I believe that as individuals we should all hold the choice to end our own life if we believe it is no longer worth living. I see this as an essential 'human right', and not one I would like removed from me. I believe that this 'choice' should be informed, and reached with capacity and consideration. However, many people have come to see me as a counsellor who have talked of wanting to end their own life but who, in my view, did not have the capacity to reach that decision clearly or in an informed way. That is to say, their level of distress was such that it was difficult or impossible for them to see beyond their distress. They had lost a sense of hope, and my role, as their counsellor, was to hold that hope for them in the event of change. I believe that mental health distress, or mental illness if you choose to call it that, can impinge on capacity and that as a counsellor I should provide my clients with opportunities to make *informed* rather than impinged decisions.

Of course, this logical argument becomes entirely redundant when applied to my own friends and family. Can I defend this contradictory stance, this ridiculous incompatibility between these two positions? No, clearly I can't. My position evidently has 'one rule for one, and a different rule for another'. It is hypocritical and nonsense. However, it is true for me ... at the moment. Such is the nature of our own positions *vis-à-vis* suicide that we all must work through what they are, and the contradictory places we might take ourselves. The fact is that it is probably impossible to stand in a concrete place until we know what that place might be. Certainly, for many, spiritually or religiously held beliefs will be profoundly important in reaching a 'position' on suicide. The task of managing these dynamics when working with a suicidal client can be daunting.

2 Historical Perspectives on Suicide and the Emergence of the Medical Model

---

Chapter overview

Given that a counsellor's own views and beliefs about suicide are important in how they respond to and intervene with suicidal clients, it is helpful to place current perspectives on suicide in a historical context. Suicide has not always been seen as fundamentally and inextricably linked with 'madness', yet the development of psychiatry and the emergence of the medical model have seemed to reinforce this link. This chapter will provide a brief overview of changing perspectives on suicide, the emergence of the medical model, and how these now shape and inform current responses to suicidal people.

It is important to place our current work with suicidal clients in some historical perspective. Attitudes towards and beliefs about suicide have changed over the centuries; our current perspectives are informed by factors that are only relatively recent. Later in this book, particularly in Chapters 14 and 15, 'The Counsellor and Suicide Risk: Personal Perspectives and Professional Actions' and 'Potential Dangers and Difficulties', I argue that the counsellor's perspective on suicide is centrally important in how they then work with and respond to suicide risk in counselling sessions. Understanding the context of that perspective in historical terms can be helpful.

Here I will provide a brief overview of how attitudes towards suicide have changed over the centuries, and latterly how the emergence of psychiatry and the dominance of the medical model have affirmed suicide inextricably in the realms of 'madness'. There is insufficient space to fully explore the dimensions and dynamics in the changing face of suicide. For that, I would recommend Minois's (1999) work, *History of Suicide: Voluntary Death in Western Culture* (translated by Cochrane), which provides a thorough consideration of suicide through the ages. Also helpful in writing this chapter, I would recommend Pritchard (1995) and O'Connor and Sheehy (2000).

Changing views on suicide

O'Connor and Sheehy (2000) note that the term 'suicide' has only a relatively recent history, with no recorded use before 1634. Previously the act of suicide was referred to in various forms, but included 'self-destruction' or 'self-killing' for example. In the Old Testament and New Testament of the Bible, there are several examples of 'self-killing' described. Barraclough (1990) noted that these instances were purely descriptive, with no positive or negative interpretations applied. We might therefore assume that the act of suicide at this time was not, in itself, viewed as morally repugnant. It seems that suicide has, over the centuries, been viewed differently at different times by society: sometimes as sinful, at other times not.

For the ancient Greeks, suicide was seen as acceptable if it were undertaken for reasons that were viewed as justifiable, such as grief or to avoid dishonour. Ancient Greek society was less tolerant of suicide for reasons less than these. Suicide was therefore seen as an acceptable death 'provided it was reasoned and reasonable' (O'Connor and Sheehy, 2000: 2). The Romans too viewed suicide without judgement, and instead saw it as an acceptable means of death in the context of 'justifiable reasons', similar to the ancient Greeks. O'Connor and Sheehy note that some suicides were not tolerated and were outlawed by the Romans, but these were usually related to suicide being seen as a loss of property, e.g. suicide of a slave or soldier.

From around AD 400, the Christian Church began to express disquiet about the act of suicide, and in AD 566 the Council of Bragga 'prohibited masses to be said for the souls of those dying by suicide and the comfort for them of a Christian burial in hallowed ground' (Pritchard, 1995: 10). The last 'unhallowed' burial took place in Britain as late as 1823, according to Wymer (1986). There were exceptions to the condemnation of suicide, principally when the person was viewed as 'deranged', or when 'honour' was at stake, such as the victim of rape taking her own life. In 1330 the priory for the sisters of the Order of the Star of Bethlehem became a hospital, to be known as the Bedlam Hospital (now the Bethlem Royal Hospital, although in a different location), and in 1357 it began to admit patients who were 'deranged', offering them sanctuary and care; it became a full psychiatric hospital later.

In the fifteenth century suicide led to severe sanctions, partly due to the influence of the Christian Church, including loss of absolution, loss of property and entering Dante's Third Circle of Hell. The Church's moral objection to suicide seemed to centre on what was believed to be a loss or rejection of hope, and thus taking a 'stand' against God. However Donne's prose work *Biathanatos*, written in 1608 and published in 1644, argued that suicide and faith could be compatible, citing examples such as Samson, Saul and Iscariot.

The corresponding development of psychiatry as a discrete discipline within medicine brought suicide into the realm of illness once again. However, from the sixteenth century onwards, perspectives on suicide have continued to shift, influenced by literature and art. Pritchard (1995) notes three main contributors to these changes, namely Shakespeare (1564–1616), Donne (1571–1631), who we have already briefly considered, and Burton (1577–1640) who in 1621 wrote *The Anatomy of Melancholy*. Much of the work of these writers and poets challenged the accepted beliefs of suicide as 'them and us' (still prevalent today perhaps), and called for greater tolerance and care. It might be argued that some of their writing was so progressive that it would still be experienced as challenging by those working with suicidal people today. Burton wrote in *The Anatomy of Melancholy*, 'His picture keep still in thy presence: Twixt him and thee there's no difference' (Burton, 1883).

Perhaps one of the most influential writers on suicide was Durkheim (1951 [1897]). The French sociologist asserted that suicide did not take place in isolation, but was instead a consequence of interplay between the individual and societal pressures and influences. In his writing he proposed four 'types' of suicide:

- *Egoistic suicide.* Suicide occurs due to marginalization, with little social support and a sense of estrangement from society. The greater the disconnection between individual and society, the greater the risk of suicide.
- *Altruistic suicide.* It might be accurate to describe altruistic suicide as the opposite of egoistic suicide, in that suicide occurs when the individual has become too integrated within society. That is, the experience of societal expectation and pressure becomes too great, with the individual feeling unable to meet these demands.
- *Anomic suicide.* An individual is in need of stability – to be in equilibrium with his or her state (and status) within society. External change, such as redundancy or loss of status, causes emotional distress for the individual, who no longer has a sense of containment and clarity regarding their role. O'Connor and Sheehy (2000) make the link between this type of suicide and the increase in suicides during times of economic recession, for example.
- *Fatalistic suicide.* Opposite to anomic suicide, fatalistic suicide occurs when an individual feels excessively controlled, with little or no sense of control over their own future or destiny.

While the specific theories of suicide as proposed by Durkheim were important, what was of equal importance was the principle on which they were based: that suicide might be the consequence of external pressures, as opposed to simply being psychopathological. Durkheim exerted a major influence over the understanding of suicide for a long time, and his work is still considered to have relevance to current thinking.

Suicide has prominence in other cultural and spiritual beliefs. In the Hindu faith, views are heavily influenced by gender. Suicide is not seen as acceptable for males, whereas for females the idea of suicide as honourable is held, for example, following bereavement. Pritchard (1995) questions whether in the UK this is an important factor in the higher rates of suicide amongst Hindu women compared with Hindu men. Pritchard also notes that the Koran contains three very specific sanctions against suicide or 'self-killing', and that the Prophet Mohammed 'assigns suicides to the third or lower levels of Hell' (1995: 11).

The emergence of psychiatry and the medical model

Greek and Roman sources can be seen to be heavily influential on Western beliefs about mental health and functioning. Causation of mental ill-health, and cure, was typically seen as coming from the gods. Additionally, a belief persisted of insanity being the result of moral failure, the former being the punishment for the latter by the gods. During the sixth and fifth centuries BC there was a move against this relationship between madness and the gods, and during the fourth century BC the work of Hippocrates became heavily influential. He believed that mental illness resulted from imbalance in the four bodily humours – blood, black bile, yellow bile and phlegm, corresponding to the four basic qualities of matter, namely heat, cold, moisture and dryness – and was specifically a disturbance of black bile, or melaina chole, later melancholia; hereas hysteria was related to movement of the uterus, for example (Merkel, 2003).

Consequently, treatment of mental illness focused on restoring balance in the humours, through diet, vapours, baths and purges. Aristotle, building on the work of Hippocrates, suggested a division between mind and body, arguing that bile mediated between mind and body; whereas Plato instead considered a division between mind/soul and body. The work of Hippocrates and his influence on medicine continued well into the seventeenth century.

Galen (AD 130–200), a Roman physician, described several 'syndromes', including dysthymia, paranoia and hysteria, linked to sexual tension and anxiety. As opposed to Hippocrates's view of mental illness as being imbalance in the body humours, Galen instead proposed a view that it was due to an imbalance between aspects of the soul, 'which had rational, irrational and lustful parts' (Merkel, 2003: 3). Treatment centred on confinement, reading, education, and decreased exposure to stimuli. However, Hippocrates's influences can still be seen, with sufferers undertaking purification and dietary changes and using substances to induce sleep.

During the Middle Ages, sin became central in the view of mental illness, with the rise of the dominance of the Church. Mental illness alienated the sufferer from God, and, as has already been highlighted, suicide was seen as a rejection of God because of a rejection of hope. The centrality of the Church in mental illness saw the use of monasteries as venues for treatment through the practices of confession and penance.

During the later Middle Ages, Islamic culture influenced what was happening in the West. As opposed to the Western Church view that the mentally ill were against God, the Koran taught that they were important to God, with the establishment of asylums in the eighth and ninth centuries. Merkel describes these asylums as providing 'a calm and relaxed environment, with fountains, gardens, and the use of soothing baths, perfumes, music and special diets' (2003: 4). From Plato's mind/soul and body separation came a further separation of mind and soul, with the mind being associated with the Greek 'psyche'.

The fifteenth and sixteenth centuries saw a movement towards science and a steadily declining influence of the Church. Descartes (1596–1650) proposed a division between the soul and mind, with the soul having spiritual aspects and the mind mental ones, although he did acknowledge an interaction between the two. According to Merkel (2003), the body was seen as primarily mechanical, materialistic and quantifiable, whereas the mind was seen as unbounded, non-material and limited to the realm of consciousness and thought.

In the 1600s there was an increasing awareness of the body as a mechanical 'entity', with greater use of anatomical studies. Thomas Sydenham (1624–1689) wrote of hysterical and neurotic disorders, thus reinforcing ideas that mental illness had clinical rather than spiritual origin. This continued into the seventeenth and eighteenth centuries, with greater numbers of people seen as mentally ill. Merkel (2003) speculates whether this was due to an actual increase in numbers, or the loss of traditional supports. Additionally perhaps might be the idea that mental illness was increasingly being viewed within clinical and therefore diagnosable constructs.

During the nineteenth and twentieth centuries further important developments occurred. Attempts were made to end witchcraft trials and greater efforts were made to differentiate people with mental illness in institutional settings. Such institutional settings were also viewed as opportunities to treat the mentally ill, as opposed to just accommodate them. Battie (1704–1776) was a key figure in these reforms.

New understandings of mental illness continued, with a greater acknowledgement of possible organic as opposed to environmental causes. Treatment included restraint and control. Psychiatry, an emerging discipline within medicine, began to focus on categorization of mental illnesses, with less emphasis on new treatment development. In Germany there was a growing linking of mental illness and physiology. The German school of experimental psychology became interested in consciousness, perception and memory. Key figures in the development of psychiatry include Kraepelin (1856–1926) and Janet (1859–1947). Kraepelin developed concepts such as incidence, anatomy and outcome – furthering the clinical standing of psychiatry. His work focused on psychosis, while Janet instead was interested in neurosis.

Merkel (2003) notes that by the nineteenth century, two schools of understanding of mental illness had emerged: the somatic and the psychic. The former saw mental illness as rooted within physical causation, e.g. brain disturbance, whereas the latter school, the psychic, linked mental illness to emotional stress. Interestingly, these two divisions are still debated amongst mental health professionals today: whether mental illness is more symptomatic of physical causation, or whether mental illness instead originates in psychological functioning. Clients often ask me whether I think their depression is 'psychological or physical' – so this dichotomous thinking has been internalized by us all.

Psychiatry has therefore developed from several strands: psyche verses soma debates; the humoral ideas of Hippocrates; and the development of psychoanalytic theories, heavily influenced by Darwin, Freud, Adler and Jung, for example. The latter theories, with which as counsellors we will be more familiar, focus on 'illness' as instead the manifestations of interpersonal relationships, attachment, the unconscious and the meaning of these things. Psychiatry has tried (and arguably continues to try) to integrate these ideas.

Psychiatry as practised today is still heavily influenced by its past, although perspectives and treatments have continued to develop significantly. The categorization of mental illness was formulated into diagnostic manuals, two of which are still central to psychiatric diagnosis: the *International Classification of Diseases and Related Health Problems* (World Health Organization, 1992; currently in its 10th revision, and first published in 1893 as the *International List of Causes of Death*), and the *Diagnostic and Statistical Manual of Mental Disorders*, published by the American Psychiatric Association (1994) (currently in its fourth revised edition). These manuals inform all diagnostic decision making, and are therefore pivotal in understanding 'disorder' models.

Counsellors will accept or disregard these models depending upon their own theoretical orientation. For example, the humanist movement and the work of psychotherapists such as Rogers would reject the notion of mental illness, and not take into account diagnostic understanding in their work. I discussed the importance of counsellors having at least a general understanding of diagnostic categories in Chapter 1.

The medicalization of suicide

In considering the changing views of suicide over the centuries, the changing explanations for mental illness, and the emerging discipline of psychiatry and the medical model, it becomes clearer how suicide has been increasingly framed within the culture of mental illness. Szasz (1971) disputed the idea that suicidality always equates to mental illness, and in doing so questioned the prevailing assumptions of the time. The naming of social and interpersonal factors as important and potentially relevant in suicide research provides further momentum for such questioning. It has been argued that the prevailing assumptions at an intervention level with suicidal people have been the preference for hospital admission and/or psychotropic medication to 'treat' suicidality (Newnes et al., 1999). By including social and interpersonal factors in the theoretical construct of suicide, other treatment options, such as counselling and psychotherapy, have greater validity.

While in the US suicide is intrinsically linked with mental illness (in that anyone reporting suicidal thoughts can be hospitalized), in the UK this is not the case. It is essential that counsellors keep in mind that under UK legislation suicidality does not *necessarily* mean that the client is suffering from mental illness. This is discussed more fully in Chapter 7, 'Confidentiality, Capacity and Consent'. It is difficult to determine how responses to suicide risk and policy development might have been shaped differently without writers such as Szasz, but some studies provide scope for talking-based approaches to be considered alongside more traditional treatments such as medication. The outcome of anti-psychiatry practitioners such as Szasz might be that suicidal thoughts cannot be dismissed necessarily as the product of an insane mind and, as such, suicide prevention and intervention strategies need to include bigger considerations.

Discussion questions

1 How relevant do you consider historical influences are in shaping what we understand about suicide now, and how we respond?
2 What do you consider to be the influences of religion and medicine in how suicide is currently constructed?
3 What role does the counselling profession have in informing and influencing society's views on suicide?
4 What role do you have as an individual counsellor in informing and influencing views on suicide amongst other professional groups, if any?

3 Suicide Trends and Statistics

Chapter overview

This chapter discusses the difficulties in accurately recording suicide, and the implications for analysing UK and international suicide statistics. An overview of current UK and international suicide trends is presented, with a discussion as to their relevance for counsellors.

The Mental Health Foundation (1997) stated that in 1995 suicide in the UK accounted for 4315 deaths, which averaged at approximately 12 suicides per day. With the inclusion of 'undetermined deaths' of 2185 where suicide cannot be ruled out as a possibility, these numbers rise to 6500 suicides or an average of 18 deaths per day.

The *National Service Framework for Mental Health* (NSF: Department of Health, 1999b) states that whilst suicide rates in England have fallen by more than 12% since 1982, there are still over 4000 deaths by suicide in England every year. As a context for setting targets for suicide reduction, the NSF states that:

- Men are three times more likely than women to commit suicide. Young men are at a particularly high risk.
- Men in unskilled occupations are four times more likely to commit suicide than are those in professional work.
- Among women living in England, those born in India and East Africa have a 40% higher suicide rate than those born in England and Wales.
- More than one in ten people with severe mental illness kill themselves.
- People with depression, those who have experienced a major loss, and those who misuse drugs/alcohol and have previously harmed themselves are at a greater risk (1999b: 77).

The World Health Organization (2009) cites the following information on its website:

- In the year 2000, approximately one million people died from suicide: a 'global' mortality rate of 16 per 100,000, or one death every 40 seconds.
- In the last 45 years suicide rates have increased by 60% worldwide. Suicide is now among the three leading causes of death among those aged 15–44 years (both sexes); these figures do not include suicide attempts which are up to 20 times more frequent than completed suicide.
- Suicide worldwide is estimated to represent 1.8% of the total global burden of disease in 1998, and 2.4% in countries with market and former socialist economies in 2020.

- Although traditionally suicide rates have been highest among the male elderly, rates among young people have been increasing to such an extent that they are now the group at highest risk in a third of countries, in both developed and developing countries.
- Mental disorders (particularly depression and substance abuse) are associated with more than 90% of all cases of suicide; however, suicide results from many complex sociocultural factors and is more likely to occur particularly during periods of socioeconomic, family and individual crisis situations (e.g. loss of a loved one, employment, honour).

Bertolote and Fleischmann (2002) state that based on current trends, and according to WHO estimates, in 2020 approximately 1.53 million people will die from suicide, and 10–20 times more people will attempt suicide worldwide. They suggest this represents an average of one death every 20 seconds, and one attempt every 1–2 seconds.

Suicide statistics are in some ways difficult to interpret given the problems in the classification of 'suicide' as a cause of death. While on many occasions it may be very apparent that the cause of death was suicide, perhaps when a suicide note has been left, or when no other possible explanation exists, too often there is sufficient doubt to confidently conclude suicide as the cause. The consequence of this is that suicide statistics as compiled and published almost certainly under-report the actual numbers of suicides, or as Leenaars states, 'statistics ... are, at best, only a representation of the true figures' (2004: 40).

Another important factor that influences the reliability of suicide statistics is how data are recorded. Hawton and van Heeringen (2002) note that while in the UK a coroner classifies suicide, in other countries this is very different. For example, in Germany a general practitioner may classify the cause of death, whereas in Australia eight systems exist (reflecting the six states and two territories). Stanistreet et al. (2001) report on the difficulties of the classification of suicide as a cause of death in coroner's hearings, particularly when self-destructive behaviour might have been a causal factor.

For a UK coroner to classify a death as suicide, they must be beyond reasonable doubt that:

- the event which caused the deceased's death must have been self-inflicted, self-enacted and self-administered; and
- the intention of the deceased in initiating the fatal event must unequivocally have been to bring about his or her death. (McCarthy and Walsh, 1975, cited in O'Connor and Sheehy, 2000: 15)

WHO compiles suicide statistics on a country-by-country basis. A working group of WHO (World Health Organization, 1982) concluded that statisticians could be confident in the use of international statistics. Other organizations also provide reliable statistical data on suicides, such as the Office for National Statistics and the Centre for Suicide Research in Oxford, both based in the UK. Statistics can provide important overviews of trends and changes, and can help inform policy and service development; however, many of the currently available suicide statistics are a few years old due to difficulties in collation. The *National Suicide Prevention Strategy for England* (Department of Health, 2002) set a target for the reduction of suicide of one-fifth by 2010. The *Fifth Annual Report on the Strategy* (Department of Health, 2007) noted that

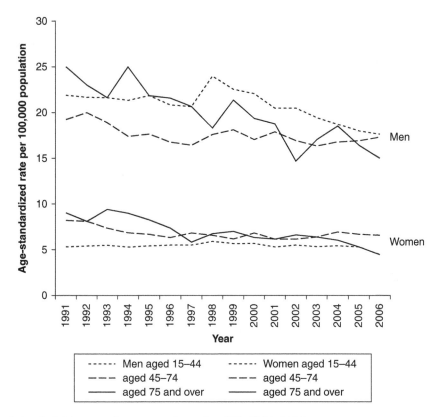

Figure 3.1 Suicide rates by age and gender, UK, 1991–2006
Source: National Office of Statistics: www.statistics.gov.uk, accessed January 2009 – reproduced with permission

the very high suicide rates amongst young males had shown a reduction over recent years, although the overall rates remained high against other population groups.

Suicide trends

I will present a general summary of the latest available suicide statistics here in relation to demographic and psychopathological factors that I think might be of particular interest to counsellors.

UK suicide trends

As can be seen from Figure 3.1, there is a steady reduction in suicide rates across the age ranges for both men and women. Men aged 75 years and over had the highest suicide rate two decades ago, but in the late 1990s there was a sharp rise in the rates for younger men aged 15–44. In males this age group has continued to represent the highest risk group, even though numbers have been falling. In women, again the 75 and over age group represented the highest risk group, whereas by 2006 this group had been overtaken by the 45–74 age group.

24 Counselling Suicidal Clients

Table 3.1 Age-standardized suicide rates for men by age group, UK, 1991–2006

	15 and over		15–44		45–74	
	Rate per 100,000	No. deaths	Rate per 100,000	No. deaths	Rate per 100,000	No. deaths
1991	21.0	4672	21.8	2755	19.3	1591
1992	21.1	4720	21.8	2723	19.9	1688
1993	20.5	4594	21.5	2671	19.0	1636
1994	19.9	4498	21.3	2646	17.5	1527
1995	20.2	4564	22.1	2729	17.6	1537
1996	19.2	4385	20.8	2577	16.8	1499
1997	19.0	4320	20.8	2561	16.4	1461
1998	21.1	4799	24.0	2951	17.7	1576
1999	20.7	4749	22.7	2798	18.1	1631
2000	19.9	4581	22.1	2729	17.1	1556
2001	19.3	4469	20.5	2544	17.8	1631
2002	18.7	4347	20.5	2560	16.8	1552
2003	18.1	4267	19.6	2463	16.3	1523
2004	18.1	4288	19.0	2401	16.8	1576
2005	17.5	4192	18.1	2304	16.9	1604
2006	17.4	4196	17.7	2264	17.3	1667

Source: National Statistics website: www.statistics.gov.uk. Crown copyright material is reproduced with the permission of the Controller Office of Public Sector Information (OPSI)

Table 3.2 Age-standardized suicide rates for women by age group, UK, 1991–2006

	15 and over		15–44		45–74	
	Rate per 100,000	No. deaths	Rate per 100,000	No. deaths	Rate per 100,000	No. deaths
1991	6.7	1645	5.3	658	8.3	749
1992	6.7	1658	5.5	683	8.2	757
1993	6.5	1618	5.5	687	7.3	683
1994	6.1	1547	5.3	652	6.9	655
1995	6.1	1520	5.4	662	6.8	638
1996	6.0	1492	5.6	686	6.4	603
1997	6.1	1496	5.6	684	6.8	649
1998	6.2	1555	5.9	733	6.6	632
1999	6.0	1506	5.7	714	6.2	597
2000	6.2	1543	5.8	716	6.8	647
2001	5.8	1463	5.3	676	6.4	614
2002	5.8	1479	5.5	689	6.1	598
2003	5.8	1464	5.3	671	6.3	614
2004	6.0	1562	5.4	682	6.9	682
2005	5.8	1479	5.2	660	6.7	663
2006	5.3	1358	4.4	565	6.6	659

Source: National Statistics website: www.statistics.gov.uk. Crown copyright material is reproduced with the permission of the Controller Office of Public Sector Information (OPSI)

The Office for National Statistics provides a more detailed breakdown of suicides across age groups according to gender per 100,000 of the population. The statistics for males can be seen in Table 3.1, and those for females in Table 3.2.

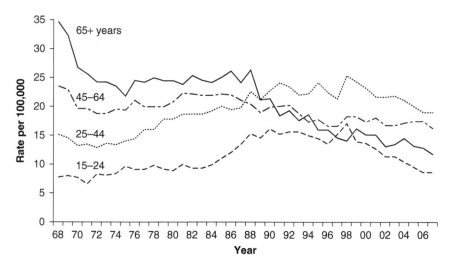

Figure 3.2 Rates of suicides and open verdicts for men in England and Wales, 1968–2007

Source: Centre for Suicide Research in Oxford: http://cebmh.warne.ox.ac.uk/csr, accessed January 2009 – reproduced with permission

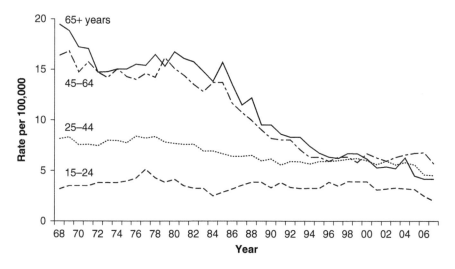

Figure 3.3 Rates of suicides and open verdicts for women in England and Wales, 1968–2007

Source: Centre for Suicide Research in Oxford: http://cebmh.warne.ox.ac.uk/csr, accessed January 2009 – reproduced with permission

Figure 3.2 provides the rates of suicides and open verdicts for males between 1968 and 2007. Figure 3.3 provides the same information for females. As can be seen from both figures, the rates for males and females have been generally falling since the late 1960s, and continue their downward trend over the last decade.

26 Counselling Suicidal Clients

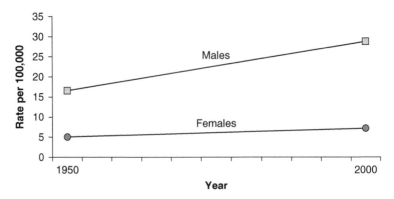

Figure 3.4 Evolution of global suicide rates, 1950–2000
Source: WHO: www.who.int/mental_health/prevention/suicide/suicide/prevent/en accessed January 2009 – reproduced with permission

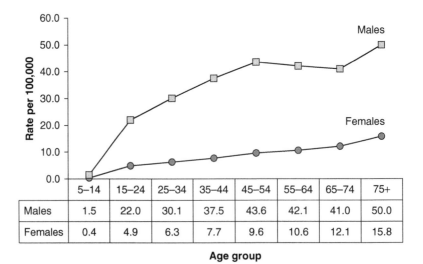

	5–14	15–24	25–34	35–44	45–54	55–64	65–74	75+
Males	1.5	22.0	30.1	37.5	43.6	42.1	41.0	50.0
Females	0.4	4.9	6.3	7.7	9.6	10.6	12.1	15.8

Age group

Figure 3.5 Distribution of global suicide rates by gender and age, 2000
Source: WHO: www.who.int/mental_health/prevention/suicide/suicide/prevent/en accessed January 2009 – reproduced with permission

Global suicide trends

WHO provides extensive reporting on international suicide statistics per country. For a detailed view see its website at: www.who.int/mental_health/prevention/suicide_rates/en/index.html.

As can be seen from Figure 3.4, there has been a steady increase in global suicide rates between 1950 and 2000, when considered per 100,000 population. While figures have risen for both males and females over this period, rates for males have increased more quickly.

Figure 3.5 provides a snapshot of the distribution of suicide rates per 100,000 for gender and age in 2000. It is evident that males present at higher suicide risk

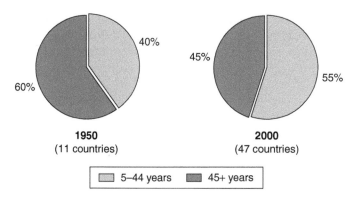

Figure 3.6 Changes in the age distribution of global cases of suicide, 1950–2000
Source: WHO: www.who.int/mental_health/prevention/suicide/suicide/prevent/en accessed January 2009 – reproduced with permission

across the age ranges than females, with an increase for both males and females in the over 75 years age group.

Figure 3.6 shows how the distribution of suicide across age had changed by 2000 from 1950. It is important to note when considering these figures that, the number of countries for which data were available increased from 11 in 1950 to 47 in 2000. It is difficult therefore to assume simply that more suicides occurred in the 5–44 years age group in 2000 than in 1950, as these figures might be skewed by the demographic profile of the additional countries for which data became available.

Suicide rates and psychopathology

Psychiatric diagnosis is strongly correlated with higher suicide risk across virtually all diagnostic categories. Bertolote and Fleischmann (2002) reviewed 31 research papers published between 1959 and 2001 to consider the relationship between psychiatric diagnosis and suicide. They suggest that over 90% of people who kill themselves have a psychiatric diagnosis. Mood disorders, and particularly depression, were strongly correlated with suicide, with other disorders including schizophrenia, substance-related disorders, personality disorders, psychotic disorders and organic mental disorders.

Baby et al. (2006) demonstrated similar findings in their study. Adjustment disorders formed the highest group, followed by depression, alcohol-related problems, schizophrenia and anti-social personality disorders. Many other studies repeat similar findings, all affirming the link between psychiatric diagnosis and completed suicide.

Suicide statistics and counselling

Suicide statistics provide important contextual information for policy makers and suicidologists. It is, of course, possible to drill down further into the data and obtain a detailed picture of the distribution of suicides across geographical locations, for example. Internationally, WHO provides detailed information on a country-by-country basis, and in the UK the Office for National Statistics provides suicide-based data for all English, Scottish, Welsh and Northern Irish regions and local authorities.

The pertinent question here is the relevance of this information for counsellors. It is undoubtedly true that there are counsellors who are also statisticians who will be interested in this information for its own sake. At the other end of the continuum will be counsellors who cannot see any relevance to their work of these numbers and trends. I personally would take a position somewhere in the middle of these two end-points. I am not a statistician; however, I can see how this information has a place in my work as a counsellor. I would argue this point from a macro or systemic perspective, believing that it is only really possible to understand my client if I can place them in the context of their own world; such statistics help to achieve that to some degree.

They are an important part of a jigsaw puzzle that helps create the bigger view of suicide, along with policy, research, counsellor experience, client experience and organizational influence. Knowing that males present at higher suicide risk across all age groups than females, or that particular age groups present at higher risk than others for both males and females, is important in understanding our client in context. As will be discussed in later chapters, statistics are insufficient in themselves to inform a complete assessment of suicide risk, but they can provide an important background in understanding our client's story. The challenge therefore for each counsellor is to find their way of integrating statistical information into their professional knowledge. By achieving such integration we help ground ourselves for working with prediction and, in all reality, best guess.

Discussion questions

1. How might you integrate statistical information about suicide into your work with suicidal clients?
2. Using your practice experience with suicidal clients, how might you understand what statistics about suicide tell us, e.g. that men are more likely to kill themselves than women?
3. How can statistical information about suicide inform your assessment of suicide potential with clients?
4. Do you notice any important differences between UK suicide trends and those internationally?

Part II

The Prediction-Prevention Model, Policy and Ethics

4 Suicide Risk Factors and Assessment

> **Chapter overview**
>
> This chapter provides an overview of the research that has, for several decades, informed suicide risk factors and subsequently the development of risk assessment tools. More pertinently for counsellors, the chapter then considers the relevance of this information for counsellors in their work, and how they can integrate such knowledge into their therapeutic relationships with suicidal clients.

The challenge for counsellors who work with suicidal clients is to find a way of integrating into their practice a diversity of information that might help them assess risk and respond appropriately. For example, post-discharge care, employment status, gender and psychopathology appear to have relevance to the likelihood of heightened suicide risk, and therefore such information might help, in part, inform an assessment of risk. However, how and whether such information is integrated into an understanding of individual presentation is more difficult to determine.

The nature of living and dying is difficult to define. For many centuries, writers, theorists, philosophers, and latterly clinicians have worked to reach a general understanding of suicide as an intrapersonal and interpersonal communication that is essentially individual. Researchers have explored different possible explanations for such thinking. Range et al. (1997) state that the process of suicide is sufficiently complex that, while our current understanding helps us predict trends of risk within certain population and demographic groups, we still do not understand enough to predict specific risk with individuals. Jenkins et al. note that 'the process whereby suicide risk is assessed is often taken for granted and rarely is it described in detail in clinical texts which tend to assume that the effective evaluation of risk necessarily follows once helper and suicidal individual meet together' (1994: 46). The difficulties facing the practitioner in working with suicidal potential are clearly articulated by Jenkins et al. Much of the literature talks about the need to assess for risk, and generic risk factors are offered as a means of facilitating that assessment. However, counsellors still need to find a way of integrating this disparate knowledge into their own working paradigm.

Suicidology can be defined as the 'study of suicide and its prevention' (*Oxford English Dictionary*, 1989). As such, a great deal of research conducted into suicidality centres predominantly around prevention. An investigation into suicide-related literature typically produces a wealth of studies that examine different factors which might help explain heightened suicide risk, therefore increasing predictability for suicide prevention. As is discussed in other chapters, however, suicide prediction is notoriously difficult. As Shneidman states, 'Most people who commit suicide talk about it; most people who talk about suicide do not commit it. Which to believe?' (1998: 57).

In attempting to increase the predictability of suicide risk, the focus of research has tended to be informed by Leenaars's (2004) 'bump on the head' metaphor. Underlying this premise is the assumption that if it were possible to strongly correlate a factor or combination of factors with suicidality, prediction would become a more efficacious task. If we could look for the 'bump on the head' as an indicator for suicide potential, prediction would be much easier. If practitioners can identify specific factors with an individual that have been demonstrated to correlate with a heightened suicide risk, then predicting the likelihood of actual suicide in that individual becomes more efficient. Research associated with risk factors for suicide conforms to this theoretical presumption. Correlations have been made between various different factors – demographic, psychopathological, occupational, etc. – yet the conundrum posed by Shneidman remains at the centre of the difficulty of suicide prediction and prevention. The 'factor driven' search for knowledge in suicidality provides greater understanding of general processes and trends in suicidology, while the bridge between general factors and individual risk remains tenuous.

However, making the assertion that research highlighting general risk factors offers little to the counsellor would fail to acknowledge important areas of understanding and learning that have emerged from such research. For example, the disproportionately high numbers of completed suicides amongst young males in the UK, as identified through statistical evaluation and research, has enabled services to target that particular group, and has therefore informed policy development in such areas. This has, in turn, arguably contributed to a reduction in numbers of suicides in that group, given the greater access of support services (Department of Health, 2007).

In considering suicide risk assessment, links between specific demographic, psychopathological and social factors and heightened suicide risk are highly relevant. Table 4.1 provides a summary of factors identified through research that have been associated with higher suicide risk. This table is based on my own review of the literature, together with a variety of other sources, including Appleby et al. (2001), Battle (1991), Battle et al. (1993), Bernard and Bernard (1985), Gilliland (1985), Hazell and Lewin (1993), Hersh (1985), Ruddell and Curwen (2008) and Williams and Morgan (1994).

While the primary factors are summarized in Table 4.1, this does not illustrate the extent to which each factor is correlated with suicide risk. For example, 'occupational factors' is an umbrella term that indicates a relationship between occupation or employment/unemployment and suicide risk. A closer analysis of the data, however, provides great variation between specific occupation groups and suicidality. Unemployment is strongly correlated with a higher suicide risk (Johansson and Sundquist, 1997), while particular occupational groups, such as those working in medicine, veterinary science and farming, show different trends in suicide potential (Hawton and van Heeringen, 2002; Kposowa, 2001).

Table 4.1 Factors associated with higher suicide risk

Gender, e.g. males generally present with greater risk across age groups
Age, e.g. males age 14–25 and people over 75 years
Relationships: single, widowed, divorced, separated
Social isolation
Psychopathology (including)

- schizophrenia
- mood disorders, including depression
- psychosis
- post-traumatic stress disorder
- affective disorders, including bipolar affective disorder
- organic disorders
- personality disorders, e.g. sociopathy, aggression

Alcohol and drug use
Hopelessness
Occupational factors, e.g. unemployment, retirement
Occupational groups, e.g. medicine, veterinary science, farmers
History of childhood sexual abuse
History of childhood physical abuse
Adult sexual assault
Specific suicide plan formulated
Prior suicide attempt and/or family history of suicide or suicide attempts
Physical illness, e.g. terminal illness, biochemical, hormonal
Bereavement or recent trauma
Significant and unexplained mood change

The same is true for psychopathological factors. Different rates of completed suicides and predictability based on the presence of psychopathological processes differ between different diagnoses. Depression and hopelessness, it is argued, are the most significant factors in suicide prediction (Schwartz and Cohen, 2001; Szanto et al., 1998), and counsellors must be sensitive in their assessment of suicide risk to the presence of these factors. As one counsellor stated during an interview, 'instead of being overwhelmed by the client's persistent hopelessness ... [we ought] to try and explore with them the meaning of what suicide is for them'. However, there is a relationship between most of the primary diagnostic criteria and a higher degree of suicidality. For example, borderline personality disorder (Kelly et al., 2000), paranoia (Saarinen et al., 1999), schizophrenia (Schwartz, 2000), affective disorders (Baxter and Appleby, 1999), and post-traumatic stress disorder (Amir et al., 1999) are all strongly correlated with a higher suicide risk.

It is helpful for counsellors to understand the relationship between risk factors and research: that is to say, how research has informed our understanding of risk factors and how that understanding has, in turn, been applied to practice. Table 4.2 provides a list of some of the principal suicide risk factors with some references to research. This list is intended not to be exhaustive of all risk factors or all research, but rather to be illustrative of the research–practice relationship.

The 'factor-based' understanding of suicidality has undoubtedly informed approaches to risk assessment. Many existing risk assessment tools and questionnaires are based around the identification and subsequent weighting of such factors by assessing counsellors. Their efficacy in identifying suicide risk and in helping to increase rates of successful prediction in general terms could be asserted; the same degree of efficacy with individuals is less clear. Lewishohn et al. (1989) reported on a meta-analysis of suicide prediction measures for use with adolescents, undertaken by the National Institute of Mental Health in the United States, concluding that out of those evaluated, only two were demonstrated to have any clinical efficacy in helping to identify suicide risk in patients. The two exceptions were the Beck Suicide Intent Scale (Beck et al., 1979) and the Lethality of Suicide Attempt Rating Scale (Smith et al., 1984).

Table 4.2 Suicide risk factors with illustrative research

Research overview	Authors
Occupational factors	
Unemployment is an important social variable that is associated with an increased suicide risk	Johansson and Sundquist (1997)
Unemployment and occupation are closely correlated with an increased suicide risk. This study additionally contradicts earlier research that had only suggested a link between male suicide risk and unemployment and instead suggests a more enduring relationship for females and unemployment	Kposowa (2001)
Gender/age-specific factors	
Suicidal ideation seemed to be more frequently expressed by females rather than males at both mild and moderate levels of depression amongst adolescents	Allison et al. (2001)
Within the psychiatric population, suicide risk is more than 10 times higher in both genders in comparison to a non-psychiatric population	Baxter and Appleby (1999)
Men who are experiencing severe depression are at a greater risk of suicide than women with the same diagnosis	Blair-West and Mellsop (2001)
Older adolescent males are more likely to die in a suicide attempt than younger males due to the lethality of the suicide method chosen	Brent et al. (1999)
Age and gender are important factors when assessing for the appropriateness of hospitalization with suicidal patients	Hirschfeld (2001)
Gender is an important factor when assessing for increased suicide risk	Qin et al. (2000)
Male patients with bipolar affective disorder with significant depressive features were more likely to attempt suicide	Oquendo et al. (2000)
In almost all industrialized countries, males over 75 years have the highest suicide rate amongst all age groups	Szanto et al. (2002)
Moderate levels of depression can be associated with suicidal ideation, particularly in females	Watt and Sharp (2001)
Gender is an important factor when considering suicide risk amongst adolescents	Woods et al. (1997)
Psychopathology	
Depression/hopelessness	
Depression is strongly correlated with a higher suicide risk	Angst et al. (1999)
Severe depression is linked with a heightened suicide risk and should be included as a factor in an assessment of risk	Blair-West and Mellsop (2001)
Depression is a particular risk factor for higher suicide risk, especially when linked with anxiety and agitation	Fawcett (2001)

Research overview	Authors
Hopelessness should be a factor in considering hospitalizing suicidal patients	Hirschfeld (2001)
High numbers of suicidal patients within the French mental health system are also receiving treatment for depression	Lejoyeux and Rouillon (1996)
When considering the established link between depression and suicide, clinicians must also note that a suicide attempt may be an 'ecstatic' rather than a 'melancholic' act. This needs to inform risk assessment	Maltsberger (1997)
Clinicians encountering patients with depressive disorders should be proficient in the assessment and treatment of depression with suicidality	Nemeroff et al. (2001)
Bipolar disorder, when associated with significant depressive episodes, was correlated with a higher risk of suicide	Oquendo et al. (2000)
It is important to consider depression and the existence of depressive symptoms when assessing for suicide risk	Schneider et al. (2001b)
Depression is an important risk factor in the assessment of risk of suicide	Schwartz (2000)
Depressive symptoms correlate most closely with higher suicide risk	Schwartz and Cohen (2001)
Hopelessness and depression correlate closely with higher suicide risks	Szanto et al. (1998)
Depression is the most common diagnosis amongst suicidal older people	Szanto et al. (2002)
Moderate levels of depression can be associated with suicidal ideation, particularly in females	Watt and Sharp (2001)
Depression is strongly linked with a heightened adolescent suicide risk	Woods et al. (1997)
Personality disorder	
Borderline personality disorder can be seen as a 'high suicide risk' diagnosis within a psychiatric population and needs to be considered when assessing suicide risk	Baxter and Appleby (1999)
In assessing suicide risk, a history of deliberate self-harm and the presence of comorbid psychiatric and personality disorders are particularly important	Hawton and van Heeringen (2002)
Patients with personality disorders are most likely to act out suicidal thoughts by comparison to patients with major depression and comorbid major depression	Kelly et al. (2000)
Aggressive personality traits and a diagnosis of borderline personality disorder are strongly linked to a higher suicide risk in adolescents	Marttunen and Pelkonen (2000)
One in 10 patients with a personality disorder diagnosis complete suicide, and hospitalization is of 'unproven value' in preventing suicide within this group	Paris (2002)
Self-harm	
In assessing suicide risk, a history of deliberate self-harm and the presence of comorbid psychiatric and personality disorders are particularly important	Hawton and van Heeringen (2002)
Identifies self-destructive processes as important factors in understanding suicidality	Orbach (1997)
Paranoia	
Withdrawal from personal relationships together with an increased severity of paranoia are high factors for increased suicide risk in individuals with schizophrenia	Saarinen et al. (1999)
Mood disorders	
There is a strong link in the research literature between mood disorders and suicide risk	Angst et al. (1999)
Mood disorders show a strong link to adolescent suicide	Marttunen and Pelkonen (2000)

(Continued)

Table 4.2 (Continued)

Research overview	Authors
Bipolar disorder, particularly when associated with depression, was a significant factor in heightened suicide risk	Oquendo et al. (2000)
Mood disorder can indicate higher suicide risk	Sharma et al. (1998)
Mood disorder is associated with suicide risk	Sher et al. (2001)
The first 7 to 12 years from the onset of bipolar disorder represents the highest risk period for suicide	Tsai et al. (2002)

Schizophrenia/psychosis

Schizophrenia is significantly correlated to a higher risk of suicide	Baxter and Appleby (1999)
Individuals with schizophrenia and schizo-affective disorder are at increased risk for completed suicide and suicide attempts	Harkavy-Friedman et al. (2001)
Psychosis is an important factor when assessing for the appropriateness of hospitalization for suicidal patients	Hirschfeld (2001)
Schizophrenia is an important risk factor that mental health professionals should consider in the assessment of suicide risk	Schwartz (2000)
Patients diagnosed with schizophrenia often use more violent means of attempting suicide. As such, psychiatric hospitals should be located so that the availability of such means is reduced, i.e. away from train lines, motorways	Shah and Ganesvaran (1999)

Affective disorders

Affective disorders are associated with a higher risk of suicide	Baxter and Appleby (1999)
Anger strongly correlates with increased suicide risk amongst an adolescent population	Cautin et al. (2001)
In the 12–15 age group, regular perpetrators of violence were also strongly represented in a higher suicide risk population	Evans et al. (2001)
Impulsivity is a significant risk factor associated with a higher risk of suicide	Fawcett (2001)
Students who have been known to commit violent acts should be adequately assessed for violence exposure and symptoms of psychological trauma, with special attention given to the suicide potential of violent females	Flannery et al. (2001)
Expressed anger can be an important indication for heightened suicide risk	Hodapp et al. (1997)
Clinicians need to consider the role of impulsivity and its relationship with suicidality when considering predictive factors	Horesh et al. (1997)
Impulsivity is an important factor for clinicians to consider when assessing suicide risk in adolescents	Woods et al. (1997)

Anxiety/panic disorders

Anxiety, panic attacks and agitation are all closely correlated with a heightened suicide risk	Fawcett (2001)

Comorbidity

Comorbidity and psychopathology can be closely correlated with suicide risk amongst adolescents	De Hert et al. (2001)

Post-traumatic stress disorder

PTSD patients present with high suicide risk and those involved in offering interventions to such patients should focus on problem-solving strategies	Amir et al. (1999)
Suicide risk is significantly higher in PTSD patients, with higher numbers of suicide attempts made by patients with a PTSD diagnosis but without	Ferrada-Noli et al. (1998)

Research overview	Authors
evidence of depression. Depression can act as a mediating factor against suicide in PTSD patients	
In assessing risk, practitioners must acknowledge any diagnosis of PTSD but additionally pay careful attention to perceived levels of impulsivity and to social support, which was identified as helping to reduce levels of risk	Kotler et al. (2001)
War veterans can present with a higher degree of suicide risk	Lambert and Fowler (1997)
Demographic and biographical factors	
Personality	
Life dissatisfaction is an important influencing factor on the risk of suicide	Koivumaa-Honkanen et al. (2001)
Aggressive personality traits are strongly linked to adolescent suicide risk	Marttunen and Pelkonen (2000)
Personality traits, background factors, phenomenological states, self-destructive processes and pathological states can be important personality factors in understanding suicidality	Orbach (1997)
Family history of suicide and/or psychiatric problems	
Clinicians should consider whether there is a family history of suicide, given its link with a higher suicide risk	Sharma et al. (1998)
History of child sexual abuse and/or adult sexual assault	
A history of child sexual abuse is an important factor when assessing suicide risk	Grilo et al. (1999)
Child sexual abuse can lead to an increased level of suicide risk	Plunkett et al. (2001)
Childhood sexual abuse and adult experience of sexual assault were indicators for possible increased suicide risk	Stepakoff (1998)
It is important to consider a history of child sexual abuse and adulthood sexual violence in the assessment of suicide risk	Thakkar et al. (2000)
History of physical abuse	
Physically abused adolescents experienced a combination of risk factors related to increased suicidal thoughts, attitudes, and behaviours	Kaplan et al. (1999)
Sexuality	
There is strong evidence to suggest that an association exists between suicide risk and bisexuality or homosexuality in males	Remafedi et al. (1998)
Sexual orientation can be a correlating factor with higher suicide risk amongst adolescents	Russell and Joyner (2001)
There is evidence to suggest that young lesbian and gay men have a higher risk of suicide than other young people	Warwick et al. (2001)
Social isolation	
Withdrawal from personal relationships together with an increased severity of paranoia are high factors for increased suicide risk in individuals with schizophrenia	Saarinen et al. (1999)
Prisoners	
The highest risk period for a new prison inmate is immediately following admission and two months following for prisoners on remand. For long-term prisoners, suicide risk correlates with the length of sentence and slightly increases with the time of custody	Frottier et al. (2002)

(Continued)

Table 4.2 (Continued)

Research overview	Authors
Suicide rates in a prison population are 11 to 14 times greater than within the general population	McKee (1998)
Medical and physical factors	
Physical illness	
There is a strong correlation between organic dementia and heightened suicide risk	Schneider et al. (2001a)
Within three to five months of a diagnosis of cancer, higher levels of suicide risk were found amongst Japanese cancer patients. The authors highlight the importance of considering psychological wellbeing as a consequence of physical ill-health when considering suicide risk	Tanaka et al. (1999)
Identify heightened suicide risk and patients who have suffered a stroke	Teasdale and Engberg (2001)
Biochemical factors	
Changes in body biochemistry can be directly linked with violent suicidal behaviour, with intervention needing to focus on rebalancing biochemical dysfunction	Brunner and Bronisch (1999)
Genetic factors	
Suggests a genetic contribution to suicidal behaviour based on twin studies	Roy (2001)
Expressed thoughts of suicide	
An expressed intention to act on suicidal thoughts is an important factor when considering hospitalization for suicidal patients	Hirschfeld (2001)
If psychiatric chart notes include expressed suicidal intent by the patient, this is a strong indicator for a current increased risk of suicide	Sharma et al. (1998)
Previous attempts at suicide	
Prior suicide attempts are a strong indicator for possible future suicide risk and need to be considered by clinicians in their assessments	Marttunen and Pelkonen (2000)
Previous suicide attempts can indicate a higher risk of suicide	Sharma et al. (1998)
Alcohol or substance abuse	
Particularly amongst males, but for both genders generally, substance abuse is a significant risk factor for suicide in a psychiatric population	Baxter and Appleby (1999)
Substance abuse shows a strong link to adolescent suicide	Marttunen and Pelkonen (2000)
Psychiatric illness and substance abuse are strongly correlated to suicide risk	Torre et al. (2001)
Substance use is strongly linked with a higher suicide risk in adolescents	Woods et al. (1997)
Availability of method	
Intent and availability of means of suicide are important considerations in assessing for hospitalization	Hirschfeld (2001)
Availability of firearms can significantly increase the level of suicide risk	Kaplan et al. (1999)
Patients diagnosed with schizophrenia often use more violent means of attempting suicide. As such, psychiatric hospitals should be located so that the availability of such means are reduced, i.e. away from train lines, motorways	Shah and Ganesvaran (1999)

The identification of factors that can be positively correlated with a higher risk of suicide helps develop understanding of the generalities of suicide risk. It could be argued, however, that the subsequent development of risk assessment tools, questionnaires and measures, etc., based on the identification of factors, creates an expectation within organizations and counsellors that suicide risk prediction is much more possible. For those counsellors who complete a risk assessment measure with a client who then goes on to kill themselves, the expectation–outcome deficit becomes more difficult to comprehend. If the subtext of factor-based suicidology is that suicide potential is predictable through the application of general trends to individual situations, getting it 'right' or 'wrong' becomes an understandable fear for counsellors.

The application of knowledge

For some counsellors, assessment is an integral and daily aspect of their work: from an initial 'intake' interview, through to regular review and reassessment of client presentation and need. For others, the concept of 'assessment' presents significant philosophical and theoretical challenges that appear to contradict with core beliefs. I have discussed the benefits of collaborative assessment strategies elsewhere (Reeves, 2008). McLeod (2003) identifies other benefits of a pre-counselling assessment. I would additionally argue that many of these factors remain relevant for assessment during counselling, and for an assessment of suicide risk:

- establishing a rapport
- making a clinical diagnosis
- assessing the strengths and weaknesses of the client
- giving information
- enabling the client to feel understood
- arriving at a case formulation or plan
- giving hope
- gathering information about cultural needs and expectations
- explaining the way that therapy works; obtaining informed consent
- providing opportunity for the client to ask questions
- giving a taste of the treatment
- motivating the client; preventing non-attendance
- arranging for any further assessments that might be necessary (e.g. medical)
- selecting clients for treatment
- selecting treatments or therapists for the client
- giving the client a basis for choice of whether to enter counselling
- making practical arrangements (time, place, access)
- providing data for research or audit (2003: 330).

In Table 4.3, I reproduce what I believe to be some key general assessment areas that can considerably help inform the definition and focus of counselling with clients.

It is perhaps in the area of risk, and the application of factor-based approaches to suicide risk prediction, that counsellors can struggle most. While some counselling approaches encompass the administration of tools and questionnaires with clients, a great many others do not. However, counsellors are

Table 4.3 Outline structure for assessment at the beginning of counselling

Presenting problems

- What is the client's problem/difficulty? How do they define it?
- How long has the client experienced problems for?
- How severely do they experience their problems (0–10 scale often helpful) and does this change? If so, what factors make things worse or better?
- Are the problems specific or do they cause difficulties in other areas of the client's life?
- Have they tried any strategies to improve things? If so, have these been successful?

Functioning and social support

- Is the client experiencing any problems with sleeping, appetite, sex, concentration, motivation, energy levels? If so, are these problems new or long-standing?
- What support does the client have, e.g. family, friends, colleagues?
- Does the client feel able to access support at particular times of difficulty? If not, what inhibits them talking to someone about things?
- How does the client feel they are coping with daily demands, e.g. job, studies, other responsibilities?

Family and relationships

- Who is in the client's family (sometimes helpful to draw a genogram – a pictorial representation of the client's family – to quickly highlight important relationships and dynamics that might be relevant to the client's problems)?
- How much contact does the client have with family, friends, colleagues? Is the client socially isolated?
- How would the client describe the quality of their personal relationships?
- Is there a history of previous significant relationships?

Medical/psychiatric history

- Has the client ever experienced emotional/psychological difficulties previously? If so, when, and what was their nature?
- Does the client use alcohol or drugs to cope with their problems? If so, how does this affect the client's mood or perception of themselves?
- Is the client taking any prescribed medication for their problems? If so, how does this medication affect the client's mood or perception of their problems?
- Has the client experienced, or does the client experience currently, any medical conditions that they attribute meaning to in relation to their psychological distress?
- Has the client ever been given a diagnosis in relation to their psychological distress?

Sense of self

- How would the client describe their degree of self-confidence?
- How would the client describe their sense of self-esteem? Do they like who they are?
- Does the client feel valued by others?
- How does the client feel/think about their physical self (their body image)?

Risk

- Does the client have any thoughts of suicide? Are these long-standing, impulsive or persistent?
- How does the client manage their thoughts of suicide? How do they not act on them?
- Does the client hurt themselves in any way as a means of coping with their problems?
- Has the client ever hurt anybody else or feel as if they might want to hurt someone else?
- Does the client appear to be looking after themselves or self-neglectful?

Psychological mindedness

- What has brought the client to counselling now?
- What does the client understand about counselling?

- What does the client hope for from counselling? What do they want to change?
- How does the client relate to you in the session, e.g. eye contact, understanding questions? Does the client have an 'emotional language'?
- Might the client benefit from short-term, long-term and/or group therapy?
- Do you have the capacity and experience to work with this client and their presenting problems, e.g. do you need to refer to other specialist services or for another form of therapy?
- Does the client appear wiling and able to engage in the therapeutic process?

Source: Reeves, 2008: 67–68

increasingly required by their employing organizations to use such tools in the assessment stages of counselling, as a means of identifying high suicide risk clients early on. In the UK, the Clinical Outcome in Routine Evaluation outcome measure (CORE-OM: CORE Systems Group, 1998) is such a tool. Developed with the intention of benchmarking services, it is increasingly being used to help identify the presence of risk factors and to provide measurement of those factors. This was never an intention in the development of CORE-OM. Counselling services increasingly make allocation decisions based on CORE-OM risk data in isolation, sometimes without further counsellor assessment of risk (Reeves and Coldridge, 2007).

However, while CORE-OM has undoubted positive qualities both for benchmarking and in the therapeutic process itself, caution must be exercised when using CORE-OM risk data without further dialogic exploration with a client. As Reeves and Coldridge (2007) highlight, risk data do not necessarily present the full picture of suicidality. One counsellor articulated this well during an interview when she said, 'if something comes up on the CORE I will discuss it with them and find out what it means. I've had a couple of CORE forms that have been filled in and given to me and the risk looks quite high, but when I have actually discussed it with clients it turned out to be 5 years ago when they had an attempted suicide, and there's actually nothing now but they didn't quite understand. It is worth checking out.' More worrying is the opposite of this scenario: when clients score zero on CORE-OM for risk, but on further exploration are identified by the counsellor as being at high risk of suicide. This is not a problem with CORE-OM *per se*, but rather reflects that clients may choose not to disclose risk on forms. This is an inherent problem with all questionnaire-based suicide risk identification and assessment tools.

One of the perceived advantages of suicide risk assessment tools is that they do provide 'evidence' that risk was explored at all. One counsellor said, 'It's that justification and validation isn't it, of why you did this, this and this – and it has greatly affected my practice and how I am thinking about what is best for the client but how it would knock on to the establishment here and the families – if something was to happen, you would then go back – that's so important about beginning to validate why you took that step.'

Instead, counsellors are able to use appropriate records of sessions to fully note the nature and degree of suicide risk presented by a client, and how that risk was responded to. This arguably provides a more accurate account of the assessment of risk undertaken by the counsellor, how the client responded, and what was agreed between them as to the best intervention to safeguard their wellbeing. This is discussed in more detail in Part VI, 'Key Aspects of Counselling with Suicidal Clients'.

It is important that counsellors consider how to use generic risk factors when working with individual potential. It is difficult and demanding to work with risk in an ongoing way whilst, at the same time, keeping in mind a client's potential to kill themselves. *Luke* is an interesting example of this difficulty.

Luke	Risk factors
Luke is a *22-year-old* university student. He presents at the university counselling service. During assessment it transpires that he is *socially isolated* with few friends. He has little contact with his family and has *very few* sources of support. He uses *recreational drugs* regularly and *drinks heavily*. He is not enjoying his course and has *little motivation* for many other activities. He spends a great deal of time in his room. He has come to the counselling service following the recent *breakdown of a relationship*. He has a history of *self-injury*, though says that he is not injuring himself currently. Says he has no plans to kill himself, though sometimes *wishes he could go to sleep 'and not wake up'*. Luke feels embarrassed and does not want anyone to contact his general practitioner.	Young Male Socially isolated No support Drug/alcohol use Loss of motivation/interest Relationship breakdown History of self-harm Suicidal ideation

Luke's presentation is, in all likelihood, not uncommon in counselling services for young people. That is to say, whilst Luke's story is unique to him, it has elements that will be familiar to counsellors. The difficulty with Luke's presentation is this: in the brief information available, it is possible to identify 10 risk factors that would correlate with a higher suicide risk potential. The risk for Luke is that, despite stating he has no intention to kill himself, under the influence of alcohol or drugs (both reducing important inhibitions that might otherwise prevent him from acting on his suicidal ideation) he makes an impulsive attempt on his life. Given that young males are more likely to choose methods of high lethality, according to research, there is a high chance that if Luke tried to kill himself, he would succeed.

Many counsellors may feel that there are insufficient grounds to break Luke's confidentiality at this point, and will contract for him to reattend for ongoing counselling. Therein lies the difficulties for the counsellor: the risk is defined by Luke's subsequent actions beyond the boundaries of this particular session. If Luke returns for his next counselling appointment, the counsellor will consider their rationale for maintaining confidentiality to be sound. In the tragic event of Luke's suicide, the counsellor may fear repercussions on the grounds that the research evidence pointed to the likelihood of that outcome. The 'wisdom' of the counsellor's decision in response to Luke's presentation to maintain confidentiality will only be affirmed or otherwise by Luke's actions at a later stage.

How the counsellor responds to Luke will also be strongly shaped by the organization in which they work. For example, a counsellor seeing Luke in private practice or other non-statutory setting might feel more inclined to contract with Luke for further counselling, and not seek referral. However, a counsellor working in a statutory setting, such as in health or social care, may feel more pressure to refer from organizational expectation or policy. Risk factors are framed not only by their meaning for each client concerned, but also by the context in which they are being interpreted.

The 'risk' for the counsellor lies not only in Luke's ongoing wellbeing, but also in playing Russian roulette with risk factors. Shneidman's words take on a greater degree of professional menace: 'Most people who commit suicide talk about it; most people who talk about suicide do not commit it. Which to believe?' (1998: 57).

When we consider Josh later in this book, we will discuss how it is possible for counsellors to make use of risk factor research to help inform and support their decision making processes, as opposed to becoming anxiety driven. The danger is that counsellors, fearing litigation and blame, move to a position where they refer clients sooner, or make decisions to break client confidentiality as a defensive strategy. This is not conducive to facilitative counselling, and both client and counsellor suffer in this process.

Discussion questions

1. How many of the risk factors identified in this chapter could be found in your current client work?
2. Are there any risk factors listed in this chapter that would apply to you? How 'at risk' are you? What does this mean?
3. As a counsellor, how can you effectively make use of risk factors in (a) your assessments with new clients and (b) your ongoing counselling?
4. How would you respond to Luke, given the suicide risk he presents with?

5 The Influence of Policy and the Prediction–Prevention Culture

> **Chapter overview**
>
> This chapter examines recent UK policy on suicide reduction and its implications for counselling with suicidal clients. Key UK prevention strategies are outlined in: the *Suicide Prevention Strategy for England* (Department of Health, 2002); *Choose Life: A National Strategy and Action Plan to Prevent Suicide in Scotland* (Scottish Executive, 2002); *Protect Life – A Shared Vision: The Northern Ireland Suicide Prevention and Action Plan* (DHSSPS, 2006); and *Talk To Me: A National Action Plan to Reduce Suicide and Self Harm in Wales 2008–2013* (Welsh Assembly, 2008). The concept of the *prediction–prevention culture* is introduced and discussed.

The meaning of suicide has been a source of exploration and enquiry by writers, philosophers and theorists for centuries. Over the last few decades, and particularly since Durkheim's seminal text *Suicide: A Study in Sociology* (1951), suicide has increasingly been investigated through positivist study, with less research investigating existential or individual meaning (Leenaars, 2004). In searching for understanding, greater emphasis has been placed on the *who* of suicide as opposed to the *why*. Researchers have attempted to discover particular demographic or sociological profiles that might help identify who is more likely to take their own lives in an attempt to inform prevention; the meaning of suicide has become less significant than the trends surrounding suicide.

In the UK, the policy imperative over the last two decades has been suicide reduction (Thornicroft, 2000). Several key policy documents, including *Saving Lives: Our Healthier Nation*, the *National Service Framework for Mental Health* and the *Suicide Prevention Strategy* (Department of Health, 1999a; 1999b; 2002), have presented an integrated framework within which suicide reduction is a key factor. The reduction and prevention agendas contain key principles for all involved in mental health provision. This stated policy does not engage in a debate as to whether suicide should always be prevented. Thus, the shades of grey, which are predominant in any discussion around suicide, are not included, and individual free will around the choice to end one's life instead becomes a prevention priority. It is within this policy context that counsellors undertake clinical practice with clients, some of whom will experience suicidal thoughts or intent.

High suicide rates and how they are perceived by the media to negatively reflect upon the care offered by mental health services is a widely recognized political difficulty (Hallam, 2002). The *National Service Framework for Mental Health* and the *Suicide Prevention Strategy for England* set targets for suicide reduction of 20% by 2010; the NSF stated that this reduction would prevent 4000 deaths (Department of Health, 1999b; 2002).

The available literature demonstrates that this trend within policy development in the UK has been paralleled at an international level (Jenkins and Singh, 2000; Weiss et al., 2001). National and international policy development clearly places prevention as a central philosophical strategy in responding to suicide. Several factors identified in the literature indicate possible reasons why suicide prevention has been the policy imperative. These include:

- The relatively high numbers of suicidal clients seen by mental health practitioners (Rubenstein, 2003).
- The high rates of suicides and suicide attempts at an international level (World Health Organization, 2003).
- The increasing rates of suicide in specific demographic groups such as young people (Appleby et al., 2001).
- The public criticism in the media following homicides involving people with mental health problems and government 'reaction' to this (Hallam, 2002).
- Practitioners' fear of litigation and of 'getting it wrong' (Baerger, 2001).

In 1996 the National Confidential Inquiry into Suicide and Homicide by Patients with a Mental Illness was established in the UK. The purpose of this inquiry was twofold:

- To collect detailed clinical data on people who die by suicide or commit homicide and who have been in contact with mental health services.
- To make recommendations on clinical practice and policy that will reduce the risk of suicide and homicide by people under mental health care (Appleby et al., 2001: 11).

This was a major study that collected together clinical and practice data to help inform suicide (and homicide) prevention strategies. Recommendations followed across a number of practice areas, which included: the need for a broad-based suicide prevention strategy in each country; patients identified as needing priority intervention; developments in the existing care programme approach (a multidisciplinary planning strategy to identify and coordinate post-discharge care plans); the need for training in risk assessment (every three years); specific recommendations regarding ethnic minorities and the criminal justice system; and ways of reducing the stigma of mental illness. Additionally, the report *Safety First* identified 12 points for a 'safer service'. These were:

- Staff training in the management of risk – both suicide and violence – every three years.
- All patients with severe mental illness and a history of self-harm or violence to receive the most intensive level of care.
- Individual care plans to specify action to be taken if a patient is non-compliant or fails to attend.
- Prompt access to services for people in crisis and for their families.
- Assertive outreach teams to prevent loss of contact with vulnerable and high risk patients.
- Atypical anti-psychotic medication to be available for all patients with severe mental illness who are non-compliant with 'typical' drugs because of side-effects.
- Strategy for dual diagnosis covering training on the management of substance misuse, joint working with substance misuse services, and staff with specific responsibility to develop the local service.
- Inpatient wards to remove or cover all likely ligature points, including all non-collapsible curtain rails.

- Follow-up within seven days of discharge from hospital for everyone with severe mental illness or a history of self-harm in the previous three months.
- Patients with a history of self-harm in the last three months to receive supplies of medication covering no more than two weeks.
- Local arrangements for information sharing with criminal justice agencies.
- Policy ensuring post-incident multi-disciplinary case review and information to be given to families of involved patients (Appleby et al., 2001: 10).

Following the report *Safety First*, major prevention strategies were put forward in England, Scotland, Northern Ireland and Wales. Already published are the *National Suicide Prevention Strategy for England* (Department of Health, 2002); *Choose Life: A National Strategy and Action Plan to Prevent Suicide in Scotland* (Scottish Executive, 2002); and *Protect Life – A Shared Vision: The Northern Ireland Suicide Prevention Strategy and Action Plan, 2006–2011* (Department of Health Social Services and Public Safety, 2006). At the time of writing the Welsh Assembly had issued a consultation document as part of their suicide prevention plan, *Talk To Me: A National Action Plan to Reduce Suicide and Self Harm in Wales 2008–2013* (2008).

National Suicide Prevention Strategy for England

The *National Suicide Prevention Strategy for England* outlines six goals (Department of Health, 2002: 5–6):

Goal 1: to reduce risk in key high risk groups. Actions to be taken include:

- Local mental health services will be supported in implementing 12 points to a safer service; these aim to improve clinical risk management.
- A national collaborative system is being established for the monitoring of non-fatal deliberate self-harm.
- A pilot project targeting mental health promotion in young men will be established and evaluated for national roll-out.

Goal 2: to promote mental wellbeing in the wider population. Actions to be taken include:

- A cross-government network will be developed to address a range of social issues that impact on people with mental health problems, e.g. unemployment and housing.
- The suicide prevention programme will link closely with the NIMHE substance misuse programme to:
  - Improve the clinical management of alcohol and drug misuse among young men who carry out deliberate self-harm.
  - Make available training in suicide risk assessment for substance misuse services.

Goal 3: to reduce the availability and lethality of suicide methods. Actions to be taken include:

- NIMHE will identify additional steps that can be taken to promote safer prescribing of anti-depressants and analgesics.

- NIMHE will help local services identify their suicide 'hotspots', e.g. railways, bridges, and take steps to improve safety at these.
- NIMHE has since been replaced by the National Mental Health Development Unit (NMHDU).

Goal 4: to improve the reporting of suicidal behaviour in the media. Actions to be taken include:

- A media action plan is being developed as part of the mental health promotion campaign, Mind Out for Mental Health, which will include:
  - Guidance on the representation of suicide into workshops held with students at journalism colleges.
  - Round table discussion sessions with leaders in mental health and senior journalists.
  - A series of roadshows at which frontline journalists can discuss responsible reporting.
  - A feature on suicide in media journals, e.g. *Press Gazette, Media Week, British Journalism Review.*

Goal 5: to promote research on suicide and suicide prevention. Actions to be taken include:

- A national collaborative group will oversee a programme of research to support the strategy, including research on ligatures used in hanging and suicides using firearms.
- Current evidence on suicide prevention will be made available to local services through NIMHE's website and development centres.

Goal 6: to improve monitoring of progress towards the Saving Lives: Our Healthier Nation *target for reducing suicide.* Actions to be taken include:

- A new strategy group of experts and other key stakeholders will be established.
- The new strategy group will regularly monitor suicides by age and gender, by people under mental health care, by different methods and by social class.

Choose Life: A National Strategy and Action Plan to Prevent Suicide in Scotland

The *Choose Life* strategy outlined seven main objectives (Scotstish Executive, 2002: 21):

- *Objective 1: early prevention and intervention.* Providing earlier intervention and support to prevent problems and reduce the risks that might lead to suicidal behaviour.
- *Objective 2: responding to immediate crisis.* Providing support and services to people at risk and people in crisis, to provide an immediate crisis response and to help reduce the severity of any immediate problem.
- *Objective 3: longer-term work to provide hope and support recovery.* Providing ongoing support and services to enable people to recover and deal with the issues that may be contributing to their suicidal behaviour.

- *Objective 4: coping with suicidal behaviour and completed suicide.* Providing effective support to those who are affected by suicidal behaviour or a completed suicide.
- *Objective 5: promoting greater public awareness and encouraging people to seek help early.* Ensuring greater public awareness of positive mental health and well-being, suicidal behaviour, potential problems and risks amongst all age groups and encouraging people to seek help early.
- *Objective 6: supporting the media.* Ensuring that any depiction or reporting by any section of the media of a completed suicide or suicidal behaviour is undertaken sensitively and appropriately and with due respect for confidentiality.
- *Objective 7: knowing what works.* Improving the quality, collection, availability and dissemination of information on issues relating to suicide and suicidal behaviour and on effective interventions to ensure the better design and implementation of responses and services and use of resources.

Protect Life – A Shared Vision: The Northern Ireland Suicide Prevention and Action Plan, 2006–2011

The key objectives of the Northern Ireland plan are (Department of Health, Social Services and Public Safety, 2006: 19):

- To raise awareness of mental health and wellbeing issues.
- To ensure early recognition of mental ill-health, and to provide appropriate follow-up action by support services.
- To develop coordinated, effective, accessible and timely response mechanisms for those seeking help.
- To provide appropriate training for people dealing with suicide and mental health issues.
- To enhance the support role currently carried out by the voluntary/community sectors, bereaved families and individuals who have made previous suicide attempts.
- To support the media in the development and implementation guidelines for a suitable response to suicide-related matters.
- To provide support for research and evaluation of relevant suicide and self-harm issues.
- To restrict access, where possible, to the means of carrying out suicide.

The specific targets set by the plan were (2006: 20–21):

- To reduce the proportion of people with a potential psychiatric disorder by a tenth by 2010.
- To obtain a 10% reduction in the overall suicide rate by 2008.
- To reduce the overall suicide rate by a further 5% by 2011.
- To change public attitudes towards mental health and suicide.
- To develop and roll out suicide/depression awareness training across a range of professions.
- To improve accuracy in suicide and self-harm data collection.
- To reduce self-harm.
- To improve the availability of services for people who have self-harmed in all trusts.
- To develop and increase the uptake of bereavement/community support services.

Talk To Me: A National Action Plan to Reduce Suicide and Self-Harm in Wales 2008–2013

Like the English, Scottish and Northern Irish strategies, the Welsh consultation document identifies a set of objectives or commitments (Welsh Assembly, 2008: 9–12):

Commitment one: to help people feel good about themselves by:

- Encouraging people, particularly young people, to talk openly about their problems and feelings.
- Removing the shame linked with emotional problems and mental illness.
- Developing healthier schools, colleges and workplaces.
- Reducing poverty and social inequality.
- Improving awareness and understanding among the public and professionals.
- Developing healthier and safer prisons and secure environments.
- Making sure children and young people feel safe and looked after.

Commitment two: to ensure early action is taken by:

- Encouraging people to ask for help as soon as they are feeling stressed, considering harming themselves or having suicidal thoughts.
- Providing more support services.
- Making it easy to get information about people who can help.
- Improving the way we diagnose and help people suffering from depression and other mental illnesses.
- Providing more help and better treatment for people with drug and alcohol problems.
- Providing support to those in prisons and custody so they do not harm themselves.
- Making sure specialist services respond more quickly to those most in need.

Commitment three: to respond to crises in people's lives by:

- Making sure people know about mental health services and how to contact them.
- Improving professionals' understanding and response to people who harm themselves.
- Monitoring services received by people to ensure they are meeting their needs.

Commitment four: to deal with the effects of suicide and self-harm by:

- Improving the care and support offered to people who have lost someone to suicide.
- Improving the care and support offered to families who are coping with the distress of someone harming themselves.
- Improving the support offered to professionals dealing with suicide.
- Making sure support services are available to help communities cope with the fall-out of suicide.

Commitment five: to increase research and improve information by:

- Encouraging research and making sure information about suicide and self-harm is available.
- Learning lessons that inform future prevention plans.

- Monitoring rates of self-harm and suicide to ensure organizations can meet the needs of the communities they serve.
- Establishing a national group to look at the needs of people who harm themselves.

Commitment six: to work with the media to ensure sensitive reporting on mental health and suicide by:

- Discussing mental health issues with the Welsh media.
- Encouraging the media to improve how suicide is reported.
- Promoting national media guidance by working with the Samaritans and government departments in the UK.
- Using the media to deliver positive mental health messages and raise awareness of suicide and self-harm in a sensitive manner.

Commitment seven: to restrict access to things which could be used for suicide by:

- Ensuring that, where possible, access to things that could be used for suicide is made difficult for those at risk.
- Ensuring all prison, custody and mental health settings are safe.

As can be seen, all four strategies follow similar lines, primarily around reducing stigma, increasing education, improving prevention strategies, reducing the availability of means and promoting responsible media reporting. Similar strategies have also been published internationally, including in New Zealand, Norway, the USA and Australia, for example. However, some important philosophical questions remain unanswered in the drive towards prevention. Recent UK policy documents have addressed prevention and reduction in suicide rates almost exclusively, while not engaging in a discussion about whether suicide should always be prevented. The discourse appears to be that a completed suicide represents a failure at an individual or institutional level and that practitioners should, wherever possible, prevent it. Whilst there is acknowledgement that suicide risk assessment is an inexact science and therefore cannot be predicted with any degree of accuracy, the discussion about whether suicide should always be prevented is broadly not attended to.

To some degree this is understandable. It is difficult for any policy document to incorporate views and perspectives that might on one hand offend some at a moral or philosophical level, while on another be seen to be condoning or encouraging suicide or sanctioning behaviour that risks contravening local legal parameters. However, by not acknowledging the shades of grey in human experience, policy documents create a prediction–prevention culture. Szasz (1986) notes the coercive power of mental health professionals in suicide prevention, arguing that psychotherapists are 'double agents'. This point is also made by Aldridge, who states that, 'While overtly claiming to serve the patient, the psychotherapist also serves society, reflecting societal concerns and diverting from threatening construings' (1998: 266).

The prediction–prevention culture

The task defined by UK and international mental health policy is for all mental health workers to recognize and assess suicide risk and to intervene and prevent suicide when confronted with it in practice. The consequence of policy development failing to incorporate the multi-dimensional nature of suicidality might cause dissonance for those practitioners who view suicide in philosophically different ways, and who personally do not subscribe to the notion of prevention.

The prediction–prevention culture dominates primary and secondary care mental health delivery, and has now defined practice in other areas, e.g. the voluntary sector, further and higher education settings etc. Counselling is not immune to such cultural shifts. The tenet of the prediction–prevention culture is that as there is now sufficient knowledge to predict the likelihood of suicide, prevention becomes sufficiently efficacious to provide for reduction targets. Each suicide therefore has the potential to be viewed as a 'failure' on the part of the mental health practitioner to utilize available knowledge effectively; had they done so, the suicide might have been prevented.

Leenaars (2004: 105) writes that suicide research has often looked for the 'bump on the head' that will unambiguously identify those individuals with a propensity for suicidality. The search for the 'bump on the head' seems to be driven by a hope that it will be possible to isolate one particular characteristic or feature of human experience that will flag suicide risk. In the context of positivist scientific endeavour, that research might objectively identify a definite precursor, 'agent' or catalyst for heightened suicide risk in the same way that genetic or biochemical 'markers' have proved significant in the identification, treatment and prevention of cancer. This comparison is pertinent given that suicide reduction targets were initially identified in *Saving Lives: Our Healthier Nation* (Department of Health, 1999a), alongside treatment targets for cancer, heart disease and stroke, for example.

The assessment of suicide risk is based around three principles: primary, secondary and tertiary prevention (Caplan, 1964). These are now more commonly referred to as prevention, intervention and postvention. Prevention (primary prevention) refers to the development of good mental health practices at both a personal and a professional level. Such practices might include training and self-care strategies. Intervention (secondary prevention) refers to the responses and treatment offered during crisis to the individual who is suicidal; whilst postvention (tertiary prevention) refers to activities following suicide with those bereaved or affected by it, such as the provision of psychological help (Leenaars, 2004).

The circumstances in which an individual may contemplate suicide are too varied to concisely describe. Suicide may be contemplated in response to interpersonal or intrapersonal crisis, psychopathology, existential crisis, trauma or physical illness, for example. Some believe that as individuals we always retain the right to end life. For others, suicide can never be morally, spiritually or philosophically justifiable; whilst others again hold different views in response to different situations. Suicidal ideation in response to advanced terminal illness may be viewed differently by many to suicidal ideation in response to a relationship breakdown or bullying, for example. The prevention discourse arguably fails to incorporate the many uncertainties of human experience of suicidality, instead attempting to create concretely defined areas of thought and behaviour. The presumption seems to be of mental illness, whereas this might not necessarily be true.

Areas of policy debate that are discordant with prevention strategies tend to be separated from mainstream discussion. For example, the public debate surrounding euthanasia touches on the central premise of whether an individual has a right to choose the timing and circumstances of their death. The debate however is more typically located within the role of the medical profession, treatment options, professional ethics and liability, rather than the individual's right to choose suicide (Snyder et al., 2001).

In this context, practitioners must consider difficult legal, ethical, professional and personal factors in response to working with suicidal clients, that include prevention and intervention versus individual rights and autonomy. Szasz (1986: 808) noted that the term 'suicide prevention' is a misleading 'slogan' characteristic of the therapeutic age. The polarizing of suicidality within policy development and research is perhaps substantiated by a prevailing view that suicidal ideation is invariably the product of psychopathology or irrationality. Suicidal intent within this context can never be seen as an informed choice. This view was highlighted and challenged by Szasz, who stated that, 'there is neither philosophical nor empirical support for viewing suicide as different, in principle, from other acts, such as getting married' (1986: 808).

If social policy is a barometer of social thinking, it appears that society continues to find suicide an expression of distress and hopelessness that it cannot tolerate. The dissonance between individual choice and society's duty to intervene with suicidal clients is enacted within the counselling frame, and is a dynamic that counsellors must tolerate for the sake of their client and themselves. The cost of this burden can be high. Perhaps societal discomfort with death, loss, grief and suicide is passed down the line: from society to policy makers, from policy makers to organizations, from organizations to managers, from managers to teams, from teams to the individual. Ultimately that is where responsibility seems to be located; no one wants to be holding the parcel when the music stops.

Discussion questions

1. In general terms, what international, national or local policies are you aware of and what do you understand of their influence on your practice?
2. What do you know of UK suicide prevention strategies?
3. How might the concept of the *prediction–prevention culture* be experienced in your work with suicidal clients?
4. What actions could you take either individually or collectively to help shape future policy development?

6   The Ethical Imperative of Suicide

> **Chapter overview**
>
> The purpose of this chapter is to consider how counsellors work with suicidal clients within an ethical context. Using the British Association for Counselling and Psychotherapy's *Ethical Framework for Good Practice in Counselling and Psychotherapy* (2007) as a benchmark for ethical standards, the chapter will consider aspects of the *Ethical Framework* as a means of constructing principles for good practice.

A large number of counsellors who work in the UK will be members of a professional association. At the time of writing, counselling and psychotherapy are not statutorily regulated professions, although it is anticipated that within the next five years this will take place. For many years professional organizations have supported practitioners in developing good standards, and have attempted to protect clients from poor or abusive practice through the development of complaints procedures and codes of conduct. For the purposes of ease, the BACP's *Ethical Framework for Good Practice in Counselling and Psychotherapy* (2007; hereafter the *Ethical Framework*) will be referred to throughout this chapter as a benchmark for good practice in working with suicidal clients. That is not to say that similar documents from other professional organizations are insufficient or less regarded, but simply to acknowledge that the larger numbers of counsellors who are members of BACP as a professional organization provide a good rationale for using their framework as a reference point.

The development and implementation of the *Ethical Framework* saw an important redefining and restructuring of the basic principles and philosophies that are seen to underpin ethical therapeutic practice. The membership of BACP are expected to work within the *Ethical Framework* and to implement its meaning in the implicit and explicit aspects of their work with clients. The *Ethical Framework* identifies six principles of counselling and psychotherapy (BACP, 2007: 3):

- *fidelity* – 'honouring the trust placed in the practitioner'
- *autonomy* – 'respect for the client's right to be self-governing'
- *beneficence* – 'a commitment to promote the client's wellbeing'
- *non-maleficence* – 'a commitment to avoiding harm to the client'
- *justice* – 'the fair and impartial treatment of all clients and the provision of adequate services'
- *self-respect* – 'fostering the practitioner's self-knowledge and care for self'.

These principles are said to point to the important ethical responsibilities of practice.

Within counselling terms, the *Ethical Framework* helps to identify good practice in a number of important areas, and attempts to respond to 'changes in the range of issues and levels of need presented by clients' (2007: 5). The increasing complexity and severity of client presentation, including suicide risk, mean that counsellors look to such guidance to help them consider their management and responses in such difficult areas.

The *Ethical Framework* states that 'situations in which clients pose a risk of causing serious harm to themselves or others are particularly challenging to the practitioner' (2007: 6). This challenge poses a number of important professional and personal considerations that need to be attended to in ensuring safe and appropriate practice. Research evidence points to the significant impact that working with suicidal clients can have on the counsellor, including guilt, anger, anxiety, and a sense of professional incompetence (Reeves and Mintz, 2001; B. Richards, 2000). These feelings potentially have a significant influence on how each professional gauges their own competence and how that, in turn, influences direct work with clients.

These are important areas for self-reflection and discussion in supervision, given how such powerful feelings might transitionally or permanently impair a counsellor's ability to practise. Even the transitional quality of these feelings can alter a counsellor's ability to be with and hear a client, and this must not be underestimated. The *Ethical Framework* places great emphasis on the importance of counsellors working within their own level of competence. In practice, this means considering limitations based on training and experience. The picture internationally is that practitioners are generally poorly prepared for working with suicidal clients by their training experiences, as is discussed more fully in other chapters of this book (Kleepsies et al., 1999; Neimeyer et al., 2001). Competence in this area is usually achieved through gaining day-to-day experience of working with clients, and processing that work in supervision. The necessity to consult with a supervisor regarding concerns for, and responsibilities towards, clients is additionally highlighted, although this is not necessarily a requirement outside the UK. Increasingly, supervisors are seeking specific training to support themselves in that role; however, given that supervisor training generally does not attend to working with suicide risk (in the same way that counsellor training tends not to address it in any depth or detail), an experience–practice deficit can occur (Reeves et al., 2004a).

Confidentiality

Confidentiality, the *Ethical Framework* states, is a 'fundamental requirement for keeping trust' (2007: 7). It is within this area, and the management of those boundaries with clients at risk of suicide, that counsellors face many of the practice dilemmas. Whether or not to break confidentiality when harm to self is suspected is, quite rightly, a major dilemma that requires much consideration. The *Ethical Framework* states that breaking confidentiality without the explicit consent of the client requires 'commensurate consideration'. Additionally, 'practitioners should be prepared to be readily accountable to clients and colleagues if they override a client's known wishes' (2007: 7).

These waters are further muddied by whether a client's 'known wishes' are necessarily those based on an informed and competent reasoning by that client. The duty of care lies with the counsellor assessing, as far as possible, whether the client is making informed choices for themselves, or whether their judgement is temporarily or permanently impaired by mental health distress. These considerations are further influenced by any organizational expectations in the management of confidentiality by the counsellor.

This area of practice highlights specifically the delicate dilemma of managing the client's wishes and respecting their autonomy and right to make life choices, versus the duty of care that is inherent within a counselling relationship that limits confidentiality to *risk to self or others*. The *Ethical Framework* encompasses this dilemma in the statement, 'The aim should be to ensure for the client a good quality of care that is as respectful of the client's capacity for self-determination and trust as circumstances permit' (2007: 6). The three words 'as circumstances permit' belie the labyrinth of possibilities that the counsellor must try to work their way through while holding on to what they believe to be ethically sound and in the best interests of the client. The counsellor must be able to clearly articulate the *circumstances* that informed their decision when being *readily accountable* to clients and colleagues if a client's known wishes have been overridden.

Alan

Alan is a 47-year-old shop worker who comes to counselling following a serious sexual assault. He feels profoundly shamed by what has happened to him, and talks of being angry and helpless at his situation. He talks of being depressed since the attack, and of having suicidal thoughts. During one session he talks more specifically of wishing he were dead. He says that he has had thoughts of hanging himself, though is not sure whether he could 'go through with it'. He does not want you to talk to his GP or anyone else about his thoughts, as that would make him 'more ridiculous'. He appears agitated and uncomfortable in response to talking about his suicidal thoughts.

- How might you balance Alan's capacity for self-determination against the risk he presents with?
- Considering the setting in which you work, what factors specifically influence your thinking? How might this be different if you worked in another setting, e.g. independent practitioner versus primary care?

Record keeping

Good practice expects that records are maintained in accordance with the requirements of data protection and other relevant legislation, and that they are respectful of the client's autonomy and dignity. Notes should be securely maintained, concise, as objective as possible, and accurate. The *Ethical Framework* encourages counsellors to keep adequate records of their work with clients. Maintaining careful notes with suicidal clients not only allows the counsellor to fully record both their interventions and the reasons for them, but also provides an important reflective opportunity to revisit therapeutic dynamics, transferences and countertransferences, as well as to take to supervision.

In practical terms, notes should state clearly what aspects of the client's presentation led the counsellor to believe that the client was a risk to themselves through suicide, and how those aspects of risk were specifically responded to. A decision to continue within the context of a confidential relationship with a suicidal client might in many instances be an appropriate course of action, but in line with the *Ethical Framework*, 'practitioners should be prepared to be readily accountable' for their decisions, and accurate and ethically maintained notes can help considerably in that process. A useful discussion of note taking in counselling can be found in Bond and Mitchels (2008).

> **Sharma**
>
> Sharma is a 23-year-old veterinary science student. She has experienced suicidal thoughts for many years, following early sexual abuse. She generally manages her thoughts using self-developed strategies, such as relaxation and distraction. She came to counselling to explore her experiences of abuse, believing that she needed to attend to these feelings to enable herself to 'get on' with her life. However, she has been surprised by the intensity of her feelings, and the heightened suicidal thoughts she has had. She has additionally cut herself for several years as a means of coping. She has asked you not to make any reference to her self-harm or suicidal thoughts in your counselling notes, even though she is aware that it is your agency policy to maintain notes. She is fearful that if such details were written down, it might prejudice her future veterinary career and raise concerns about her fitness to practice.

- Would you include in your notes Sharma's thoughts of suicide and self-harm? If so, how would you discuss this with her?
- What might be the risk for you (and Sharma) of not recording these details?

Working with colleagues

The *Ethical Framework* also addresses fully the implications for counsellors in working in multi-professional settings. Such teams can be found in many settings, including primary and secondary care, and in education settings where counselling is often integrated within a student service network – sometimes sharing reception facilities.

While there are many advantages of working in multi-professional team settings, dangers can include, on one hand, the dilution of concerns over sharing personal client information, and, on the other, an intransigent retreating into professional roles where the notion of 'team' instead becomes simply a collection of disciplines working in the same space. Neither of these positions is conducive to ethically sound practice with clients at risk of suicide.

Colleagues need to be fully informed and understand the contracts of confidentiality that are agreed with clients. Additionally, such contracts need to reflect the ways in which teams need to work together. If this situation is achieved, counsellors are more able to support themselves in their work, to consult appropriately and professionally, and to continue to be client focused rather than anxiety or defensively driven.

> **Denise**
>
> You have been working with Denise for two months. She is a 30-year-old mother of two who has experienced postpartum depression. She has had suicidal thoughts on occasion, and during one session handed you a bottle of anti-depressants which she had intended taking an overdose of. You work in a family centre alongside child protection staff, youth worker staff, and child and family social workers. A colleague with whom you have a good working relationship approaches you. They say that they want to talk to you 'off the record' about Denise, as they have concerns about her risk of suicide.

- How much information would you be willing to share 'off the record' with your colleague?
- How might your confidentiality policy facilitate or hinder communication with other colleagues?

Probity in professional practice

The *Ethical Framework* states that probity in professional practice is important both for individual clients and for the standing of the profession as a whole. How counsellors respond to their most vulnerable clients is one of the ways by which other professions and society as a whole make judgements about the integrity of the profession. Probity would clearly include how or whether counsellors are competent to carry out practice demands that are integrated into the counselling contract. For example, if a counsellor contracts with a client an agreement of confidentiality that is limited by the safety of the client in the event of suicidal ideation, they need to ensure that they are sufficiently experienced and/or supported to assess suicide risk in an appropriate informed way. Additionally, the client not only needs to be informed that risk to self is a boundary of confidentiality, but more importantly needs to understand what that means in practice, so that the client can give informed consent for the counselling to take place in the terms described.

> **Edward**
>
> Edward is a 54-year-old client who has been seeing you for counselling following the breakdown of his relationship. At times he has been profoundly distressed, and has more recently talked of feeling suicidal. These thoughts have increased in intensity, he reports. At a recent session you asked his permission to speak to his GP, and said that you needed to talk to his GP about his suicidal thoughts because of the risk you felt he

> presented with. Edward is angry with you when he returns the following week as he says he feels manipulated by you into him giving you his consent to speak to his GP. He says he was not aware of the requirement to speak to a GP.

- How might you respond to Edward's concerns?
- How might you ensure that your client is fully aware of (a) the details of your confidentiality agreements, and (b) why you feel a GP consultation is necessary?

Self-care and personal development

'The practitioner's well-being is essential to sustaining good practice' (BACP, 2007: 10). Burnout and vicarious trauma are destructive dangers for all counsellors; the impact of working with suicidal clients, as has already been described, might be a significant contributory factor to burnout occurring. Counsellors must therefore ensure that they give themselves plenty of opportunities to consider the implications of the issues of suicide on them, both personally and professionally. This is discussed in much more detail in Chapter 17, 'Good Practice for Self-Support'.

> ### John
>
> John is a 25-year-old counsellor who works for a young person's agency. He has a busy, full-time caseload. Several of his clients have talked of their suicidal thoughts, and one recently took an overdose. John feels trapped, angry, distressed and tired. He is aware of feeling angry with his clients, and blaming them for how he feels.

- What is the best course of action for John? Why and how should he achieve this with respect to the clients he is currently seeing?
- What might John do to help support himself in the future?

The development of the *Ethical Framework* has provided counsellors with an important tool when reflecting on practice. It does not prescribe practice and, as such, aims to be flexible in responding to the diversity that is now found in counselling practice and provision. This is a laudable attempt at mapping the baselines by which we can all consider our work. The *Ethical Framework* does not, however, provide the 'specific' and the 'concrete' that counsellors often look towards at times of uncertainty and difficulty. It has the potential to become a hall of mirrors – reflecting back a reality but also showing many dimensions and perspectives, leaving different alternatives often ambiguously defined. However, while the *Ethical Framework* does not help us assess the risk of suicide, it does provide a structure into which we can integrate risk assessment knowledge that can be obtained elsewhere, while keeping in focus the important principles of counselling.

Discussion questions

1 How much do you understand of your own professional organization's ethical statements in relation to your work with suicidal clients?
2 What steps do you take to ensure that your work with suicidal clients remains ethical at all times?
3 Is it impossible to really balance the rights of your clients with your professional responsibilities and duties with respect to suicide risk?
4 How might you use supervision to benchmark ethical practice?

7 Confidentiality, Capacity and Consent

Chapter overview

The work of counsellors is determined not only by professional codes of practice and ethical requirements, but also by legislative considerations. Working with suicidal clients can be particularly demanding for the counsellor in ensuring they maintain a balance between respecting a client's rights to autonomy and confidentiality and ensuring their safety. This chapter aims to provide an overview of three aspects of working with suicidal clients that can be particularly problematic: confidentiality, capacity and consent.

As is discussed throughout this book, the work of counsellors with suicidal clients is influenced by many factors: the presentation of the client; the countertransferential responses of the counsellor; the organization in which counselling takes place; any procedural or guidance documents of that organization pertaining to risk; the ethical requirements of any professional organization which the counsellor may be a member of; national policies that set benchmarks for good practice in mental health and suicide; and legislation.

Within this context counsellors must sometimes make difficult decisions about how best to respond to clients when suicide potential becomes apparent, mostly with the cooperation and consent of the client but occasionally, if necessary, without it. This latter scenario can be both challenging and stressful, in that it contradicts much of what counselling is about: the empowerment of the individual in the context of their world. The prospect of breaking confidentiality, which for many practitioners remains the cornerstone of a trusting counselling relationship, is a profoundly difficult decision.

Confidentiality is not a professional nicety that counsellors simply choose to afford their clients. It is enshrined in law, and it is essential that counsellors consider carefully any situation in which they are considering breaking a client's confidence. The potential for the client to act on their suicidal thoughts is one of those situations that might be justifiable under law; however, counsellors still need to be sure that they are able to clearly articulate their rationale for such an outcome.

This chapter will provide an overview of some of the legislative areas that particularly challenge counsellors in their work with suicidal clients. There are some excellent resources that provide for an in-depth discussion, including Bond and Mitchels (2008), Bond (2009) and Jenkins (2007), and I would recommend them to counsellors who wish to know more about the subject.

Confidentiality

The *Ethical Framework* (BACP, 2007) makes the following statement about confidentiality:

> Respecting client confidentiality is a fundamental requirement for keeping trust. The professional management of confidentiality concerns the protection of personally identifiable and sensitive information from unauthorised disclosure. Disclosure may be authorised by client consent or the law. Any disclosures should be undertaken in ways that best protect the client's trust. Practitioners should be willing to be accountable to their clients and to their profession for their management of confidentiality in general and particularly for any disclosures made without their client's consent. (p. 6)

The *Ethical Framework* clearly places the importance of confidentiality as central to the counselling process, in that it is a 'fundamental requirement for keeping trust'. Most counsellors would understand the importance of confidentiality in terms of the therapeutic process and the rights of the client for privacy, but it is sometimes less clear that confidentiality is a legal as well as a professional duty.

It is worth noting at this point that the *Ethical Framework*, and other such codes of practice issued by professional bodies and associations, are not legal requirements, but instead provide benchmarks within which ethical practice can be located. As such, these documents remain voluntary and are applicable only to members of those bodies. This raises difficulties when complaints against a counsellor are made, in that the counsellor can decide to resign membership of their organization, and therefore no longer be deemed accountable to its guidelines. Statutory regulation of the profession of counselling and psychotherapy in the UK is likely to change this situation dramatically, with registration becoming dependent on an adherence to ethical professional parameters.

The *Oxford English Dictionary* (1989) defines confidential as '1. intended to be kept secret. 2. entrusted with private information: a confidential secretary'. Bond and Mitchels suggest that professional confidentiality is 'protecting information that could only be disclosed at some cost to another's privacy in order to protect that privacy from being compromised further' (2008: 4). They note also that in more general terms, 'confidentiality occurs when two people decide to restrict the communication of information to between themselves in order to prevent it being communicated to a third person or more people' (2008: 4).

The client has a general right to expect confidentiality within a professional relationship, but this is not an absolute legal right, since confidentiality is always subject to the requirements of the law. For example, in certain situations like terrorism, compulsory disclosures must be made. Confidentiality should always be negotiated as part of the contract between therapist and client. The client should be informed of any limitations on confidentiality before counselling commences, and the counsellor should ensure that the client understands and agrees these limitations.

This again is covered in some detail in Bond and Mitchels, but they state, 'counsellors and psychotherapists owe their clients a legal duty of confidentiality. Any personally identifiable information is to be protected. It does not appear to matter whether the disclosure of information is favourable or unfavourable to the person concerned. Any unauthorised disclosure may be damaging to the client' (2008: 15).

Confidentiality will apply to all aspects of the counselling process. The clearest way of applying this would be to what the client tells the counsellor during counselling, but confidentiality will equally apply to any records that are maintained (in addition to data protection directives), and to the fact that the client is having counselling at all. This last case is often tested in institutions where counsellors can receive calls from others enquiring as to whether the client has attended. In further and higher education settings, for example, it is not uncommon for counselling services to receive calls from worried tutors or parents asking whether their student or child has attended counselling. Confidentiality applies in these situations, and the counsellor must politely inform the enquirer that such information is confidential.

Capacity

One of the factors important for counsellors to consider is whether or not their client has 'capacity' to make informed decisions. The Mental Capacity Act 2005 came into force in 2007, and in Scotland the Adults with Incapacity (Scotland) Act 2000 applies. The following principles are contained in the Mental Capacity Act 2005 section 1:

- A person must be assumed to have capacity unless it is established that he lacks capacity.
- A person is not to be treated as unable to make a decision unless all practicable steps to help him to do so have been taken without success.
- A person is not to be treated as unable to make a decision merely because he makes an unwise decision.
- An act done, or a decision made, under this Act for or on behalf of a person who lacks capacity must be done, or made, in his best interests.
- Before the act is done, or the decision is made, regard must be had to whether the purpose for which it is needed can be as effectively achieved in a way that is less restrictive of the person's rights and freedom of action.

These principles are important because they clearly state that all people over the age of 16 are assumed to have capacity. It is not lawful to assume that someone lacks capacity simply because we do not agree with decisions they might make. It should be noted that young people over the age of 16 and under the age of 18 *with mental capacity* have the right to refuse medical treatment, even if that refusal might result in their death. However, it is possible for the High Court or Court in Session to overrule a refusal of consent by any young person under the age of 18 to undergo any medical or psychiatric treatment which is essential for their health and welfare, and where that refusal could result in death or serious harm to the young person. This is clearly pertinent to work with suicidal clients in counselling, which will be discussed a little later.

The Mental Capacity Act 2005 section 2 makes the following statement about incapacity:

- For the purposes of this Act, a person lacks capacity in relation to a matter if at the material time he is unable to make a decision for himself in relation to the matter because of an impairment of, or a disturbance in the functioning of, the mind or brain.

Confidentiality, Capacity and Consent 63

- It does not matter whether the impairment or disturbance is permanent or temporary.
- A lack of capacity cannot be established merely by reference to

    (a) a person's age or appearance, or
    (b) a condition of his, or an aspect of his behaviour, which might lead others to make unjustified assumptions about his capacity.

- In proceedings under this Act or any other enactment, any question whether a person lacks capacity within the meaning of this Act must be decided on the balance of probabilities.

This section of the Mental Capacity Act 2005 makes reference to a person being 'unable to make a decision'. The Act section 3 states the following in this regard:

Inability to make decisions

- For the purposes of section 2, a person is unable to make a decision for himself if he is unable

    (a) to understand the information relevant to the decision,
    (b) to retain that information,
    (c) to use or weigh that information as part of the process of making the decision, or
    (d) to communicate his decision (whether by talking, using sign language or any other means).

- A person is not to be regarded as unable to understand the information relevant to a decision if he is able to understand an explanation of it given to him in a way that is appropriate to his circumstances (using simple language, visual aids or any other means).
- The fact that a person is able to retain the information relevant to a decision for a short period only does not prevent him from being regarded as able to make the decision.
- The information relevant to a decision includes information about the reasonably foreseeable consequences of

    (a) deciding one way or another, or
    (b) failing to make the decision.

This then clearly lays out the circumstances in which a person may permanently or temporarily be defined as not having capacity. These are whether the person can understand the information relevant to a decision, remember it (even if for a short while), use the available information to help inform a decision, and communicate it to others.

A person may be deemed to lack capacity for both physical and psychiatric reasons. Capacity is important at all stages of the therapeutic process: for example, whether the client has the capacity to make a decision to enter into counselling in the first place. The Mental Capacity Act 2005 requires that before commencement of care or treatment, an assessment of capacity should be made. A counsellor should ensure that such an assessment is made, and in most instances this will be relatively simple. However, when in doubt, or with vulnerable adults, young people or children, it may be necessary to consult with other professionals, e.g. a general practitioner or a psychiatrist. A distressed client may temporarily lack capacity, as long as the above criteria are met. In instances of dispute about capacity, the matter may be referred to the High

Court or Court in Session where a ruling may be made. Again, this is highly pertinent to working with suicidal clients.

Consent

The Ethical Framework makes a number of references to the term consent. For example, it states:

> Practitioners should ensure that services are normally delivered on the basis of the client's explicit consent. Reliance on implicit consent is more vulnerable to misunderstandings and is best avoided unless there are sound reasons for doing so. Overriding a client's known wishes or consent is a serious matter that requires commensurate justification. Practitioners should be prepared to be readily accountable to clients, colleagues and professional body if they override a client's known wishes. (BACP, 2007: 6)

Explicit in this reference is the need for counsellors to ensure that the provision of therapy, and any subsequent action that takes place during counselling (and in most instances following the end of counselling when actions relate to that counselling relationship), are conducted with the client's consent. Consent is closely linked with the concept of capacity, as a client is only able to give consent, or informed consent, if they have the capacity to do so. For example, entering into counselling with a client who the counsellor suspects does not have capacity (temporarily), perhaps because they appear to be under the influence of drugs or alcohol, would not be ensuring that the client's informed consent had been obtained. It would be impossible for the client to consent to counselling if, either temporarily or permanently, they lacked capacity to do so.

Bond and Mitchels (2008: 118) identify the following useful questions counsellors might consider in determining whether a client has capacity to give valid consent:

- For what action is consent being sought?
- Have all the potential benefits, risks and consequences of taking or not taking that action been fully explained and understood?
- Has the person retained the information long enough to properly evaluate it when making their decision?
- Can the person clearly communicate their decision (with help as appropriate) once it is made?
- Is the consent sought for the individual concerned, or is it for the treatment of another person?
- If consent is sought for another person, is that person an adult or a child?
- If consent is sought for a child, does the person giving consent have parental responsibility for the child?

As can be seen, the concepts of confidentiality, capacity and consent are central to any decision making process with regard to suicidal clients. However, even though these terms are clearly defined in law, the application of law does not necessarily mean that decisions become any easier. A counsellor working with a suicidal client instead has to weigh a large number of factors in: (a) ensuring they act for the well-being of the client; (b) ensuring they act in line with any contractual aspect of their employment; (c) ensuring they act ethically in line with any ethical guidance to which they have subscribed; and (d) ensuring they act within the law.

The legal implications for working with suicidal clients

It is important for counsellors to know that in the UK there is no legal requirement to report concerns about suicide. Some counsellors I have spoken to work under the misconception that the law places a duty on counsellors to pass on concerns of suicide risk when they become apparent in a counselling session; this is not the case. Perhaps this misunderstanding comes from confusion around debates on assisted suicide and euthanasia, which have received prominent media coverage over recent years following some high profile cases. Employers may require that counsellors employed to deliver a therapeutic service on their behalf should pass on concerns of suicide risk to a GP, for example, as outlined in organizational procedures, etc. Any specific aspects of working with suicide risk, particularly around confidentiality, should be clearly communicated and agreed with the client as part of the therapeutic contract at the outset of counselling. A fuller discussion of this is contained in Chapters 8 and 9, 'Counselling Suicidal Clients in Organizational Settings' and 'Developing Procedures and Guidance'.

The Suicide Act 1961 decriminalized suicide in the UK. The effect of this was that anyone who had attempted suicide and survived would no longer be prosecuted. However, the Act section 2 does state:

> A person who aids, abets, counsels or procures the suicide of another, or an attempt by another to commit suicide, shall be liable on conviction on indictment to imprisonment for a term not exceeding fourteen years.

This means that a counsellor is liable to prosecution under the Suicide Act 1961 if there is sufficient evidence that they aided or abetted another's suicide. Simply knowing that the client was suicidal but not breaking confidentiality may not come under the terms of the Suicide Act 1961 as aiding or abetting the suicide of another.

Clients have a right under law to expect that a counselling relationship remains confidential. This includes clients who may express suicidal thoughts to their counsellor. In Chapter 2, 'Historical Perspectives on Suicide and the Emergence of the Medical Model', we explored how suicide has increasingly (and wrongly) become associated with mental illness: that is to say, anyone who is suicidal must also be suffering from a mental illness. While higher suicide risk is strongly correlated with mental illness, it would be very wrong to assume that anyone expressing suicidal thoughts is also mentally ill. As we will discuss using several scenarios throughout this book, that simply is not the case. As such, it would be wrong to assume that a client expressing suicidal thoughts or intent did not have capacity under the Mental Capacity Act 2005.

This point often causes some debate; many hold with the view that a person must be suffering from mental illness if they are suicidal. However, I would suggest that this position is likely to be more informed by the counsellor's view of suicide, rather than an accurate reflection of the true legal position in the UK. It would be essential that any counsellor considering breaking confidentiality, in the event of concerns about the client's wellbeing as a consequence of suicide risk, should also consider whether the client is suffering from an underlying mental health problem. It may well be the case that increased suicidality stems from mental illness, or from a strong mental disturbance which affects that person's mental capacity, and further specialist assessment/intervention may be required. As stated previously, an increased risk of suicide is strongly correlated with psychopathology.

However, as will be demonstrated using several case vignettes throughout this book, some clients may be suicidal and not be suffering from mental illness. We might not like their decision to end their own life, but legally they may have the mental capacity to make that decision. Clearly other aspects that help define the boundaries of the counselling relationship will inform counsellor action, such as the contract of confidentiality agreed at the outset of counselling, the context in which counselling is offered, the age of the client, and any mental illness or condition which may impact on their mental capacity and decision making process.

The Mental Capacity Act 2005 (and in Scotland the Adults with Incapacity (Scotland) Act 2000) applies to individuals over 16, with the possibility of decisions being overruled by the courts for persons aged between 16 and 18. However, the position with respect to children (defined by the Children Act 1989 as anyone under the age of 18) will pose different and additional difficult legal complexities. Counsellors who work with children under the age of 16, who are not 'Gillick competent' to make their own decisions, need to ensure that consent for treatment is obtained from the person holding parental responsibility for that child. It is important that counsellors do not assume that all parents automatically have parental responsibility in law for their children and so are the right people to provide this consent. Legal proceedings following child protection concerns might also include the courts in such decisions. Further clarification on parental responsibility, 'Gillick competence' and mental capacity in decision making for adults and children can be found in Chapter 11 of Bond and Mitchels (2008).

If the counsellor believes that their adult client retains mental capacity, despite being profoundly distressed and suicidal (using the criteria specified for capacity under the Act and detailed in this chapter), they do not have an automatic right to break confidentiality in the absence of client consent, and would potentially be acting in breach of their contract with the client. Other good reasons might include evidence of mental illness, such as psychosis or depression, where the client may not have capacity temporarily; the conditions for capacity would still apply in this situation.

There are situations when breaking confidentiality would be allowed in law. These are:

1. where the law requires, e.g. legislation on terrorism
2. where the law allows, e.g. where the public interest outweighs the client's wishes
3. where the client consents.

The 'public interest' referred to in point 2 is important here. The counsellor would need to be able to justify that a breach of confidentiality in response to suicidal potential was in the 'public interest'. Certainly the situation is clearer if the proposed act of suicide involved danger to others, e.g. jumping off a bridge on to a motorway. The counsellor could justify public interest in such circumstances. The balance otherwise is how a court would respond to a situation in which a client's life was saved, versus the counsellor being seen as interfering unnecessarily and without good reason in the client's life. In articulating a justification for breaking confidentiality in response to suicide potential, the counsellor would need to pay careful attention to their duty of care to the client, and clearly outline:

- How real was the risk of harm to the client?
- How serious was the risk to the client?
- How imminent was the risk to the client?

Obtaining consent

Wherever possible counsellors should attempt to gain their client's consent to pass on concerns to a third party, e.g. general practitioner, mental health team. Where consent is obtained, it is preferable for it to be in writing, perhaps using a pro forma document that details date, who would be releasing information and to whom, signed by both client and counsellor. An example of this can be found in Figure 7.1.

This provides both parties with protection in the event of disagreement or dispute. It is important (and good practice) for counsellors not to assume that once consent has been given to share information with a third party, this then becomes a 'blank cheque', that is an ongoing permission from the client to do so. Counsellors need to ensure that valid consent (written wherever possible) is obtained for *every instance* where contact with a third party is considered, for example discussing concerns with the client's GP. A client may give consent for contact, but retains the right to withdraw consent if they change their mind. Clearly, if written permission has been obtained and contact with the third party has already taken place, the counsellor is more likely to be able to demonstrate that the client was willing for contact to have taken place.

However, as stated previously, client permission *in and of itself* is insufficient grounds to justify disclosing confidentiality information about a client when considered from an ethical position. While consent is required to release information, it is good practice for the counsellor to be able to support their request for consent from the client with a clear rationale as to why that request was made. It is important for the counsellor to be able to clearly articulate the reasons for their concerns and need to disclose information, in addition to having client consent to do so. Other chapters of this book look in more detail at what information is pertinent in helping a counsellor make a judgement about confidentiality, and how to explore those concerns in more detail with their client.

From my own experience in working with suicidal clients, in secondary care (psychiatric) and higher education settings, I believe that in most instances it is possible, with care, patience and respect, to obtain client consent to act on concerns. If clients understand the rationale for concerns, and more importantly what might happen as a consequence of passing on information sensitively and appropriately, they are more likely to be willing to work collaboratively with the counsellor. This provides for the best outcome, as the client can fully participate in the care they

---

Consent to Release Information to a Third Party

Counselling is based on a confidential relationship. That is, the fact that you are receiving counselling, and what is discussed in sessions, will remain confidential between you and your counsellor (or the agency) at all times. The only limits to this were explained in the leaflet 'Information About Your Counselling' that you received and signed at the beginning of your sessions, and by your counsellor in the first session.

Occasionally your counsellor might consider it necessary or helpful to speak to another person about your care, e.g. your general practitioner, a mental health team, or another person. Your counsellor would explain fully to you why they believed this to be necessary or helpful, and ask for your consent to do this. This form indicates that you are happy for your counsellor to release information about you to another person, either in writing (by letter or email), or verbally (face to face or by telephone). Once you have read this information, and it has been explained fully and clearly to you, please sign below to indicate that you are happy for your counsellor to release information about you.

Date

I _____ (name of client) give consent to my counsellor _____ (name of counsellor) to release information about me. My counsellor has fully explained to me why they feel this to be necessary or helpful, and I am happy for them to do so.

I have agreed for my counsellor to release information to _____ (name of person or agency) on this occasion only. I understand that should my counsellor believe it be necessary or helpful to release information about me in the future, I will need to give consent by signing another form if I agree.

Signed	(Client)
Signed	(Counsellor)
Date	

Figure 7.1 Release of information form

receive and is less likely to trigger more formal mental health interventions, and the counselling relationship can be protected for future work.

It is essential that counsellors pay due care to how confidentiality agreements are contracted from the outset of counselling. Such agreements need to clearly state any limits to confidentiality, which in the UK in respect to harm to self usually include a statement to the effect of 'immediate risk to self through suicide' (and some might include self-harm). Some counselling services or individual counsellors build into their contracts the right to consult (a supervisor, or a member of the counselling team) in the event of concern. Other services make clear that confidentiality is between client and counselling agency, as opposed to individual counsellor, e.g. 'the confidentiality that applies to counselling will be between you (client) and the counselling team. No information will be passed on to any third party outside of the service without your written consent.' All confidentiality agreements should ensure that potential damage to the client's rights and autonomy is avoided.

Other factors that might influence whether or not a counsellor breaks confidentiality with a suicidal client will be the nature of the organization for which the counsellor works. For example, if a counsellor works in a setting such as primary or secondary care, prisons or other mental health teams, they may be required by their organization to manage situations involving suicidal clients in prescribed ways.

Challenges to the counsellor

The fear of many counsellors is that their actions will be challenged at some stage. With respect to working with suicidal clients, this might mean proceedings taken by the client on the grounds of breach of confidentiality, and the subsequent 'damage' the client believes they have suffered accordingly, e.g. to reputation, earnings, etc. Or, perhaps the worst feared scenario, the counsellor may have to defend a case of negligence in the event of client suicide.

For a case of negligence to be made, a duty of care must be seen to exist between counsellor and client. Cristofoli states that, 'It is generally accepted and has been found in case law that this duty of care exists' (2002: 28). The *Bolem case* is the test for negligence, and Cristofoli states that, 'It is necessary in negligence to demonstrate that the treatment fell below the standard of a reasonably competent therapist occupying that particular post' (2002: 28).

To defend an action of negligence, the counsellor must demonstrate that 'a substantial body of reputable practitioners would have acted in the same way as the defendant in those circumstances' (2002: 28). However, it is also vital that a counsellor is able to clearly demonstrate the rationale for their actions, the details of their concerns, and why they either went against the client's known wishes, or did not refer for specialist mental health assessment or consult with the client's GP, for example, in the event of client suicide. Chapter 9, 'Developing Procedures and Guidance' pays attention to what information might be usefully recorded in client notes when risk is identified. Bond and Mitchels (2008) provide a more detailed discussion of the issues surrounding keeping client records, including working within the requirements of the Data Protection Act 1998.

In summary, despite apparent clarity in legal terms, working with suicidal clients in the context of legislative expectations remains complex and challenging. The following points are important to remember:

- There is no duty in the UK to report concerns of suicide risk.
- While suicide as an act was decriminalized by the Suicide Act 1961, an offence is committed by anyone who 'aids, abets, counsels or procures the suicide of another, or an attempt by another to commit suicide'. Any counsellor found doing so would be liable to criminal prosecution.
- The client has a general right to expect confidentiality, but this is not absolute, since confidentiality is always subject to the requirements of the law. Confidentiality should be negotiated as part of the contract between counsellor and client. The client should be informed of any limitations on confidentiality before counselling

commences, and the counsellor should ensure that the client understands and agrees these limitations.
- Counsellors need to ensure that a client has the mental capacity to consent to counselling prior to counselling commencing.
- Being suicidal does not automatically mean that a client lacks mental capacity. This would only be the case if there were other evidence of mental illness or other significant impairment.
- If a client lacks capacity, either temporarily or permanently, as defined under the legislation, the counsellor may consider it appropriate to break confidentiality if they believe the client presents at high risk of harm through suicide, and no alternative intervention is possible or appropriate to safeguard their wellbeing.
- If the client is suicidal and has the capacity to make an informed decision on suicide, counsellors must be very wary of breaking confidentiality. Wherever possible, they should work to obtain client consent. Clients with capacity have the right to make decisions about their lives, even if those decisions might lead to their death. The only factor that might mitigate such circumstances is where counsellors are employed in settings, or are working within procedural guidance or previously agreed contracts of confidentiality, that might provide them with an opportunity to consult, without client consent, if high suicide risk is suspected.

The complexity of this situation demands that, wherever possible, counsellors should always aim to consult with supervisors, colleagues or other experts to help them determine the best course of action. Bond and Mitchels (2008: 41) provide an excellent 'checklist' to consider when facing such dilemmas:

- What is the likelihood of serious harm in this case?
- Is this serious harm imminent?
- If I refer, what is likely to happen?
- If I do not refer, what is likely to happen?
- Do the likely consequences of non-referral include any serious harm to the client or others?
- Is there anything I (or anyone else) can do to assist in preventing this harm to my client or others?
- What steps would need to be taken to implement such assistance?
- How could the client be helped to accept the assistance or proposed action?
- Does my client have the mental capacity to give explicit informed consent (or refusal of consent) at this moment in time?
- If the client does not have mental capacity, then what are my professional responsibilities to the client and the public interest?
- If the client has mental capacity, but does not consent to my proposed action (e.g. referral to a GP), what would be my legal and professional situation if I went ahead and did it anyway?

This chapter can only provide the simplest overview of the legislative complexities when working with suicidal clients. It is apparent not only that what we do as counsellors is informed by ethical requirements, but also that legal imperatives exist to ensure that certain parameters in counselling are attended to, e.g. confidentiality, capacity and consent. Counsellors should ensure that they take appropriate steps in seeking professional and specialist guidance on a case-by-case basis to help ensure that their work is both ethical and legal.

The following two vignettes provide an opportunity to consider actions in the light of the discussion in this chapter.

Angie

Angie is a counsellor who works for a university counselling service. She has been seeing Jo, a 19-year-old client, for several weeks. Jo is currently estranged from her family and is clear that she does not wish anyone to know that she is attending counselling, nor does she want her family to know her home address. Angie comes into work and takes a telephone call from Jo's parents. They are upset and anxious about Jo's wellbeing. They say that they are concerned for her, and do not know how to locate her. They ask Angie whether Jo is attending the counselling service.

1. Should Angie let Jo's parents know (a) that she is okay and/or (b) that she is safe and attending counselling?
2. What is the rationale for your decision?

Jack

Jack is a 17-year-old client with 'mild learning difficulties'. He has been attending counselling because of depression, and is accompanied by a support worker who brings him to the sessions, and waits in the waiting room while Jack is in his session. Jack explains that he has been feeling 'very low', and has had thoughts of killing himself. He does not think that he would act on these thoughts, but is sufficiently worried about them to talk to you. He does not want you to talk to his support worker about how he feels, as he feels the support worker would be disappointed in him.

1. Would you talk to Jack's support worker without his permission to safeguard his safety?
2. What legislation would inform your thinking, and what information would you need to know to support your decision?

Discussion questions

1. What steps do you take to ensure that, at the commencement of counselling, your client has the capacity to give informed consent to enter into counselling?
2. How do you ensure that your client fully understands any contract of confidentiality that applies to the counselling? What adjustments would you make, as expected by the Mental Capacity Act 2005, to ensure that information was provided in such a way that the client could understand it?
3. Specifically, how do you ensure that your client understands your responsibilities and potential actions towards them if you were concerned about their risk of suicide?
4. How do you ensure that you act within the law when making decisions about responding to suicide risk?

Part III

Organizations

8 Counselling Suicidal Clients in Organizational Settings

> **Chapter overview**
>
> How a counsellor works with suicidal clients will be strongly influenced by the setting in which counselling takes place. For example, independent practitioners will face different dilemmas and challenges to counsellors who work in health care settings or social services. This chapter aims to consider the challenges that can be faced by counsellors when working in organizations and responding to suicide risk.

Kinder writes that, 'Workplace counselling is different to traditional counselling or therapy in the sense that whenever a client is seen, there is one other "person" present – the organisation' (2005: 22). It could be argued that this is true not only for organizations, but for any counselling that is located within and funded by an organization. Kinder uses the term 'workplace counselling' very specifically here in referring to counselling designed to support the needs of a workforce. However, the issues relating to working with suicide potential can be seen as wider than that specific role, while also including it. It is also important to view independent practice as an 'organization' of sorts, in that the counsellor will exert some control over the client in terms of fees, availability, and where counselling takes place, and the client has to essentially work within these parameters.

Since I began training as a counsellor, the place of counselling in organizations has changed considerably. While counselling was strongly embedded within voluntary organizations, it was rare to find such provision in primary or secondary care, other health-based services, social services or schools, for example. The last two decades have seen great changes in both how counselling is viewed, and where it is now located.

It is now unusual for primary care services not to include counselling provision; the same is true for secondary care services, such as psychiatry and physical health services. Counsellors are increasingly found within multi-professional mental health teams and, over the last few years, are now increasingly common in school settings. This undoubtedly offers greater choice for clients who previously might have only had more traditional options available to them, e.g. psychopharmacology. It might also be assumed that as more people access counselling in different contexts, the greater is the potential for counsellors to find themselves working with clients who are experiencing suicidal thoughts.

As is discussed in detail in other chapters, counsellors might often find themselves having to work in ways that respond to organizational expectation, but are in conflict with either personally held views, or what they consider to be the practice and philosophy of counselling. McLeod (2003: 419) identifies a number of ways in which counsellors might find themselves in conflict with their employing organization:

- Being pressured to produce results desired by the agency rather than the client.
- Maintaining confidentiality boundaries.
- Justifying the cost of the service.
- Dealing with isolation.
- Educating colleagues about the purpose and value of counselling.
- Justifying the cost of supervision.
- Avoiding being overwhelmed by the numbers of clients, or becoming the 'conscience' of the organization.
- Avoiding the threat to reputation caused by 'failure cases'.
- Coping with the envy of colleagues who are not able to take an hour for each client interview.
- Creating an appropriate office space and reception system.

McLeod notes these points in general terms about organizational working. It is helpful to consider each one separately, specifically in relation to working with suicidal clients.

Being pressured to produce results desired by the agency rather than the client

'Results' is a term hard to define in the context of counselling. The client's 'result' might be very different to the counsellor's, which in turn might be very different for the organization. For example, I have seen many clients who have decided after a period of counselling that they wish themselves, or their situation, to remain entirely unchanged. They make this decision in awareness, rather than with a lack of insight that might have brought them into counselling in the first instance. For them, making a decision to remain unchanged, but in awareness, might be a significant 'result' or outcome. As a counsellor, I have often found these to be the most difficult situations, as they have not felt to be a 'result' to me. The idea that a client might choose to leave counselling with nothing changed perhaps challenges the most basic ideas I hold about the purpose of the counselling process, or perhaps my efficacy as a counsellor. Yet, when these situations have arisen in my work, they are often profound. For the organization it may be important for funding purposes, for example, that clinical benchmarks demonstrate change between pre- and post-counselling evaluation. There is always a danger of trying to understand the complexities of client process simply through a benchmarking tool.

Suicidality can present in many different ways. For some, the option of ending life is sufficient for sustaining it. Counselling might explore the client's suicidal fantasies, and the client might gain awareness of the role their suicidality has in their life. However, counselling might end with the client continuing with the option of suicide as a means of managing their distress – an exit route if things become too onerous. This may be an important 'result' for the client and perhaps the counsellor, but does not necessarily contribute to successful positive benchmarking.

Maintaining confidentiality boundaries

This is discussed in more detail in several other chapters. Essentially this can be the biggest challenge to the counsellor when working with suicide potential. As counsellors, we agree with our clients regularly to maintain and respect confidentiality in spite of their suicidal thinking, in the belief that counselling provides the best opportunity for the client. Or perhaps the client makes a choice not to enter the world of mental health systems.

Organizations are often very wary of the dangers of client suicide in terms of the reputation of the organization, and duty of care considerations. Procedures or policies are made that expect counsellors to refer suicidal clients to more specialist services, or for additional assessment, when suicide risk is suspected. However, I can think of many situations where this would not be appropriate, in terms of the work being undertaken within the therapeutic relationship, or because the client does not wish this to happen and I do not feel that I have the right to override their expressed wishes at that point. What is to be done?

The reality often is that organizations never really 'know' of these decisions, because risk is ultimately safely contained within the relationship. The client returns to counselling and the process of therapy continues through the crisis. The risk for counsellors is of client suicide, when suddenly it transpires that the counsellor has been working outside of the organizational policy and, as such, is left exposed. It is possible for the counsellor to support themselves in positive risk taking with clients through supervision and record keeping, and this is discussed in more detail elsewhere. The implications of working within such procedural parameters are discussed more in the next chapter, 'Developing Procedures and Guidance'.

Justifying the cost of the service

Counselling services, even when based within larger organizations, can often be subject to financial scrutiny and threat of closure. It is difficult to clearly account for the work of the service because positive client 'outcome' does not necessarily relate to financial gain. Organizations can sometimes see counselling services as purely a financial drain, offering little in return. There is now an increasing body of research evidence that refutes this presumption by demonstrating the benefits of counselling within organizations (McLeod, 2008).

Suicidal clients are often not 'cost effective' clients to see, in that it is not always possible or appropriate to contain the work within the usual parameters of brief therapy, and thus more sessions are needed. Counsellors seeing suicidal clients should (ideally) have allowance made to their caseloads (perhaps by reducing the overall numbers of clients they see for a period of time) to respond to the increased complexity or challenge that suicide potential brings. Also, there may be times when additional consultation or supervision is required to ethically support the counsellor in their work, with cost implications.

Dealing with isolation

It is imperative that any counsellor working with suicidal clients should be well supported. In independent practice this should mean good supervision, but additionally peer support from other colleagues. In other organizations the same is true, and yet counsellors can often feel isolated in their role, with little opportunity to appropriately discuss concerns about client safety. Paradoxically, it seems sometimes the larger the organization, the greater the propensity for isolation. For example, counsellors working in schools might find themselves to be a lone counsellor, with little immediate support for their work. It can often not be possible for counsellors to find other members of the team or staff group who have sufficient knowledge of the theory or process of counselling to help explore a difficult situation.

Educating colleagues about the purpose and value of counselling

During my research I have had a great deal of contact with counsellors working in a variety of organizational settings. Often counsellors can feel misunderstood by other professional colleagues, and not sufficiently empowered to feel confident about engaging in a dialogue of education and awareness raising. I have argued throughout this book that I believe counselling has something positive to contribute to work with suicidal clients, by virtue of our integration of theory and philosophy into a dialogic-relational approach that, regardless of orientation, is client centred.

There may be a number of interpersonal and intrapersonal dynamics that the counsellor needs to disentangle in their work around suicidality. It can be difficult to achieve this with colleagues who come from different theoretical, conceptual or ethical standpoints. Some counsellors have reported that they are sometimes reluctant to speak with colleagues about their concerns for a suicidal client, or indeed refer for further assessment, as they do not always have confidence that it will be handled well. In my own study, a counsellor talked of these fears by saying, 'I feel as if I am letting a client down. I also feel that sometimes when I have to break confidentiality that it is not dealt with appropriately. If it was dealt with appropriately then I think that I may feel happier about breaking confidentiality – especially in terms of suicidal clients' (participant, Reeves and Mintz, 2001).

Justifying the cost of supervision

As discussed earlier, working with suicidal clients can sometimes demand extra supervision time, or additional consultation in deciding on the best intervention. In general terms organizations can fail to understand the need for supervision at all. It has been said to me on more than one occasion that I shouldn't need supervision if I was 'competent to do the job'. Alas, the argument about good practice and ethical requirement sometimes still falls on ears that do not want to hear. It can therefore be extremely difficult for some counsellors to justify the need for additional supervision, when working in the context that supervision at all is seen as a self-indulgent nicety.

Avoiding being overwhelmed by the numbers of clients

Working with suicidal clients takes time, energy, emotional resourcefulness and capacity. Counsellors too often have to engage in such work in the context of a caseload that is full. I recall supervising a counsellor working in a primary care setting expected to see seven clients a day, five days a week. At any given time the counsellor estimated that approximately half of her clients were actively suicidal, or had talked of suicidal thoughts in some form. The stress of working under such conditions was evident for the counsellor. The implications for the clients on her caseload can only be imagined, as she often felt overwhelmed, exhausted, angry, distressed and ultimately depleted.

The ideal of course is that, through supervision and line management discussion, the counsellor is able to manage casework in such a way that it allows for particular demands and stresses. If the counsellor is carrying a 'heavy' caseload, an adjustment should be made as an allowance; this will ensure that the counsellor is able to continue to work competently and ethically, and that the clients seen receive a competent and ethical service. This so often is not the case.

Becoming the 'conscience' of the organization

As will be discussed in greater detail in the next chapter, 'Developing Procedures and Guidance', organizations often struggle to acknowledge the reality of suicide. They can deny its existence at all, preferring instead for a counselling service to be the 'container' into which everything unpalatable is placed. In large organizations such as in higher or further education, this can often be seen. The aim of the institution is the educational, personal and professional development of its students. Therefore, student distress can be experienced as a profound contradiction to that philosophy or ethos; it becomes the job of the counselling service to 'mop up' and hold this distress on behalf of the institution.

This isn't necessarily always a negative aspect. My own experience as a counsellor in a university setting is that the counselling service has been able to provide the institution with an alternative perspective in response to difficult situations, or to 'contain' the distress of the institution until it is able to recover from an event or a crisis. However, counsellors and counselling services must be aware of the dangers of this too, in that organizations can sometimes need to annihilate the 'container' at a later point.

Avoiding the threat to reputation caused by 'failure cases'

As highlighted in Chapter 5, 'The Influence of Policy and the Prediction-Prevention Culture', one consequence of the policy imperative around suicide reduction, and the absence of any engagement around the discussions of *whether* to prevent suicide always, has been a danger that any completed suicide will be viewed as a failure on behalf of the practitioner to use available knowledge competently. That is, if the practitioner had used available knowledge appropriately, then the suicide might/could/should have been prevented.

In this context, the organization can see client suicide as a failure of the counsellor, thus causing damage to reputation. The antecedents of suicide are many and varied. It might be true that the counsellor had 'failed' to hear the needs and distress of the client, acting out personal conviction of the right to die, for example. Alternatively, the suicide might have been entirely unpredictable. I recall elsewhere in this book my work with a young man who had developed multiple sclerosis, and who informed me of his intention to end his life while he still had the physical capacity to do that. Some months later he died following an overdose. Whether that situation represented personal empowerment on his part, or a failure on mine for not preventing it, will be dependent upon your personal views of suicide. It is difficult to integrate such complex ethical and moral thinking at an organizational level, and my suspicion is that, for many organizations, such 'outcome' would be viewed as a 'failure case'.

Coping with the envy of colleagues who are not able to take an hour for each client interview

I currently work in a 'dedicated' counselling agency, so consequently we all work to the same practice parameters of time. However, much of my working life has been spent in multi-professional settings where the world of the counsellor sits in stark contrast to that of other non-counselling colleagues. I was based for many years in a secondary care assessment and therapy service, where individual and group therapy were the preferred interventions for people with long-term, complex mental health needs. We offered an alternative to hospital admission, while at the same time working closely with inpatient colleagues. Referral to our service came via community-based workers in mental health teams, such as psychiatric social workers, community psychiatric nurses, psychiatrists etc.

There was a significant difference between the type of service we could offer clients, based around the 50-minute hour for individual therapy, or one-and-a-half or two hours for group sessions, and that of the referring community workers who might be managing caseloads in excess of 100 people – all of whom were presenting with complex mental health needs and high suicide potential. The conditions for envy were well in place.

In such a situation, it is easy to begin to lose sight of the importance of therapeutic parameters, and feel apologetic for the way in which we work. However, this is a dangerous road to travel as it can easily lead to compromised ethical practice, a poorer service for clients accessing help, and a sense of counsellors forever chasing a point at which colleagues' envy might be assuaged, not realizing that this is a bit like chasing a pot of gold at the end of the rainbow. Instead, it is important that counsellors remain focused on the professional aspects of counselling that ultimately are in place to protect both client and counsellor, and to provide the conditions for the best possible outcome. Certainly, when working with suicide potential, the boundaries and containing aspects of counselling parameters positively contribute to a dialogic exploration of suicide ideation.

Creating an appropriate office space and reception system

Any counsellor will know of the importance of ensuring that the 'systems' that support counselling are ethical and appropriate; for example, how the client can contact the counsellor, how appointments are arranged or changed, how clients are greeted when they arrive for sessions, how their confidentiality and autonomy are respected throughout this process. All of these administrative elements are integral to ethical practice.

While this is true for all clients at all times, it is particularly true if a client arrives for counselling in a distressed state, or leaves distressed, or requires additional space while waiting for their counsellor to access other services or additional information should the client present at risk of suicide. There have been a number of occasions in my work when I have needed a space for clients to wait privately while I have contacted a GP or mental health team, when they have not wanted to be present when I make the phone call.

For many organizations space is at a premium, and counsellors can sometimes experience difficulties in arguing for confidential space for their clients. Working in higher and further education is a case in point, where some institutions are moving to 'one-stop shops', i.e. where students can go to one point to access a range of student services, including counselling. Many services have expressed concerns over this trend, in that the privacy of counselling clients is not always accounted for in planning. Of course, there are many examples of this type of service working well, particularly when the counselling team have been able to contribute to the planning and design, to ensure that the particular needs of counselling clients are catered for. However, the outcome is not always so positive.

It is perhaps helpful to consider a case vignette from different organizational standpoints.

> **David**
>
> David is a 27-year-old plumber. He talks of very low self-esteem, self-confidence, poor body image and social anxiety. He finds the thought of relationships terrifying, and avoids social situations as much as he is able. He feels increasingly desperate about his situation; he wants to 'change and feel better' about himself, but cannot imagine how he might achieve this. He has been prescribed anti-depressants by his general practitioner, partly to help lift his mood, and partly to help with his social anxiety. He does not feel that these are helping, but feels uncomfortable talking to his GP about how he feels. He has started to use counselling to explore suicidal thoughts, saying, 'I know what I'd do. Sometimes it feels really pressing y'know ... hard to resist. Sometimes that's all I can think of and I don't know how I don't do it. It's just getting worse and worse, those thoughts there all the time.' David does not want you to talk about his feelings to anyone else.

Consider your responses to David as his counsellor, thinking about how the organization in which you work might influence those:

- You see David in independent practice; he pays £40 per week for weekly sessions. You have agreed an open-ended contract with no limits to the number of sessions available.
- You see David in a voluntary agency where counselling is free, with no limits to the number of sessions available. The organization has no policy regarding suicide, leaving it to individual counsellor assessment.
- You see David in a voluntary agency where counselling is free, with no limits to the number of sessions available. The organizational policy states that all suicide risk must be disclosed to the agency manager, who will then refer the client to their GP.
- You see David as a primary care counsellor. You work in the same building as David's GP. Your work is restricted to six sessions.

1. In thinking about these scenarios, what factors that might influence how you respond to David are the same across all settings, and what are different?
2. How might these different contexts influence how you feel about your work with David?
3. How do you imagine each setting will influence David's use of counselling?

The points above highlight some of the difficulties that counsellors might experience when working with suicidal clients in organizational settings. Independent practitioners might have more control over some of these issues, as opposed to those working in larger institutions where finding ways of inputting into decision making processes might be difficult. The truth for many counsellors might be that they have little input into or control over their working environment, so any discussion otherwise seems to be a fanciful luxury.

It is essential in the face of such pressures and expectations that counsellors continue to try to help their organizations understand the 'hows' and 'whys' of counselling. Through better understanding it might be possible to ensure that aspects of counselling that are considered the cornerstone of any work, e.g. confidentiality (appropriate to the setting), privacy for clients, outcomes that are contextually relevant, supervision that is ethically sound, and accessible consultative support, are put in place and protected. In that way, even in an imperfect system, the needs of suicidal clients and their counsellors can remain a priority.

Discussion questions

1. What is the relationship between you as a counsellor, the counselling you provide, and the organization in which it takes place?
2. What organizational aspects facilitate this relationship?
3. What organizational aspects hinder this relationship?
4. How do you or have you managed the difficulties of organizational working highlighted in this chapter?
5. How is your work with suicidal clients influenced by the organization in which you are based?

9 Developing Procedures and Guidance

> **Chapter overview**
>
> Many counsellors who work in organizations see suicidal clients in the context of an organizational policy or guidance document. This chapter considers the benefits and difficulties that may arise through the existence of such documents, and identifies elements that might usefully be included in procedural guidance to help support practice.

Given that most, if not all, counselling organizations will offer support to clients who present at suicide risk at some point, there is an increasing trend for those organizations to develop policy or procedural guidance to inform their employees when working with suicide risk. Statutory services, such as health trusts or social services, have traditionally worked to clear policy around risk. However, the development of suicide risk policy can also be seen in non-statutory agencies, such as in voluntary organizations. Some counsellors working privately from home also develop guidance to support their practice.

It might be argued that this move towards self-regulation through policy documents is in response to organizational anxiety around suicide; the fear is that in the event of client suicide, the organization might be held accountable by family, or be judged to have failed in their duty of care to the clients using their service. Certainly, as we have already highlighted, given the level of anxiety that can be experienced by the individual practitioner when working with suicide risk, it is fair to assume that this anxiety will also be experienced at an institutional level.

Organizational expectations of counsellors when working with suicide potential can present those counsellors with difficult ethical dilemmas. For example, where organizations insist on a referral to more specialist intervention for any client who expresses suicidal ideation, this can often be in conflict with how a counsellor might alternatively choose to work with suicide risk. Some counsellors feel that their employing organizations expect them to work in ways which are inconsistent with the perceived ethos of counselling, or perhaps with personally held views. For example, one counsellor said, 'Just by knowing that I need my job and that if I don't abide by [policy] then I am likely to be looked at very closely, for using my own personal view as opposed to what their wishes are.' Another said, more pragmatically,

> There is a conflict between my view and what I am expected to do about it. But I respect the right of the organization to expect that from somebody who is working for them. My personal view has to be put aside ... And there is a reality to the fact that

when working in a large organization like this or a small organization that is part of it, our practice is prescribed to some extent and we all have that tension every time we go in the room, don't we?

Putting personal views aside can be extremely difficult, even though the organization's requirement or expectation is well known. For example, a counsellor who strongly believes that their client has to right to make decisions about their suicide, and to act on those thoughts if they so wish, might experience great difficulty when the policy centres on prevention and intervention.

The fear of litigation, or of being perceived to have failed in their duty of care to a client, can often drive organizations to develop detailed procedures for counsellors to follow. Sometimes this can take the form of 'if client says A, then the counsellor will do B', and so on. Some organizations have started to make use of 'at-risk registers', similar to child protection procedures. The aim of such registers is to help ensure that all clients who present at risk of suicide are 'flagged' and monitored. However, unlike child protection where careful procedures are in place to safeguard the rights and autonomy of the child/family, this tends not always to be the case with adult suicide 'registers'. There are instances of clients not knowing their name has been 'flagged' in such a way, and consequently with little right of reply or appeal. It is therefore important that if organizations adopt such a register, careful consideration is given to ensuring clients' confidentiality and reputation are respected.

I believe there are inherent dangers in being too prescriptive over responses to suicidal clients in risk procedures. Human beings are simply not that straightforward or predictable. It is important that the vagaries of human behaviour, and the unpredictable nature of suicide potential, are incorporated into any policy or procedure document. In essence, it is important that those developing such policies consider carefully what they would like to achieve by having such a policy in place. There are a number of reasons why developing a risk policy might be beneficial, including:

- To ensure a consistent and equitable response to all clients using the service.
- To ensure that clients are protected from counsellors 'acting out' a personal agenda about suicide, e.g. 'I believe it is everyone's right to kill themselves', or 'I don't approve of suicide.'
- To ensure that all counsellors are aware of services to call on in the event of high suicide risk.
- To communicate clearly with clients how the organization will support them in the event of them being at risk.
- To provide an opportunity to consider/discuss how suicide potential should be responded to.
- To make clear to all employees the organization's expectations when they are working with suicide risk.
- To help protect the organization and/or counsellors in the event of client suicide.

In short, therefore, a policy or guidance that achieves a balance between clearly stating options in supporting clients who are suicidal, and avoiding becoming too prescriptive and therefore tying counsellors' hands behind their backs, can be extremely supportive and containing.

Achieving the right balance

Essentially, any policy should support, contain and guide counsellors, without overly directing practice. The following points might be worth considering when developing a new policy, or reviewing an existing one:

1. Does the policy appropriately reflect the parameters of the service offered, i.e. taking into account the experience of the counsellors, supervision contracts, the capacity of the service to work with risk, the profile of the client group?
2. Does the policy provide sufficient guidance to counsellors in the event of suicide risk, without becoming too prescriptive?
3. Is the policy clear, accessible and easy to communicate to all involved? That is to say, if a policy already exists, are the counsellors aware of it and do they understand the implication of it for their practice?
4. Is the policy realistic? Does it provide counsellors with options, rather than set up unrealistic and often unachievable expectations?
5. Does the policy provide a safe containment for the work with vulnerable clients?

In my view, the best policies provide guidance for counsellors and affirms trust in their assessment and intervention skills. They make clear statements about not expecting counsellors to have all the answers, or to be able to predict the future. Too many policies run the danger of hoisting the organization by its own petard. If instructions are too prescriptive, counsellors will inevitably run the risk of falling short of procedural expectations in trying to manage a difficult or unpredictable level of risk. Once this happens, both the counsellor and the organization become vulnerable if practice needs to be defended. Given that one question likely to be asked in the event of client suicide is 'Did the counsellor follow the organizational lead or instruction?', it is important to ensure that it is reasonably possible for counsellors to do so.

Table 9.1 represents a sample guidance document for working with risk. This guidance document contains a number of important elements:

- definitions
- acknowledgement of uncertainty when working with suicide risk
- discrimination between 'thought' and 'intent'
- encouragement to talk to clients about suicide
- practice direction (but not prescription)
- placing decision making process in context of consultation
- expectations regarding record keeping
- post-suicide support options.

Policies or guidance need to be developed in such a way that they reflect the culture and specific responsibilities of each organization. Suicide potential can raise considerable anxiety in counsellor and organization alike; the explicit or implicit intention sometimes is to try to define practice in such detail that the uncertain becomes certain, or the unknown becomes known. As is the case for individual counsellors, a successful organizational approach to working with suicide potential is as much about being able to tolerate the unknown and uncertain as it is about getting the detail right. If counsellors can feel supported

Table 9.1 Sample guidance document for working with suicidal clients in organizational settings

Definitions	The aim of this guidance document is to help clarify how you might respond in a situation where you feel a client presents at risk. For this purpose, risk is usefully defined in the context of the confidentiality agreements that are made between the client and the Service when they register for counselling. The Service confidentiality policy is stated in the leaflet 'Information About Your Counselling' which all clients receive when registering for counselling. Risk would be viewed as a client expressing an intent to commit suicide, or where self-harm is severe enough to suggest that it might be immediately life threatening. Risk to others would include child protection (physical, sexual, emotional or neglect), or an expressed intent by the client to harm another person or commit a terrorist act.
Acknowledgement of uncertainty when working with suicide risk Discrimination between 'thought' and 'intent' Encouragement to talk to clients about suicide	It is acknowledged that working with clients at risk is difficult and it is not possible to accurately predict possible client actions in the future. In working with clients at risk, being able to talk to your client openly and honestly about their feelings or their situation will offer the best possible opportunity to decide upon how best to proceed. Any response to a suicidal client at risk needs to be mediated with an acknowledgement of the difference between 'thought' and 'intent'. For example, an expressed thought about suicide does not necessarily communicate intent. It is important to feel sufficiently confident to talk explicitly with your client about their thoughts, to help gauge intent. The general guidelines for responding in such situations are:
Practice direction (but not prescription) Placing decision making process in context of consultation	• If you are concerned about the immediate safety of your client or another person, it is important to consult with your manager and/or another member of your team, and where possible your supervisor – if possible before your client leaves the building. However, if your client wishes to leave the building before you have been able to consult, they must be permitted to do so. Wherever possible inform your client before they leave the building of what you intend to do, e.g. contact their GP, the police (in emergencies), etc. In the event of terrorist concerns, it is not appropriate to discuss these concerns directly with your client. It is important however to speak with the Head of Counselling Service as soon as possible. • Wherever possible, every intervention or contact with a third party regarding the client should be undertaken with the client's explicit permission. In exceptional circumstances we may need to initiate contact with a third party to help safeguard the client's wellbeing without their consent, but with their knowledge. This would only happen after consultation with your supervisor or a member of the core team. • The aim of consulting with your supervisor or another member of the team is to ensure that all possible options are explored fully and that you are supported in your work and not left in an isolated position either professionally or personally. The Service acknowledges that working with clients at risk is a difficult and stressful process; the aim is to ensure that you are fully supported at all times. Additionally, as a counsellor, you are not expected to undertake psychiatric diagnoses or to be able to predict the future actions of your client: risk assessment is an inexact and subjective process. It is, however, important to respond to your own concerns both with the client directly and within the Service team.

Table 9.1 (Continued)

Expectations regarding record keeping	Ensure that you record accurately and fully in the client notes your concerns and how you responded to those concerns, paying particular attention to the following: – the *specific* nature of the risk identified – any relevant discussion between client and counsellor regarding the risk(s), including client responses. – any agreements made with the client in response to the risk, or any other specific actions taken, including consultation with supervisor or other senior counsellor. If a decision is made to break confidentiality against the client's expressed wishes, but with their knowledge, notes should include the following information: • The reasons why the counsellor believed breaking confidentiality was in their client's best interests. • What the purpose of breaking confidentiality was, e.g. referral for psychiatric assessment. • Why it was not possible to gain client consent. This may be because the client was unable to give their informed consent at that point due to the level of their emotional and/or physical distress, or they had already left the Service building and were not contactable.
Post-suicide support options	In the event of a client suicide or other serious incident involving a client, the Service acknowledges that in addition to procedural management within the organization, it is very important to offer support and help to all those directly involved. In addition, this acknowledgement will include the implications for the wider team. The nature and extent of such support will be influenced by the expressed needs of those directly involved, but might include: • The need for those involved to remain in the Service for support/debrief. • The need for those involved to leave the Service but have a defined point of contact with someone in the Service. • Organized time with the supervisor, senior counsellor or Head of Service. • The management of other ongoing client work and the needs of existing clients. • An opportunity for the team to meet and discuss other responses needed. These points are in addition to existing support/debrief structures within the wider organization.

and contained by procedure, they are much more likely to be able to engage with suicidal clients in such a way that both will feel cared for.

> **Discussion questions**
>
> 1 Are you aware of any procedural or guidance document within your organization that defines practice with respect to working with suicidal clients?
> 2 If such a procedural or guidance document exists, do you feel that it supports or potentially exposes your practice?
> 3 Can you be specific about what aspects of the procedural or guidance document support or potentially expose your practice?
> 4 How might you as an individual counsellor, or counselling team, help develop existing or future procedural or guidance documents?

Part IV

The Client Process

10 Understanding Suicide

> **Chapter overview**
>
> While much research has focused on suicide risk factors, counsellors often prefer to consider the meaning of suicide for their clients in interpersonal and intrapersonal ways. This chapter aims to provide an overview of some explanations of suicidality while acknowledging that, in reality, the reasons for an individual experiencing suicidal thoughts can be so multi-faceted that any 'blueprints' of meaning can only be tentatively made.

Helping a client understand the meaning behind their suicidal intent, or finding a meaning for ourselves, can be profoundly problematic. Suicide can present in different ways, from the person who plans their own death with detail and intent, to the person who lives with the constant thought of suicide as a means of surviving in life, to the person who has no plans or intent but acts on spontaneous or impulsive thoughts triggered by a moment of crisis. Is suicide an attack only on 'self', or an attack on the 'other' too? Suicidality can be experienced by the counsellor as an attack, and also as a withdrawal from the relationship.

Leenaars states that, 'There are biological, psychological, intrapsychic, logical, conscious and unconscious, interpersonal, sociological, cultural and philosophical/existential elements in the suicidal event, to name a few. It thus seems reasonable that we would be perplexed and bewildered about answering the question "why"' (2004: 39). Leenaars offers an in-depth discussion of all these factors, which I shall summarize here.

Intrapsychic

Unbearable psychological pain
Suicide provides the client with an opportunity to escape from psychological pain that is so unbearable, and that the client fears has no end. Certainly, there are many instances from my own practice when clients have said to me that they cannot imagine their pain ever ending.

Cognitive constriction
Leenaars describes constriction as 'rigidity in thinking, narrowing of focus, tunnel vision, concreteness' (2004: 45). When present in a suicidal client, it can be experienced

such that the client sees no alternative to managing their problems other than suicide. They have lost the capacity in the moment to contemplate alternative solutions.

Indirect expressions

The suicidal client may only be aware of certain aspects of their distress, the rest being unconscious processes. Ambivalence is an important aspect of this presentation, with the suicidal client caught between contradictory aspects of their experience, e.g. living and dying, anger and passivity.

Inability to adjust

Suicidal clients might experience problems in life as so unbearable that they have no capacity to overcome them, or to adjust to manage them differently. Such problems might include psychopathology such as depression, anxiety disorders, etc. Leenaars states that, 'Having the belief that they are too weak to overcome difficulties, such people reject everything except death – they do not survive life's difficulties' (2004: 46).

Ego

Ego is 'part of the mind that mediates between the conscious and the unconscious and is responsible for the interpretation of reality and the development of a sense of self' (*Oxford English Dictionary*, 1989). As such, it becomes clear that clients with a diminished ego are more likely to be at risk of acting on suicidal thoughts, as the client is likely to present as quite vulnerable with a diminished capacity to cope with difficulties or resist unconscious impulses.

Interpersonal

Interpersonal relations

Clients who are suicidal are likely to struggle with developing or sustaining relationships with others; this may be related to attachment difficulties. In the absence of satisfying interpersonal relationships, the client is left reflecting on persistent unmet needs – suicide is seen as the only alternative. Bell offers some interesting thoughts on unmet needs from a psychoanalytic perspective, suggesting that suicide can result from an intolerance of frustration, linked with an awareness of 'needs or desires unsatisfied [which] precipitates serious mental difficulties' (2008: 49). The physicality of such awareness means that the body becomes the point of attack.

Rejection–aggression

Stemming from the 1910 meeting of the Psychoanalytic Society in Vienna, the rejection–aggression hypothesis has developed further since. Essentially, it is proposed that loss or rejection lies at the centre of suicide, in that the client's rejection is experienced as abandonment. This traumatic 'injury' leads to pain and then to self-directed anger. Leenaars explains that, 'the suicidal person is deeply ambivalent and, within the context of this ambivalence, suicide may become the turning back upon oneself of murderous impulses (wishes, needs) that had previously been directed against a traumatic event, most frequently someone who had rejected that individual' (2004: 48).

Identification–egression

An important aspect of understanding suicidality is, as Freud (1974a; 1974b; 1974c) and Zilboorg (1936) state, identification with a lost person or ideal, e.g. employment, youth. In this identification the client can experience profound distress, and seeks a means of escaping these feelings; hence suicide.

In my own analysis of the discourse of suicide as it presents within counselling sessions, I speculated on three dominant discourses that appeared to encapsulate the meaning of the narrative of suicidal clients in the study. In the discourse analysis tradition, these are referred to as interpretive repertoires. Three emerged from my analysis of transcribed video sessions with suicidal clients, and are discussed here. The full discourse analysis can be found in Reeves et al. (2004b).

Suicide ends existential crisis

The first repertoire places the discourse of suicide as a means of resolving existential crisis. The subject position of this discourse can be illustrated as follows:

> What's the point, what's the point in carrying on? I feel really alone with it all … I just feel that I don't exist – I don't belong in the life I live in [alone and abandoned; invisible and valueless; not worthy of my own existence].

This example, integrated from phraseology across all 16 transcripts analysed, suggests that the action orientation of the discourse verbalizes a dilemma faced by the suicidal individual at an internal level. The purpose of life in this interpretive repertoire is defined externally rather than having an internal intrinsic value. The 'worth' or 'pointlessness' of life lies outside the individual, and consequently their own sense of worth is lost. The individual ceases to exist as there is 'no point', and without a 'point', there is no reason to 'carry on'. The notion of 'self' is transferred from an intrapersonal phenomenon to one that is defined in relation to environment: the removal of a purpose to exist in turn removes the purpose to live, thus presenting self as out of place.

The 'task' of the counsellor in the therapeutic process is predominantly defined by the theoretical orientation from which they work. Within this discourse it might be argued that a reflective response allows the client to find further meaning and additionally enables the client to explore this existential crisis and facilitates their understanding of how it impacts on their experience of 'self'. However, it might also be true that predominant reflective responses

Table 10.1 Suicide as a means of ending existential crisis: an example from a transcript

Client	1	No, I feel like I've tried everything that I can and I need help now … I really really need help otherwise there is no point in carrying on.
Counsellor	2	It seems very bad – you see no point in carrying on.
Client	3	Yes. Not really.
Counsellor	4	Can you tell me a little bit more about that feeling of not being able to carry on?
Client	5	It just feels like I've been in the same place for so long and that things are just getting more and more difficult and it's getting more difficult to keep going – the kids take a lot of time and energy. Keith's no use and I just feel like I'm trapped and I've been trapped in the same place for a really long time.
Counsellor	6	So you're kept in one place and you can't run. It's as though you can't escape from this place.
Client	7	No, not at all.
Counsellor	8	Like a cage.
Client	9	And I've been there ages and I've been there for a long long time and it just doesn't feel like … it just feels like this is my life and it's never going to change, so what's the point.

compound the sense of loss of definition and purpose and fail to engage with an exploration of the nature and intent of the suicidal discourse. The reflective response could reinforce the client's sense of pointlessness in hearing their own words and meanings repeated back to them, thus failing to engage with a redefining process. This can be illustrated in Table 10.1.

In line 1 the client states that without help, which they 'really really need', there would be no point in carrying on. Whether there is any point in carrying on is dependent upon the client receiving help. However, the therapist's reflection in line 2 removes the tentative nature of the 'pointlessness' by stating definitively that the client currently sees no point in carrying on. The client's speculative pointlessness is brought into the present, and during the remaining section of dialogue this is reinforced by the therapist, particularly in lines 6 and 8.

The client has been moved from a point of conditional pointlessness to one of unconditionality. The reflective nature of the counsellor responses does not explore the consequence of the emerging unconditionality. At the end of this section of transcript, and also in the complete transcript, the client's desperate statement in line 1, that without help there is no point in carrying on, is not explored. It is unclear as to what 'help' the client may be looking for and what the client means by 'no point in carrying on': the nature and intent of the client's implicit reference to suicide remains untouched and uninvestigated.

Suicide removes a sense of being 'stuck' with the negotiations and manoeuvrings of life

The action orientation of this repertoire is based on a presumption implicit in the dialogue that life is essentially about movement and negotiation. The expression of suicidal thought/intent is an articulation of a sense of being 'stuck' in this

Table 10.2 Suicide as a means of removing a sense of being 'stuck' with the negotiations and manoeuvrings of life: an example from a transcript

Client	1	Maybe ... maybe – but if there isn't there's nothing for me ... there's no way forward – I can't think about –
Counsellor	2	So this hope that we can do something here and some real fear about what if this doesn't work – like being at the end of the line and ...
Client	3	Don't ... I don't ... I feel like I don't ... there's no way for me to go forward and there's nothing, and I don't like being back (slight laugh) ...
Counsellor	4	Erm, really stuck. (yes)
Client	5	I feel like I er, I don't know ...
Counsellor	6	As if something is holding you back or keeping you back from moving forward.

otherwise dynamic process. In synthesizing the presentation of this discourse from across the transcripts, the subject position of the discourse can therefore be represented as:

> I'm thinking about stopping it. I don't see what's keeping me here, or why carry on. I feel stuck and cannot see a way forward. I need to get out and go somewhere else – I need to get out of people's way and get out of this stuckness [not a willing participant; an inconvenience and an obstruction; powerless and no longer dynamic].

Here in the metaphor of movement and of being stuck, the client does not see themselves engaged with this otherwise dynamic process: whilst others move and negotiate, they 'stand still' and therefore 'get in the way' – as someone standing still will become an obstacle for a moving crowd. The client therefore needs to find a way of shifting themselves from this position. The action orientation of the discourse is centred on movement, 'stuckness' and subsequently removal.

Without the perceived possibility of movement or change, the client presents a solution to their dilemma in which suicide essentially absolves them from future manoeuvrings and ultimately 'removes' them. This discourse is illustrated in Table 10.2 where the client identifies that they feel there is 'no way forward' in line 1. The therapist in line 6 paraphrases this short statement, when the client's inability for movement is reflected. Again, the primary reflective position of the therapist (line 4: 'Erm, really stuck') restates a meaning for the client but does not explore or help the client redefine it.

Suicide ends apathy and fatigue generated by the burdensome nature of life

Here the interpretive repertoire of the discourse again externalizes the process by which suicide is explored and expressed by the client. The burdensome nature of the experienced distress is represented as 'it', with 'it' becoming an entity – separate from, but in relationship with, the client. The metaphor is developed further in that 'it' also becomes the distress itself that the client has been forced to carry and manage. When the weight of the burden of 'it' is no longer tolerable by the client, the notion of suicide enters the process. Leenaars (2004) provides an overview of psychoanalytic theories of suicide that may have some relevance in the context of this particular interpretive repertoire. Some specific elements of theory include:

- The root of suicide is in the experience of loss and rejection of a significant cathected object.
- The suicidal person exhibits an overly regressive attachment – 'narcissistic identification' – with the object.
- The suicidal person is angry at the object although the feelings and/or ideas of vengefulness and aggression are directed towards self.
- The suicidal person's organization of experiences is impaired. They are no longer capable of any coherent synthesis of experience (2004: 17–18).

While this is not a comprehensive overview of the main aspects of psychoanalytic theory regarding suicide, it does identify the importance of the object, in object-relations terms, and the suicidal individual's interaction and projection on the object. The aggressive or vengeful feelings towards the object become self-directed and suicidal. The repertoire then develops this as burdensome, resulting in fatigue and self-annihilation.

The subject position can be illustrated as:

> I just feel too tired to carry on. It feels so heavy, I don't know if I can continue to manage it any longer/further. I feel so tired and exhausted in keeping it going. I don't want people to worry about me any more. I need to take the pain away – to ease the pain [exhausted and incapable; have become other people's concern; palliative positioning].

The repertoire positions the client separately from their own intrapersonal processing. The distress that has led them to consider suicide is externalized to the product of 'it', which over time has become increasingly weighty and burdensome. In many ways this also positions the client as a victim of their distress rather than having a dynamic relationship with it. This is something that they have been burdened with, rather than their distress stemming from an intrapersonal or interpersonal struggle.

This position suggests that the focus of change ultimately needs to be on the nature of the burden that life has created, rather than on possible achievements at a more individual or relational level. While it is important to acknowledge that human distress is often the product both of a subjective world view and of societal pressures and influences, the discourse does not easily allow the client to renegotiate their position and therefore move from their current state. This is demonstrated in Table 10.3 where the therapist in lines 4 and 6 reflects suicidal thoughts without exploring them further.

Table 10.3 Suicide as a means of ending apathy and fatigue generated by the burdensome nature of life: an example from a transcript

Client	1	Its just like … I dunno … just a black, blackness …
Counsellor	2	Just as though everything is black and dark and heavy (heavy) like there is no light at the end of the tunnel in a way …
Client	3	Yeah. It's heavy. I just … I know that my mum, I know she worries about me … I sometimes just think, well she'd be a lot better off if I wasn't around. She could go off and do her thing and wouldn't have to call on me … do my shopping …or my washing … and so sometimes it seems like a good idea …you know.
Counsellor	4	So I guess you're feeling like she might be better off without you ehm …
Client	5	Yeah …
Counsellor	6	It sounds as though it's a really bad feeling when it comes … a really, really bad feeling …
Client	7	Yeah it is, yeah.

The nature of the counselling discourse is essentially different from that of a spontaneously generated conversation. The counselling process is based on the facilitation of the client by the counsellor using particular forms and styles of intervention. Regardless of the theoretical orientation of the practitioner, therapeutic skills might include reflection, paraphrasing, open questioning and challenge. The *predominant* use of reflective interventions can mean that the position of the counsellor in the discourse is essentially defined by the position of the client. The three repertoires identified here all seem to position the client as feeling powerless to change their predicament, other than through suicide. The three repertoires and the position of the counsellor within them have implications for how counsellors are then able to assess the risk of suicide in their clients and how that assessment subsequently informs interventions.

In this chapter, I have attempted to provide an outline of some of the explanations for suicidality. Perhaps so much of the available research has focused on risk factors because finding meaning in suicide is so notoriously difficult. Perhaps if we could generate blueprints of meaning, then that would provide an efficacious means of understanding distress, without having to delve too deeply. For each individual client who talks about their suicidality in sessions, there will be different meaning and experience. Certainly their risk factors may correlate with research, and it may be possible to make sense of their experience by applying general theories of suicide, as presented here. However, as Shneidman (1998) states,

> our best route to understanding suicide is not through the study of the structure of the brain, nor the study of social statistics, nor the study of mental diseases, but directly through the study of human emotions described in plain English, in the words of the suicidal person. The most important question to a potentially suicidal person is not an inquiry about family history or laboratory tests of blood or spinal fluid, but 'where do you hurt?' and 'how can I help you?' (p. 6)

Discussion questions

1. How consistent are the theories of suicide, as presented here, with your own model of practice?
2. Reflecting on your own work with suicidal clients, do any of these theories of suicide enhance the meaning or understanding of your own or your clients' experience?
3. From your own experience, in what different ways do you understand the process and experience of suicide?
4. How much do you agree or disagree with Shneidman's quotation given at the end of this chapter? What are your reasons?

11 The Use of Language in Counselling Suicidal Clients

> **Chapter overview**
>
> Understanding suicidal ideation and assessing potential require insight into the client's process around their suicidal thinking. Given that counsellors work predominantly with the client's narrative, it is important to consider whether or how clients might talk about suicide within sessions, and the implications of this for counsellors.

I was thinking about the language that clients use because I find now that I am much more aware of what clients are saying. Whereas in the past I would hear things like, 'I feel really low' and might take it at face value. Now I might think, 'well, how low' and I am much more willing to explore that and go into it and ordinarily that would just pass by' (counsellor participant in research)

The phrase 'risk assessment' within the context of human distress is widely used by a number of professional groups. However, as has been highlighted in other chapters, there is an important difference between the risk-factor-based approach to assessing suicide risk, and the understanding of the individual suicidal person's thinking obtained through listening and talking. Williams and Morgan (1994) stated that,

> It would seem common sense, when faced with an individual who is suspected of being at risk of suicide, to search for demographic and clinical factors known to be associated with increased suicide risk ... this is the statistical stereotype of suicide ... they do, however, present problems in the day-to-day clinical situation. Many individuals will possess these characteristics yet not commit suicide, and suicide can occur in people of very different characteristics. (p. 19)

As we have been discussing, a number of tools and protocols have been developed in an attempt to 'quantify' levels of distress, and thus improve the likelihood of predicting the nature and extent of risk. Much of the literature that considers the assessment of suicide risk is concerned with the development and subsequent efficacy of such tools. While such research has furthered knowledge and understanding about the nature of suicide risk within specific demographic groups, counsellors are still unable to accurately predict which individuals will attempt to kill themselves or, of those, who will be successful (Range et al., 1997).

Leenaars (2004) writes that,

> It is likely that no one behaviour, including a test score or an interview, will provide all of the information needed to assess and predict suicide ... each bit of information (like a test score, an observation) will have to be placed in the context of that person's life ... all predictions ultimately depend on the skills of the clinician. In that sense, suicide prediction is a task like many others a clinician faces: a problem of understanding a number of evaluations of the same person. (p. 105)

Policy and practice development over the last few years have focused on objectifying the process of suicide assessment in the application of scientific method and positivist measurement (Beck et al., 1974; Marris et al., 1992). The degree to which a counsellor needs to assess risk in their working context is different to when such an assessment is being undertaken by others to inform a treatment regime, or when the removal of an individual's liberty under mental health legislation is being considered. Counsellors have a significant role to play in offering mental health care to clients both within and outside statutory mental health services, but they are not diagnosticians. A psychiatrist or clinical psychologist makes psychiatric diagnoses.

Within a counselling context, risk assessment is essentially undertaken to ascertain whether the client can be contained within the agreed structures of counselling, or whether the client is in need of alternative or additional specialized care. This is an important decision making process given the integral role that confidentiality has within the structure of counselling (Bond, 2009). Within counselling, discussions about the need for secondary prevention are predominantly achieved through dialogue between counsellor and client. It could be argued that this is also true for all mental health disciplines, where tools and questionnaires only enhance understanding achieved through actually listening to the client. The heavy reliance on tools and questionnaires in some settings though can sometimes appear to throw doubt on this claim.

Exploring discourse

Counsellors work with clients who have a range of presenting issues, including suicide. The existence and nature of suicide risk pose the practitioner with several ethical, moral and practice dilemmas. The counselling dialogue that takes place between client and counsellor is central to a complex interplay of discourses that aim to help the client move from a position of inter/intrapersonal distress, to a point where they are more able to function effectively on a practical and emotional level. The theoretical model from which the counsellor works will essentially determine the 'aim' of counselling, and how that aim is achieved.

As is highlighted in Chapter 15, 'Potential Dangers and Difficulties', one of the possible consequences of working with suicidality is the loss of psychological 'contact' with the client, through the counsellor's experience of fear, anxiety and self-doubts. The nature of the discourse between suicidal client and counsellor is potentially informed by many factors, including:

- The level of confidentiality agreed between client and counsellor, and the context in which counselling is taking place.
- The nature of the 'suicide discourse' of the client.
- The meaning of suicide for the client.
- The counsellor's own thoughts, feelings and understanding about suicide in general terms.
- The meaning of suicide for the counsellor.
- The counsellor's own thoughts, feelings and understanding about the individual client's expression of suicidal ideation.
- The level of 'suicide awareness' of the counsellor and their willingness and/or ability to be open to a self-exploration of that awareness and subsequent responses.
- Transferential and countertransferential issues between counsellor and client: the dynamic nature of the relationship.
- The facilitative style and theoretical orientation of the counsellor in working with suicide 'talk', and in the level/depth of exploration achieved.

Given that there is no one single expression of suicide, but instead infinite ways in which suicide might be named or alluded to by an individual, the role of language and its subsequent influence on therapeutic dynamics become integral factors in how suicide is explored. For example, the literature emphasizes the importance of mental health practitioners adopting a questioning/explorative style when working with suicide potential (Firestone, 1997; Leenaars, 2004; Lemma, 1996; Shea, 2002; University of Manchester, 2002). Clients may often be reluctant to talk about their suicidal thoughts due to a number of factors, including shame, embarrassment, and the fear of acknowledging what they perceive to be a personal 'failure' (Shea, 2002).

It is therefore helpful to consider the implications for counselling, and counsellors, when clients introduce their suicidal ideation or intent into the counselling discourse. This consideration can be helpful because it can throw some light on the *means* by which suicide can be constructed in the discourse, and *how* that positions counsellors accordingly. I shall provide an overview of findings from my own research looking at these issues. A comprehensive discussion of discourse analysis can be found elsewhere (e.g. Billig, 1997; 2001; Brown and Yule, 1993; Parker, 1992; Potter and Wetherell, 1987; Schiffrin, 1994; Van Dijk, 2003). For a full discussion of my study presented here, see Reeves et al. (2004b).

The meanings of suicide

The findings presented here are based on an analysis of videotaped assessment sessions between counsellors and suicidal clients (Reeves et al., 2004b). No one particular model of counselling is represented, with counsellors working to a range of models, including person centred, psychodynamic, solution focused and gestalt. The analysis of the transcripts concentrated on those points at which the clients talked about suicide, whether explicitly ('I feel so bad I am thinking of killing myself') or implicitly ('I just wish I could go to sleep and not wake up'). What is noteworthy is how rarely clients made explicit references to suicide; this is something counsellors need to pay attention to. That is not to say that clients will never talk explicitly about suicide, because they do. However, what seemed pertinent in my analysis was that clients often took the lead from the counsellor. That is to say, if counsellors were able to talk about suicide explicitly, to name it, then, with support, clients were able to do the same. Conversely, when counsellors did not name suicide but reflected only their client's implicit references to it, that is how it remained: not named and only alluded to.

Table 11.1 provides an overview of the primary ways in which clients talked about their suicidal ideation. It is interesting to note that 'do myself in' was probably the most explicit first reference to suicide throughout all the transcripts.

Table 11.2 shows a list of predominant counsellor responses to their clients at the point of their client making reference to suicide for the first time. What is clear is that the majority of the counsellor phrases are reflective, rather than more

Table 11.1 Ways in which clients talk about suicide

References to discursive object	Example from transcript	Contextual understanding
Stopping/stop it	'In a way, if I was on my own you know, I wouldn't be here – I would have stopped it. I would have stopped it.'	Externalization of distress – stopping 'it'
Too tired	'Yeah. If I was on my own that's what I'd do now [take tablets] cos I'm just too tired.'	Loss of energy for life; constructed metaphor of life as energy focused and therefore draining
There's nothing keeping me here	'There's nothing keeping me here … so what's the point?'	An expressed polarity of either being here or not; being present or absent
What's the point?	'It's useless, just a waste – there's no point.'	Questioning of self as having an internalized and externalized 'value'; existential dilemma, existential guilt
Black/blackness	'Its just like … I dunno … just a black, blackness.'	The metaphor of colour – polarity of light and darkness/white and blackness
Too heavy – to manage	'Its heavy. I just … I know that my mum, I know she worries about me … I sometimes just think, well she'd be a lot better off if I wasn't around.'	Life as burdensome – weight of hopelessness too great to carry any further
Do myself in	'Might get away – do myself in.'	Demolition of self – to destroy and annihilate
Just too much	'It's too much now – just too much.'	Revisiting the previous notion of life being burdensome – being overwhelmed
Carrying on	'There's no point in carrying on if this doesn't work.'	Constructing the notion that life is a forward moving dynamic process – emotional burden too great to carry on

Table 11.1 (Continued)

References to discursive object	Example from transcript	Contextual understanding
Feel really alone in it	'Yeah. [pause] I just feel really alone in it.'	Isolation and separateness – disconnection with family/friends/supporters – in the final analysis we are on our own
Way out	'It [taking an overdose] was the only way out.'	Finding a means of exit when trapped
Going somewhere else	'It's about going away from everything, and everything that is going on in your life, and being somewhere else.'	Linked with 'there's nothing keeping me here' – the act of suicide being the final removal
Continuing with it	'I don't see the point in continuing that much longer to be honest if it's going to be the same … I don't see what reason to continue at all for any of it.'	Same as 'carrying on' – the 'it' being an externalized notion of distress and despair
Don't exist	'It's kind of like there's nothing … there's a blank … it's almost like I don't exist – anyway.'	Feeling that self is invisible or not existing with any value – projected loss of self
Empty and dead	'Yeah … I feel really empty and dead inside.'	Self as an empty shell – no life
Don't belong in the life I live in	'Yeah. Feel like I'm er … I don't belong anywhere in life.'	Impostor – don't deserve the life I live in – fraud and need to get out; being somewhere when not welcome
Can't move forward – really stuck	'It just feels like I'm stuck in it and it's gone on for ages and it's going to go on for ages – there doesn't feel like there's any … any way out of it.'	Manoeuvring through life – again the dynamic shifting process of life that can no longer be negotiated

explorative. As was noted in the previous chapter, reflective responses can be profoundly powerful when working with any client, including a client who is contemplating suicide. It can be both important and facilitative for clients to hear their own words, and thus consider the meaning of them without counsellor influence or bias. However, as we have discussed elsewhere, clients may experience difficulties in naming suicide for the first time. It is important that the counsellor acknowledges the existence of the fearsome place, for the client may have learnt to disregard it over some period of time. Or, the client may be startled and frightened at the realization of its existence. In this sense, it is essential that counsellors are able to ask questions, to explore, and to be prepared to name it in the first instance: 'How bad does this feel for you? Are there times when you have considered killing yourself?'

On occasions, even when a counsellor begins an explorative route, they can easily become deflected by their own anxiety and move back to a place of their own safety. Table 11.3 is an extract from one of the transcripts that illustrates this.

Table 11.2 Predominant counsellor responses to client expressions of suicide

Can you say (tell me) a bit more about that ... (could you tell me a little bit more ...)
Wonder how you're feeling about that ... (I wonder if ...) (I'm [just] wondering ...)
I'm getting the impression ...
I guess that this is ... (I guess there's ...) (I guess you['re] ...)
Almost as if ...
Am I right in thinking ...
Can I suggest that ...
It sounds like ... (So it's sounding like ...) (It sounds as though ...) (You sound a bit ...)
It feels as though ... (You're feeling that ...)
Can you help me understand ...
I can't help noticing ...
How about you tell me ...
It seems to me ... (You seem to be ...)
So I think I'm hearing ... (What I'm hearing is that ...)
This is the sense that ... (I am sensing that ...) (I'm [almost] getting a sense that ...) (I get a real sense that ...) (I really get a sense that [of] ...)
It's almost like ...
It seems like [that] ...
Somehow though it seems ... (So it seems that you're saying)
You're saying that ...
Let me just get this right ...
Is that something you could tell [share with] me ...
So tell me ...
It seems almost as though you are saying ...
I could be wrong here but ...
I'm aware that ...

Neither the client nor the counsellor returned to the client's expressed thought (line 2) of taking an overdose throughout the rest of the session. The direct way in which the client answered the counsellor's question, 'I'd overdose', almost seemed to overwhelm the counsellor for a moment: 'So you'd take your stockpile of tablets [yes] ... right ... right ... Erm ... one of the options ... right ... right.' In counselling terms, the counsellor continues to help the client to explore their pain and the difficulties experienced by the client in fully articulating the awfulness of their situation.

As was discussed in the previous chapter, the choice of reflective responses is a common theme throughout the transcripts. In line 1, the therapist asks for more information about the client's stated intention to take their own life – a more explicit reference by the counsellor to the discursive object. The client's response to this question in line 2 provides the therapist with specific information: the nature of the suicide intent (the use of stockpiled medication) and the preferred means of suicide and availability of the 'tools' to achieve this end (an overdose with the stockpiled medication). The therapist's reflection in line 3 clarifies the

Table 11.3 Counsellor deflection and retreat: an example from a transcript

Counsellor	1	Erm ... that's something you could tell me about ... share with me ... about how you might take your life.
Client	2	Well ... the GP has provided me with more than enough tablets over the years. I've managed to just stockpile them so I've got enough ... I know how I'd do it ... erm ... and I'd overdose.
Counsellor	3	So you'd take your stockpile of tablets [yes] ... right ... right ... erm ... [pause] ... sounds like you feel pretty sure about this as a way of managing this really difficult pain.
Client	4	It's one of the options, isn't it?
Counsellor	5	Erm ... one of the options ... right ... right ...
Client	6	Feels like the only option left at the moment.
Counsellor	7	I really get a sense of how at times this pain hurts so much for you – that it's unbearable
Client	8	Well, yes ...
Counsellor	9	Can you tell me a little bit more about this kind of feeling inside of you that is unbearable?
Client	10	[sighs heavily] ... it's like I've tried and tried and tried and tried ... and it just feels like, you know ... for someone like me the world's ... just set up against me. I feel like I'm finally being realistic about my situation ... actually ... and that I don't think there is a way out ... in a way ...
Counsellor	11	It seems like in here you're really trying to tell me how desperate you feel?
Client	12	I mean ... I assume that's what you do with counsellors?
Counsellor	13	But that it is really quite hard to put into words to that ... to these feelings.
Client	14	It's kind of like there's nothing ... there's a blank ... it's almost like I don't exist – anyway.

information and offers a 'meaning-making' statement by suggesting an overdose is a means by which the client is choosing to manage 'really difficult pain'. The remaining therapist interventions in this section seem to serve a similar function to that in line 3, but do not have the explorative quality of line 1. The exception to this is line 9 where the therapist attempts to help the client explore the nature of the 'pain'. The therapist's interventions essentially reflect and facilitate the client's expression of distress but do not further clarify the imminence or likelihood of a client suicide.

In general terms the discourse represents a conversational style – turn taking within the therapeutic context, each 'turn' signalled by a number of linguistic mechanisms such as intonation, pausing, sighing, etc. Goffman's (1974) work on frame analysis has some relevance here. Frame analysis refers to the 'frames' through which people structure their experiences, such as 'serious, joking, business, chat' (Schiffrin, 1994). In this context the frame is self-annihilation.

The frames of 'therapy' and of 'suicide' structure the discourse and the participants' role in it: the 'counsellor' as listener and the 'client' as talker within a 'helping' purpose. As the client is involved in 'self' generated talk, the counsellor offers responses to help clarify understanding, further meaning and thus offer a move towards 'health'. The frame of 'suicide' thus impinges on this as the suicidal client has temporarily or permanently ceased moving towards health, and instead is verbalizing self-annihilatory thoughts. The counsellor is able to accurately reflect this conversational dynamic but does not seem to be able to explore or help develop it. Firestone (1997) describes the suicidal process as a response to a destructive 'inner voice', and states that the key to understanding suicidal behaviour lies in accessing and understanding an individual's self-destructive dialogue.

Perhaps there was an important parallel taking place, with the counsellor finding difficulties in putting into words their thoughts and feelings about their client's suicidal ideation? At the end of the session, neither the counsellor nor the client understood any further the nature and extent of the suicidality touched on in the session. In risk assessment terms, little information was made available to help the counsellor, or the client, consider the risk inherent in the process.

An example of exploratory discourse

It is worth considering at this point, in the light of how exploration can be inadvertently avoided in the therapeutic discourse, how a counsellor might use interventions appropriately to help the client consider their suicidality more specifically. One transcript was noteworthy in its different approach to the suicidal client. As opposed to using predominantly reflective responses, the counsellor instead took a questioning, explorative position. The client was asked specific questions about their suicidal thoughts, including being asked to subjectively evaluate the intensity of suicidality on a 0–10 scale. The counsellor can also be seen checking risk factors, such as social isolation, depression, availability of support, and use of alcohol. The outcome was that the counsellor and client were able to renegotiate the discourse from a position of hopelessness, and as a consequence both achieved a greater understanding of the immediacy of risk. This example of the explorative position is demonstrated in Table 11.4.

Counsellors are sometimes anxious that asking questions of a client about their suicidal thoughts might seem insensitive, or inquisitorial. The transcript in Table 11.4 perhaps demonstrates that a thorough exploration of suicide potential

Table 11.4 An exploration of suicide potential: an example from a transcript

Client	1	Getting out of everyone's way. Just making everything worse for everyone else.
Counsellor	2	That would make it better for them (yes) – have you thought about harming yourself in any way?
Client	3	I've thought about doing myself in yes. That's what I said – it's the best way.
Counsellor	4	Have you thought about how you might do that?
Client	5	Yeah – go for a walk and that …
Counsellor	6	Can you say a bit more about that …
Client	7	Like … like … alongside the park is some water – usually walk there – probably do it there. Might get away – do myself in.
Counsellor	8	How might you do that …?
Client	9	Probably hang myself – something like that. Sometimes I feel like driving the car into something
Counsellor	10	So you've thought of different ways of doing it?
Client	11	Yeah

Table 11.4 (Continued)

Counsellor	12	I wonder if you could bear with me Chris – but on a scale of 0–10 where 0 is you not likely to do it, not likely to actually hang yourself or have an accident in the car, and 10 is there is a great chance that you would do it, where do you see yourself on the scale at the moment, between 0 and 10 … 0 being you wouldn't do it, 10 being you would …
Client	13	Probably only about 5
Counsellor	14	About a 5
Client	15	You know, gets worse
Counsellor	16	So today you're not feeling quite as bad as you have in the past?
Client	17	Not really, no. I wouldn't come here otherwise.
Counsellor	18	I'm wondering if you're drinking at all to cope with it?
Client	19	I have had some cans and that – not much though.
Counsellor	20	Not much – and in the past have you harmed yourself in any way?
Client	21	No.
Counsellor	22	No. Or anybody in the family?
Client	23	No. No.
Counsellor	24	One other thing is whether you are taking any medication at the moment?
Client	25	Yeah – just anti-depressants and that.
Counsellor	26	Okay. I'm just wondering erm … what sort of support you have around you at the moment, where you get your support?
Client	27	I don't get any … well, the wife – she just gets to the end of her tether – I don't blame her – I should be able to give her a hand, but I just can't. She's fed up so … she used to be alright but it's too much now – just too much.

can be sensitive, appropriate and also collaborative. There is sometimes a concern that 'risk assessment' is fundamentally the counsellor's agenda imposed on the unsuspecting client. However, risk assessment does not have to be a formulaic, mechanical or bureaucratic exercise. As is demonstrated, the risk exploration discourse can be entirely consistent with a therapeutic discourse and, when conducted collaboratively, can enable the counsellor *and* the client to achieve a greater understanding of the nature and form of distress.

Discussion questions

1. Reflect on your use of language with suicidal clients. What aspects might facilitate an exploration, and what aspects might inhibit it?
2. How might you integrate an exploratory approach consistent with your model of practice?
3. Considering your work with suicidal clients, what is your experience of how suicidal ideation is presented in sessions?
4. What can you learn about the ways clients introduce their suicidal thoughts, and the ways in which you subsequently respond?

12 From Self-Murder to Self-Support

> **Chapter overview**
>
> Amidst the anxiety of 'getting it right' in working with suicidal clients, it is too easy to become preoccupied with assessment, intervention, prevention, policy, procedure and management, for example. However, for many clients naming their suicidal thinking in counselling sessions, there remains significant therapeutic opportunity to facilitate movement and positive change. This chapter explores some of the strategies that counsellors might use to help their clients begin to consider self-care, as opposed to self-destruction.

Regardless of the years I have worked with suicidal clients, the moment when a client begins to explore their suicidal world can still feel overwhelming. The power of the self-annihilatory process can feel immobilizing in the moment, leaving me blank and helpless. In those moments, it is almost possible to have an insight into the suicidal client's process: hopeless, deadening and blank. It is sometimes hard of think of things to say; how to respond in a way that facilitates movement, as well as acknowledging the stuckness and constriction. As is explored in Chapter 10, 'Understanding Suicide', constricted thinking can sometimes typify that of a suicidal client, when no alternative is seen. The power of the suicidal dynamic can leave us as counsellors feeling equally constricted.

Alongside this process can be our anxiety about how to manage the situation. As is explored elsewhere in this book, much policy focuses on identification and prevention of suicide, and the ways in which risk can be managed. We can too easily become preoccupied with 'what happens next', and fail to consider 'what happens now'. I suspect that in the vast majority of situations, we might briefly contemplate breaking confidentiality, but instead decide with our clients to work together and retain the privacy of the therapeutic encounter. Much of our work with suicidal clients probably falls into the category of 'positive risk taking': acknowledging the risk that exists, but making active choices to continue work, if necessary, without referral to other support options.

It is generally very rare for a client to walk into a counselling session and announce that it is their plan to end their own life. More often, clients struggle to name suicide at all, and when they do, it is a tentative, anxious and potentially shameful process. As is discussed in other chapters, the task of the counsellor is to actively facilitate this process, rather than become defined by it. With all of this going on, it is easy to forget that much can be achieved in helping clients explore their suicidality, and facilitate their move from helpless and hopeless to taking an active responsibility for themselves and their safety. This chapter therefore is about ways in which, as counsellors, we can work to harness the client's wish to live (assuming that in most cases it will be present), and expand their thinking to begin to re-encompass choices.

Responding to Crisis

Before looking at such strategies, it is perhaps helpful to locate suicidality within the context of crisis intervention. If a client is extremely distressed within a session, the first task is about helping them to be sufficiently present in the moment to enable any therapeutic work to take place. A client lost in chaos and despair will quickly lose therapeutic contact. The initial task therefore is about helping establish contact if it is not present, or to re-establish it if it is lost.

Leenaars (2004) outlines five primary tasks in crisis intervention with suicidal clients: establish rapport; explore; focus; develop options and a plan of action; and terminate.

Establish rapport

At this stage, the counsellor should focus on establishing what we might call 'psychological contact' as much as possible. This will include making use of the necessary skills to communicate to the client that you are present and interested. If the client is highly agitated, it is important and helpful to use some basic 'grounding' techniques to bring their focus back into the room. There are several strategies for achieving this, including:

- *Basic breathing techniques.* Asking the client to take one deep breath in and then blow it out as hard as possible, followed by steady breathing (perhaps using a count of three); asking the client to focus on their breath as it comes into and then leaves their body. The counsellor might need to be quite active in the early stages of this strategy, demonstrating what they mean, and talking their client through the process.
- *Noticing support.* This can include a number of different strategies, but they are all essentially about assuring the client of their safety and control. The counsellor might ask the client to pay attention to the chair they are sitting in, its solidity and strength, and the sense that they are supported by it. The counsellor might instead remind the client of their presence (which can be forgotten in high anxiety or panic) by making statements such as, 'I am here sitting with you. I'm here to support you in whatever way I can', for example.
- *Establishing contact in the room.* Highly distressed or anxious clients can temporarily lose a sense of contact with the world around them. This intervention can help bring them back into their space. The counsellor might gently invite them to look at something in the room and pay attention to it: for example, 'Can you look at the clock on the wall and remind yourself that you are safe.' Another suggestion is to establish eye contact with the counsellor; this can sometimes be too threatening for clients, so counsellors need to judge this for each occasion. For visually impaired clients, the counsellor's voice might be used to help ground the client: steady, gentle, reassuring, but strong.

If these strategies are required to help the client, it is important that the counsellor is active, rather than passive, in the process. Reflective responses can be used to good effect to reinforce the instructions of the counsellor, but instructions they must be. My own experience is that at such times, clients need a sense of strong support onto which they can anchor themselves. This demands that the counsellor is very present – perhaps sitting slightly forward in their chair – and clearly communicating to their client that they can cope. As the client begins to calm a little, the counsellor can then slowly resume their usual intervention style.

Explore

It is important to understand that if a client is actively suicidal, it is usually because in that moment they can no longer see an alternative solution. Whatever has happened to bring them to this point, they feel thwarted in finding an alternative way forward. In this instance, the counsellor can begin the process of easing the client's constricted thinking by gently exploring with the client the nature of their thoughts, feelings, and how they understand their problem. Many counsellors fear that exploring or naming suicide might increase risk; this is in fact one of the most commonly held myths about suicide. The reality is that, for the majority of clients, a sense of risk can significantly diminish simply by naming suicide, and exploring it with someone who is willing to hear, without judgement.

Again, a crisis intervention perspective can help here in that 'crisis' will be defined and experienced by the client. To the outside world, the trigger of the crisis might appear innocuous and minor. I recall, when working in a crisis service, visiting a woman who had made an attempt on her life following the breakdown of a washing machine; this was the final event in a sequence of many, and the point at which the client no longer felt able to cope. The external construction of what is a crisis needs always to be checked against the client's experience of the problem. The counsellor's role in this stage is to slowly introduce alternative ways forward, rather than passively reinforcing the client's perception of only one alternative.

Focus

This is similar to the grounding techniques described about, but is more geared to providing focus thinking/feeling for the client, as opposed to immediate crisis management. At this stage it is helpful for counsellors to ask specific questions of the client (who may need such questions to help provide an outline structure for their thinking), such as, 'What is the best way I can support you at the moment?', 'What do you need right now?', or 'What things can we put in place to help you feel safer?' The questions are centred on helping the client to begin to take responsibility for their own wellbeing, wherever possible, and again affirm that they are being contained – 'held' – in a supportive process.

Develop options and a plan of action

This stage can be subdivided into the short term and the medium term. The immediate anxiety for many counsellors when faced with a suicidal client is the end of the session; the ticking of the clock which brings the session to an end, highlighting the sense of urgency for the counsellor to make a decision. My view is that this is a two-stage process. The first stage is to help the client such that the risk is lower, and the client is able to leave the session sufficiently self-supported and aware of external support to ensure their immediate safety. The second stage is to help the client begin to address the crises that led them to a point of suicidality, to help them explore all of their options and hopefully find realistic alternative ways to move forward.

Terminate

Before ending a session with a suicidal client, it is important to ensure that their risk has been responded to and that they no longer present at high risk. There are a number of helpful factors that should be considered during this stage. These include a full discussion with the client about:

- Who is available.
- Who they could contact if the sense of crisis returned.
- Whether they would be able to contact people (and what might prevent them from contacting people).
- Whether other people ought to know, e.g. friend, family and/or general practitioner.
- Whether a more formal referral ought to be made to put additional support in place.
- Information such as crisis telephone numbers, locations of accident and emergency departments, mental health crisis teams.
- When the next counselling session might be, and whether additional sessions might be added (if possible or appropriate), or the availability of drop-in type services (which some counselling agencies offer).
- How the client was going to help themselves be safe.

Some counsellors choose to make use of no-harm contracts. These can be helpful if they complement other strategies the counsellor has used in trying to respond to the level of risk, e.g. some of the points above, but are not helpful on their own. Such no-harm contracts are usually verbal (but can be written), and affirm that the client will take steps to support themselves between sessions, rather than making an attempt on their life. When used carefully and sensitively, they can help affirm the client's autonomy and self-responsibility, and communicate the level of care between counsellor and client. However, there is always a danger of them becoming emotionally coercive, with clients left feeling that they have let their counsellor down if another crisis happens. This can sometimes prevent the client returning to counselling. Additionally, some argue that such contracts are sometimes used by counsellors as opposed to undertaking a more thorough assessment of risk (Buelow and Range, 2001; Miller et al., 1998). Counsellors need to be aware of these dangers if they choose to use such contracts.

The medium-term strategy is helping suicidal clients explore their suicidality in greater depth (once the immediacy of risk has been attended to). The particular model of counselling the counsellor uses will inform such an approach. Heard (2002: 507) however suggests that 'poor treatment compliance' and particularly 'poor attendance' are two of the biggest difficulties counsellors face when working with suicidal clients. It might be that such problems are partly influenced by the context in which counselling is set. For example, my own experience of working in secondary care reflected the problems Heard has highlighted, with difficulties in engaging and retaining more highly suicidal clients. On the other hand, in a higher education setting my experience is that clients more readily engage with the therapeutic process, regardless of their degree of risk. It is obviously impossible to generalize my own experience out to all settings.

Heard also questions whether, when the suicidal client also has a psychiatric disorder, counselling should focus on suicide, where in fact suicide might be more symptomatic of the underlying problems. This question strikes at the heart of debates around diagnosis, and how counsellors integrate such thinking into their work. My own view would be that if a client presents in counselling with suicidal thoughts, and is willing and able to explore the meaning of those thoughts, that would be a valid focus for counselling. For example, a depressed client might well talk about suicidal feelings (given the high correlation between depression and suicide), and counselling should not exclude those feelings merely as symptomatic of other problems if the client can gain benefit from attending to them.

Strategies for effecting change

A more cognitive behavioural perspective on working with suicide potential would be to help the suicidal client consider options other than, or at least in addition to, suicide. As Litman states, the role of the counsellor in working with suicide is to 'widen the scope of the view of the patient, so that the patient can see more options other than a suicide solution' (1994: 276). In addition to this underlying principle, Leenaars (2004) outlines some helpful aspects for counsellors to consider in their work. The following list is informed by Leenaars's suggestions, and my own practice experience.

1 *Importance of exploration*

   (a) Counsellors need to explore clearly, calmly and openly the nature of the client's suicidal thoughts.
   (b) This can be achieved by asking questions such as 'What are you feeling?', 'What do you want to do?', 'What are you trying to stop by killing yourself?'
   (c) Begin to help the client redefine the solution using skills such as challenge, clarification, paraphrasing, reflection.

2 *Know your options*

   (a) Ensure that you are fully aware of what referral options are available to you in your setting (or as an independent practitioner), and how to access such services.
   (b) Be willing to talk openly with your client about what additional support is available for them, and how it might be accessed, i.e. what happens next (which is often particularly frightening for clients).

3 *Provide a safe emotional 'language'*

   (a) Sometimes clients move to a suicidal place because they cannot contemplate continuing, *and* cannot find the language to fully articulate their feelings and needs.
   (b) Counsellors can tentatively begin to help clients find a language that begins to put into words the feelings that have perhaps previously been unexpressed. Naming the process can sometimes help make it sufficiently concrete for the client to begin to re-evaluate their position in relation to it.

4 *The quality of the relationship*

   (a) Most counsellors will freely acknowledge the importance of the quality of the therapeutic relationship for reparation and growth. This is particularly true when working with suicidal clients, who might be trapped within their own sense of dissociation and disconnection.
   (b) Rogers's (1997) core conditions of empathy, congruence and unconditional positive regard are of great value, regardless of the primary theoretical orientation of the counsellor, as they provide a safe base for the suicidal client to begin to re-establish their relating.

5 *Challenge constricted thinking*

   (a) The nature, form and degree of challenge with a suicidal person will be entirely dependent upon what the counsellor believes they can safely tolerate at the time. However, as discussed in Chapter 11, 'The Use of Language in Counselling Suicidal Clients', it is vital that the counsellor does not become defined by the hopelessness of the client.
   (b) In accepting and validating the client's reality, it is also important to name alternatives in an honest and realistic way. As Leenaars writes, 'Take the side of adaptation and, in a kindly way but focused way, remind the person of the fact that life often involves the choices among lousy alternatives (or pains). A wise adaptation to life itself is often to choose the least lousy alternative that is practically attainable' (2004: 216).
   (c) Gently challenge the polarized thinking that the client is likely to present, i.e. it is either this, or the other. The way forward for the client will almost certainly lie somewhere in the middle of these two extreme positions, and it is helpful to find a way of exploring the grey area with the client.

6 *Understand the client's frame of reference*

   (a) As discussed in the section above on responding to clients in crisis, it is essential to conceptualize the client's experience from their perspective (while not being defined by it).
   (b) Listen to how the client has reached this crisis point, even if on the surface it does not necessarily make sense.

7 *Remember the often transient nature of suicide*

   (a) As discussed elsewhere, suicidality may be planned, lived with, or spontaneous.
   (b) In most instances the move to a higher risk of suicide is likely to be a transient state that the client can be supported through. Even people for whom suicide is 'ever present' usually attend with some crisis or change in circumstances that has altered the nature or intensity of their thoughts.
   (c) Help the client consider the suicidal place they are currently at *in relation to* how things might change. Introduce the possibility that the intensity of their thoughts might change again.

8 *Encourage the responsibility of the client*

   (a) The client may need additional support and intervention at times of high risk.
   (b) However, the focus should, wherever possible, reinforce the client's self-responsibility and autonomy.
   (c) Encouraging this at the time of crisis, using questions such as, 'What do you think you can do to support yourself?' and 'What has helped you previously – what has kept you alive?', can affirm the client's sense of agency and sense of self.

Counsellors who work with suicide risk often look for the one single factor, or intervention, that will make the difference. When offering training, counsellors will sometimes ask at the beginning of the session for 'answers to help me to do this work'. In risk assessment, we can look toward risk assessment tools and risk factors to provide the particular nugget of information that will tell us whether our client is likely to kill themselves or not. The same is true for therapeutic work with suicidal clients, where we hope there is one intervention or approach that will tend to the suicidal mind. The reality is that no such panacea exists; the 'truth' lies in a combination of factors, grounded in familiar skills, rooted in a sound philosophical and theoretical model.

> **Discussion questions**
>
> 1 What aspects of your approach do you consider to be most facilitative when working with suicidal clients?
> 2 What aspects of your approach might hinder work with suicidal clients?
> 3 How might you integrate a crisis intervention approach into your work, when required?
> 4 What steps would you take to explore a suicidal client's safety before they left your room?

13 Suicide and Self-Injury: Annihilation and Survival

> **Chapter overview**
>
> The purpose of this chapter is to define what is meant by self-injury, consider the types of behaviours that might be seen as self-injuring, and highlight what key research tells us about the extent of self-injury. The differences and similarities between self-injury and suicidal potential will then be explored, including the implications of these differences and similarities for the counselling process, before a final discussion of the important factors counsellors need to keep in mind when assessing the risk of suicide potential in a client's self-injuring behaviour.

Understanding the differences between a client who experiences suicidal thoughts, and another who self-injures as a means of coping and surviving intolerable emotional pain, is a challenge for even the most experienced practitioner. To all intents and purposes, the risk seems as great when presented in the counselling room. Certainly in terms of making an assessment of risk, the difference between a client who takes an overdose as a means of attempting to end their own life, and a client who takes an overdose as a means of coping with the 'uncopable', can be almost indistinguishable. Yet, counsellors work with clients who experience differences in degrees of suicidal ideation, and clients who harm themselves as a means of living.

Babiker and Arnold define self-injury as 'an act which involves deliberately inflicting pain and/or injury to one's body, but without suicidal intent' (1997: 2). The National Institute for Clinical Excellence (NICE) guidelines on self-harm define self-injury as 'self poisoning or injury, irrespective of the apparent purpose of the act ... [it is] an expression of personal distress, not an illness, and there are many varied reasons for a person to harm him or herself' (2004: 7). In Babiker and Arnold's definition, the fine difference between an act with an intention to end life, and an act with an intention to sustain life, becomes apparent in the words 'but without suicidal intent'. The imperative seems to be to determine the client's motive when harming themselves, in then being able to understand whether they present at a higher risk of suicide. The NICE definition, which states that self-harm can be defined 'irrespective of the apparent purpose of the act', attends to this dilemma at one level, but perhaps not at the level which would be more relevant to counsellors. A discussion of these definitions, together with a discussion of other considerations for working with self-harm can be found in Reeves and Howdin (2008).

In practice, clients may present with a number of 'behaviours' that might constitute self-injury. Those that people will usually think of first include cutting, burning and perhaps hair pulling. However, injury might also include breaking bones and scalding, for example. If the definition is drawn more widely to include self-harm, then a whole range of other behaviours might be included: for example, sexual risk taking, dangerous or reckless driving, alcohol and/or substance misuse, over/under-eating, excessive exercise, etc. It is important that, in this context, we, as counsellors, consider how we self-harm (for we almost certainly do): if we can challenge the 'them' and 'us' distinction, this might help us achieve a greater degree of relational depth with our clients. We will touch on this again later in this chapter.

'Treatment' in primary or secondary care might often include physical treatments in response to any injuries sustained, for example, following an overdose or cut. Where the 'injury' was self-inflicted, the *purpose* of the act is less relevant in the context of such treatment. But understanding the meaning of an act of self-injury, and then its likelihood of repetition and the possible consequences if repeated, becomes much more important. We might then work on a presumption that the act of suicide is about self-annihilation and of wanting to be dead, whereas self-injury is about survival: coping with unbearable psychological pain, an expression of wanting to live. This would be an easy (albeit overly simple) demarcation of two challenging behaviours.

The story becomes more complicated when considered in the context of research evidence that links self-injury with a greater risk of completed suicide. That is to say, a person who self-injures is more likely to end their life through suicide than a person who doesn't (Harriss and Hawton, 2005; Orbach, 1997; Zahl and Hawton, 2004.) This research particularly links longer-term self-injury to a greater risk of suicide. However, in the shorter term, situations can also arise where the client does not (consciously perhaps) intend to die, but their self-injury has become sufficiently chaotic or severe that death is a probable outcome (whether desired or not). As we can see, working with self-injury and suicide in counselling can be particularly problematic if considered specifically from an *assessment* perspective.

Self-injury can be a profoundly troubling behaviour for people to understand. From the outside looking in, it can be hard to appreciate the level of intrapersonal distress, or the lack of words of sufficient magnitude to fully articulate an inner turmoil, that might lead to someone injuring themselves. All we can see is the consequence, the 'after-effect' of the behaviour. It is easy to assume that self-injury must be about attention seeking – a cry for help. While for some people this may be true, for the majority of people who self-injure this could not be further from the truth. Self-injury is often a private, hidden and secret activity, shrouded in shame and carefully covered with clothing.

It is difficult to provide accurate statistics on self-injury, precisely for the reasons just cited: self-injury is often a very private thing. As such, research that considers hospital admissions or self-reporting is likely to significantly understate the prevalence (Green et al., 2005; Hawton et al., 2002; Meltzer et al., 2001). Also, there are so many different definitions of self-injury – some that include specific behaviours only such as cutting or burning, others that are more inclusive – that comparing like with like is very difficult. However, *Truth Hurts: Report of the National Inquiry on Self-Harm in Young People* (Mental Health Foundation, 2006) offers some useful indicators as to possible prevalence. The report highlights a number of interesting research papers, such as:

- A study conducted by the Samaritans and the Centre for Suicide Research, University of Oxford (2002) estimates that one in 10 young people self-harm.
- One in five girls between the ages of five and seven had self-injured, and just under one in five adolescents (males and females) had considered self-injury (The Priory, 2005).
- If The Priory (2005) study was extrapolated to the full UK population, the *National Inquiry Report* estimates that this would mean more than 1 million adolescents have considered self-injury and more than 800,000 would have self-injured.

The act of self-injury can cause profound emotional responses amongst those in the helping professions who are on the front line in responding to its consequences. For example, health care staff can sometimes struggle to respond appropriately to self-inflicted injury in busy accident and emergency departments. Patients attending with such injuries are usually treated at a physical level, but sometimes staff do not have the necessary training to understand the emotional or psychological dynamics that led to the injury (Friedman et al., 2006). This can sometime lead to an escalation of the self-injury, as clients can be left feeling disregarded or judged. For some clients, the reaction they sometimes receive at accident and emergency departments can become part of the 'self-harming process'.

That is not to say that health care professionals in accident and emergency departments are uncaring, for this is certainly not the case. More likely, the response sometimes experienced by people attending with self-inflicted injuries is more about the countertransferential reactions to the communication of the injury. Self-injury can often be experienced as an attack, and can leave the 'attacked' feeling vulnerable, impotent and angry. These difficult feelings can then be 'acted out' in the form of rejection, or of being dismissed.

Such responses to self-injury are not exclusive to accident and emergency departments. Therapy services can also be guilty of 'acting out' against self-injury, either at an institutional level, for example by demanding that self-injuring behaviour must stop before counselling can begin, or at an individual level, in the demands made by the counsellor. This dynamic is not very different to that provoked by suicide risk.

Working with self-injury

In counselling terms, the challenges of working with self-injury are therefore similar to those of working with suicide risk. A summary of these might include the following:

- The need for careful and accessible contracting.
- An understanding of your organization's expectations of work with clients at risk.
- An awareness of some theoretical explanations for self-injury and suicide.
- An awareness of ways in which self-injury and suicide are present in the relationship.
- An awareness of a 'self-position' in relation to self-injury and suicide, and the consequences of a lack of self-insight.
- A willingness to actively engage in the discourse around self-injury and suicide.

The need for careful and accessible contracting

All counselling demands high quality contracting. As was discussed more fully in Chapters 6 and 7, 'The Ethical Imperative of Suicide' and 'Confidentiality, Capacity and Consent', it is essential that counsellors are able to contract fully with clients, not only at the commencement of counselling, but also in an ongoing way to ensure that clients fully understand the parameters of the service being offered. I'm not always sure that this is something we do very well. Let me give an example of what I mean.

Sashi

Sashi was referred to me for individual counselling by her general practitioner. At the time I was working in a mental health team, and the GP and Sashi had discussed the possibility of counselling following a suicide attempt. Sashi had experienced a breakdown in a relationship and had lost custody of her children during that process. These losses were almost too terrible for her to manage. One evening, she took her car and deliberately drove it into a wall. She sustained very serious injuries, the longer-term consequence of which was that she was no longer able to walk.

When I met Sashi she remained very distressed, although she was no longer suicidal. Since leaving hospital following her suicide attempt she had begun to self-injure by cutting her legs, which she now 'hated as they are useless'. The loss of her relationship, and the regularity of contact with her children, were now compounded by her physical losses. In our introductory session we talked about what counselling was, and I explained the nature of the contract that would inform our work, including the limits of confidentiality. Sashi listened attentively and said she understood what was meant by the contract.

Four months into the counselling Sashi's mood deteriorated, and she began to experience levels of anger towards her ex-partner that she had not allowed herself to experience previously. Her self-injury was increasing in frequency and severity. I was increasingly concerned about her, and in one session asked about suicidal thoughts: 'As we're talking, Sashi, it seems that you're experiencing some pretty powerful feelings. Do you experience any of the feelings that you had previously, when you tried to kill yourself?' Sashi broke down and talked of wanting to be dead. However, this time it was slightly different, she felt, because she wanted her ex-partner dead too. She would kill him before killing herself.

We explored her thoughts in some detail. *How* would she kill her ex-partner, and then herself? *What* methods were available to her to achieve this? *When* would she do this – imminently or was it a longer-term plan? Did she see any *alternatives* for her in the future? Did the *changes* in her self-injury have any meaning for her wishes to be dead? After discussion, and an opportunity to talk with my supervisor, I talked with Sashi about my concerns for her and the need for me to speak with her GP about these concerns so that she could be fully supported. She didn't want me to talk to her GP as she felt that people would only try and stop her from doing what she 'needed to do'. When I explained that I would prefer to have her permission to talk to her GP, but that in the light of my concerns and her apparent intentions, and the contract of confidentiality we agreed at the beginning of counselling, I felt that I needed to do this anyway, it became quickly apparent that Sashi had not really fully understood the detail *and implications* of the contract of confidentiality that I had described early on.

The learning for me was apparent: as a counsellor I might be very clear as to what I mean by phrases such as *risk to self and others*, but my client might not. Particularly when working with the risk of suicide and self-injury, it is essential that we find ways of ensuring that clients fully and clearly understand the limitations of confidentiality for their counselling, so that they are able to make an informed decision as to (a) what they talk about in sessions and (b) whether they agree to begin counselling at all.

An understanding of your organization's expectations of work with clients at risk

As was discussed in more detail in Chapter 8, *'Counselling Suicidal Clients in Organizational Settings'*, the context in which counselling is practised is likely to have a significant influence on the nature of counselling, and how counsellors can work with clients at risk of both suicide and self-injury. Just as organizations can be wary of suicide potential, for the subsequent risk it might pose to the institution itself, so too can the same be true for self-injury.

As a means of managing this organizational 'anxiety', procedures can sometimes be put in place that, while designed to tolerate and contain self-injury, can inadvertently be prescriptive and controlling, such as insisting that self-injury must stop before counselling will be offered, or suspending counselling if self-injury is disclosed. Any procedural document must be based on a sound understanding of the nature of self-injury: it is a means of surviving or articulating intense psychological pain, or a self-punishment, or the transferring of psychological pain to a more 'manageable' physical pain. Policy is much more helpfully located at the point at which self-injury might stray into suicide potential, in supporting counsellors to make difficult decisions about how best to proceed in counselling with someone whose self-injury has become such that risk to life is high.

An awareness of some theoretical explanations for self-injury and suicide

Counsellors must understanding to some extent why people may self-injure, to help inform intervention strategies or the therapeutic discourse. Without some basic understanding, it will become extremely hard for even the most empathic counsellor to fully appreciate the process of the client. Instead, the danger is that the counsellor will become self-injury focused – seeing only the physical communication and missing what else the client might be trying to communicate.

If we can 'know', intellectually, that perhaps the person sitting with us cuts themselves as a means of coping with traumatic feelings or other emotional turmoil, perhaps because they are unable or unwilling to find alternative ways of expressing those feelings, that can help us to 'know' something a little more about their pain. In 'knowing' this, we are immediately facilitated to see a bigger picture, rather than focusing on or being drawn to one particular aspect of it.

> **Joni**
>
> Joni, a 19-year-old student, said to me about her self-injury in a counselling session:
>
> Sometimes I make sense of it, and sometimes I just don't. It's kinda gone on for years, probably since I was about 10. My mum and dad were always having a go at each other, and I felt so angry and just wanted to shout ... and I felt so sad too. It all sort of gets caught up inside – there was nothing I could say or do. My friend at school used to do it and I didn't really get it. I started to cut myself on my arms, and it sort of helped. But then it didn't ... I'd feel better and didn't want to scream anymore, but then I would have this cut on my arm which was like a constant reminder of how crap I had felt. I had to keep it hidden from people so they wouldn't go mad. Then my mum saw it – took me to the doctor and ... well ... here I am. They all assumed that I wanted to be dead. It's sort of hard to explain – I don't want to be dead. In the moment there is part of me that sort of wishes I was out of the way, but then I don't want to die. It's really strange. Even though I am left with a cut, at least I feel like I can live again.

An awareness of ways in which self-injury and suicide are present in the relationship

As has been said, how pain is communicated in the counselling relationship is not always a straightforward, clear process. We understand from early in our training that clients can be facilitated to talk more about their experiences and feelings through the use of appropriate counselling skills, in the context of a safe and appropriate relationship. However, as we have explored specifically in relation to suicidal ideation, self-injury may not always be forthcoming, and clients may need their counsellor to 'give permission' to talk about it by them exploring it as a possibility, e.g. 'Are there any times when you might hurt or harm yourself as a way of coping with your feelings?'

This question is often a difficult one for many counsellors to contemplate asking, fearing that it will sound insensitive or inappropriate, or that the client will take offence at the possibility. Again, for the same reasons as when we considered this aspect in relation to suicide potential, this outcome is highly unlikely, and typically speaks more of the counsellor's anxiety than it does the client's.

An awareness of a 'self-position' in relation to self-injury and suicide, and the consequences of a lack of self-insight

Developing the previous point, more specifically why we might be reluctant to explore the possibility of self-injury with our clients, the importance of an awareness of our 'self-position' in relation to self-injury cannot be overstated. What do I mean by 'self-position'? Similarly to that around suicide, it is essential that we are open to our personal responses to self-injury as a means of understanding our responses to our client's self-injury. For example, if our assumption is that self-injury inevitably is a symptom of underlying mental illness, or that it is a 'wrong' thing to do as it contradicts spiritual or religious beliefs we might hold, we are likely to bring these positions into our work if they are not held in our awareness. Alternatively, we may diminish the severity of our client's self-injury or not consider it as relevant, if our belief is that it is something we should just accept unconditionally.

Understanding our own self-harming process is important in this respect. One of the aspects of any discourse about self-harm is how the language used is seemingly unconsciously designed to separate 'us' from 'them'. In this respect I am not referring to an unthinking political correctness that demands conformity to a kind of talk, while leaving attitudes unchanged. I am instead referring to ways in which we can absent ourselves from the relationship with clients who self-harm, and in doing so fall into the trap of 'doing to', as opposed to 'doing with', in our therapeutic work.

I would suggest that this tendency is energized by the vulnerability in all of us. Rage, hurt, wounds, sadness and injury lie in our experiences in some way, and at some level. For me, this is the biggest single relational and therapeutic challenge: how we, as counsellors, can enable ourselves to pay sufficient attention to our own pain, and our own self-harm, to achieve a true contact with the 'other'. In Buber's terms, we must consider how we work in the I–thou, as opposed to being drawn to working with the I–it.

As for language, we know the terms 'self-harmers', 'cutters' – indeed, 'people who self-harm' – that inevitably are about 'us' and 'them'. 'People who self-harm': on the face of it, this a fairly innocuous and respecting phrase intended to define a group without labelling them. Yet I would argue it is still fundamentally rooted in difference: there are 'people who self-harm', and then there's me. I cannot believe this doesn't have implications in the therapeutic process, in the same way as it has implications at a systemic level – in families, peer groups, schools, clubs, and at a wider societal level. In the difference between 'us' and 'them' perhaps lie denial, fear, shame and some embarrassment. We must remember that we separate and make such distinctions for a reason.

In all honesty, can I say that when I get home from work tired, anxious and stressed, and open yet another bottle of wine, I am not instead looking to blank out and anaesthetize something that I find uncomfortable? We all know something of self-harm, and in knowing it, important connections can be made with the individual who comes to therapy for help, and with the systems in which they live and try to function. We can use our counselling knowhow and language to separate ourselves off if we wish, but who are we really kidding?

A willingness to actively engage in the discourse around self-injury and suicide

As with suicide, self-injury is something I would ask all of my clients about in early assessment sessions. The timing of when I will do this, and how I might ask, will vary depending on the client, the story and the wider circumstances, but I will always ask. This is for several reasons:

1. To bring any self-injury into the assessment to help inform the type and nature of counselling offered.
2. To provide the client with a space to name and explore any self-injury, at whatever depth they feel appropriate at that stage.
3. To give 'permission', i.e. this is something we can talk about and I am willing to 'hear'.

4 To communicate to the client that even if they decide not to talk about it currently, it is something they might decide to bring back to counselling at a later stage.
5 To help clarify the meaning of the contract, i.e. by naming self-injury I can be clear with the client, using their own narrative, about the limitations of any confidentiality agreements offered.
6 To ensure that I am able to work within my own levels of competency and knowledge.

When self-injury comes into the counselling discourse, it is important that, as counsellors, we feel sufficiently grounded to facilitate, rather than inhibit, the discussion. The points I have already made, if sufficiently addressed, will help in this process. However, it is vital that I am able to explore the nature and process of the client's self-injury, not only to help my understanding of it, but more importantly to help the client with their own understanding of it. I might do this by considering the following types of questions:

1 How long have you been self-injuring? Can you remember when you began?
2 Has it always been the same type of self-injuring, or has it changed?
3 Can you think of what was happening for you to trigger self-injury?
4 Can you make any sense of what motivates your self-injury now, e.g. things happening in your life, feelings that you have, other experiences?
5 What do you use to self-injure, and where on your body do you injure?
6 Does this vary?
7 Can you isolate the sorts of feelings you have moments before you self-injure, i.e. physical or emotional tension, particular triggers?
8 How long might these feelings last, e.g. a few seconds, minutes, hours, days or maybe weeks?
9 How do you feel during self-injury? Are you aware of any feelings, or a lack of them?
10 How about afterwards? What is the consequence of self-injury for you?
11 Have there been any times when you have been able not to self-injure, when you wanted to?
12 What alternative strategies have you tried instead of self-injuring? Do any of these work?
13 Have you ever talked to anyone about your self-injury before? If so, was this helpful, and how?
14 Are there any times that you hope your self-injury might kill you?

The suggestion here is not that these questions are worked through sequentially; that would become a bit of an inquisition! However, they might helpfully structure thinking when self-injury becomes part of the client's narrative, particularly when reflecting on whether the client presents with any degree of risk.

Self-injury and suicide potential

The majority of clients who disclose self-injury in a counselling session will not necessarily present at a higher risk of suicide simply because they self-injure. There are obvious difficulties within this statement in virtue of the fact that the research evidence strongly suggests that self-injury is correlated with a higher risk of suicide. However, that does not necessarily mean that all people who self-injure are at a higher risk of killing themselves – in the same way that a young male is not necessarily going to kill himself simply because he is young and male.

However, in the same way that if the young male talked of suicidal thoughts we would need to hear them in the context of his demographic risk factors, the same would be true for someone who self-injures talking of wanting to be dead.

More pertinent is not to assume that self-injury is always about self-survival. In a great many cases it is, and it could be argued that in many ways the fact that the client self-injures helps them through potentially vulnerable times. However, there are times when someone's ambivalence about their living becomes enacted in their self-harming, so that their life is threatened by a strategy that might otherwise be life sustaining. Or perhaps their level of distress is such that the degree or extent of self-injuring poses real dangers to their survival.

Annabel

Annabel has self-injured for many years. Her traumatic upbringing, which included experiences of physical and sexual abuse, led her to begin cutting her arms and stomach at nine years of age. Since that time, Annabel has participated in other risky behaviour, including unprotected sex with strangers, heavy drinking, hair pulling, and taking overdoses of prescribed drugs. Annabel is supported via a 24-hour crisis line through her local health trust, in addition to weekly individual counselling.

Annabel describes her overdoses clearly as a means of self-injuring. She experiences the process of the overdose – taking the tablets, contacting emergency services, attending accident and emergency departments, receiving intrusive physical treatments, ultimately feeling criticized, judged and dismissed – as part of the self-injuring process (both physically and in terms of her self-esteem).

Her counsellor has been able to talk extensively with Annabel about this process, so they both understand and know it well. Annabel is consistently clear that she does not want to die, she just does not always know how best to live on occasions; however, as her distress increases, so does the self-injuring. A point is reached when, in supervision, it becomes clear to Annabel's counsellor that Annabel is reaching the point where she is beginning to put her life at risk, with more severe overdoses. In trying to cope with her unbearable pain, Annabel has inadvertently redefined her overdoses as potentially life threatening.

At this point, the task of the counsellor is to challenge Annabel so that she can begin to understand what has changed, and the implications of that change. The means of achieving this is not, I would suggest, more complex than addressing concerns with a client who is expressing suicidal thoughts, but similar to that process. It is important that the counsellor is able to clearly articulate the nature of their concerns with Annabel, and in doing so to begin to seek ways of managing things differently. This helps bring into Annabel's awareness the changes in her self-injury so that she can begin to reflect on these changes herself, and consider what they might mean.

Essentially, the counsellor has begun a process of risk assessment, in collaboration with the client (doing with as opposed to doing to), with a view to harnessing Annabel's desire to live more constructively. In that sense, the counsellor is bringing into Annabel's awareness how her behaviour is no longer helping her achieve what she would wish (or perhaps checking that unconsciously Annabel does not have a wish to be dead; and if this is the case, making that wish more known). By bringing thoughts, feelings and behaviours into a 'known' place, both the counsellor and the client are better placed to develop an appropriate response or support package.

(Continued)

> *(Continued)*
>
> If Annabel does not wish to be supported, the counsellor faces the same dilemma as they would in any situation: that is, the management of their professional responsibilities, set against the client's known wishes. This is discussed more fully in other chapters. What is important is that the counsellor has not allowed an understanding of self-injury as a self-supportive strategy (albeit a maladaptive one) to obscure the potential risk that might be inherent in the strategy.

Final thoughts

The similarities and differences between self-injury and suicide risk are hard to disentangle. While in many ways they serve opposite functions (a means of sustaining life in the face of overwhelming pain; a means of ending life in the face of overwhelming pain), there are sufficient overlaps and shared points to create confusion. It is important that counsellors are clear about what process they are working with alongside their client: self-survival or self-annihilation. Again, demographic risk factors and client profiles provide a little of the story; this is insufficient in the face of what can be obtained through a discourse.

There are many factors that can inhibit an honest and respectful discourse with our clients about their self-injury: the client's sense of shame, embarrassment or secrecy; the fact that much of self-injury takes place beyond the knowledge of anyone else; the counsellor's anxiety and feelings of potential incompetence in the face of something that intellectually makes sense, but emotionally is still shocking; uncertainty and confusion between self-injury that is within coping, and self-injury that becomes life threatening. The skill is simply the willingness and ability to remain open to our own fragility and inadequacy, and not be silenced by it.

Discussion questions

1. How might you ask your client about self-injury, if they have not already mentioned it?
2. In what ways might you harm yourself? What insight might this give you into another person's process?
3. If you work for an organization, is there a policy on self-injury? If so, do you feel that this supports or inhibits your practice?
4. Reflect, perhaps in supervision, how self-injury might affect you as a counsellor in your work with clients.

Part V

The Counsellor Process

14 The Counsellor and Suicide Risk: Personal Perspectives and Professional Actions

---

Chapter overview

A counsellor's views on suicide, influenced by their personal or family history, spiritual or religious views, experience of supporting family or friends, for example, will have great significance in how they subsequently respond to suicidal clients in sessions. This chapter raises some of the important issues counsellors need to consider, the dangers of not adopting a self-reflective position, and how different client needs and presentations will challenge counsellors in a variety of ways.

Counsellors are well versed in reflecting on how client work impacts upon their 'self' as counsellor. From initial training, the importance of supervision, personal counselling and continuing professional development, for example, in providing for self-care is affirmed and reinforced. Such principles are additionally enshrined within ethical frameworks of professional organizations (e.g., BACP, 2007). The concept that a counsellor might not be willing to reflect on their personal position in relation to counselling work, or perhaps that being disengaged in such a way they might additionally disengage during the counselling process, is likely to be seen as contraindicative for ethical practice. However, while some client narratives might be difficult to hear, others make additional demands on the resources of the counsellor in relation to their own 'self' and perspective. Examples of such client presentations might include those considering a termination, those involved in counselling and spirituality, and those experiencing trauma and suicide risk, for example.

A dialogue around suicide is unlikely to be a neutral one. Perhaps, like politics or religion, as a discussion it is likely to either facilitate people taking a particular 'position', or instead leave them trying to avoid any discussion at all. Indeed, during my many years of researching counselling and suicide potential, I have inadvertently stopped an emerging conversation in its tracks by mentioning the 's' word on far too many occasions. One might speculate on why this is the case. Suicide is ultimately about living and dying – about life and death. Western culture does not tolerate such polarizations lightly: life is present, active, vital, energetic, engaging – an advertiser's dream – whereas death is to be avoided, hushed, escaped from, alluded to in whispered tones. Those involved in working with bereavement know only too well the importance of talking about 'death' and 'dying', as opposed to 'going to sleep' and 'passing on', as a therapeutic means of enabling people to engage with and make sense of their grief.

Suicide falls into the latter category of secrets and shame. As was explored in Chapters 2 and 7, 'Historical Perspectives on Suicide and the Emergence of the Medical Model' and 'Confidentiality, Capacity and Consent', suicide has been decriminalized, yet the shame, disgrace and dishonour of the act continues still. Lukas and Seiden, in their work on supporting those bereaved by suicide, state that, 'Despite the fact that there has been some movement away from official stigmatizing of suicide, survivors often feel the shame that comes from neigbors, former friends, and other segments of society' (2007: 42).

As counsellors, we are not immune to these influences and dynamics. Indeed, as counsellors we are potentially more likely than many others to be witness to the overwhelming pain and despair that can characterize suicide. It will not leave us feeling neutral, but will instead seep into our 'selves', and be filtered through layers of experiences, perceptions and standpoints. The imperative for counsellors to reflect on our own position in relation to suicide is therefore high. However, our view on suicide must also be considered in the context of how we respond to our clients in more general terms.

The judging self

Whether it is possible to fully suspend judgement within the context of a counselling relationship is much debated. Some theoretical paradigms hold central the belief that a non-judgemental stance on behalf of the counsellor is essential to the development and maintenance of a therapeutic relationship. Other approaches position the counsellor *in relation to* the client; that is, through the identification and working through of transferential material. Other approaches see the role of counsellor as a facilitator of change only, with less emphasis placed on the relationship *per se*. However, it is my assertion here that as human beings we make judgements continually, and that the process of judging and assessing is ultimately the means by which we negotiate our way through the world (Reeves, 2008). That we judge is less important than what we do with those judgements in our work as counsellors. By disregarding them or maintaining that they do not exist, we increase the potential that they are acted out in our work. By acknowledging and exploring them (even if we cannot easily 'switch off' the more repugnant ones), we minimize them being present in our unconscious process.

By following this argument through in our work with suicidal clients, it is essential therefore that we fully consider our views on suicide, and how those views relate to the 'bigger picture', i.e. how we consider our world and other people in it. This reflection might sometimes unearth uncomfortable truths, where we become aware of hierarchies of acceptability that challenge our position of all-accepting counsellor.

We can ultimately be drawn into making judgements on life and death. For example, consider the following brief scenarios.

Duncan

Duncan is an 84-year-old male who has recently been diagnosed with terminal cancer. His partner died three years previously and his family, who live locally, care for him. Duncan has always been proud of his independence, but feels emotionally shattered by his diagnosis, and the rapid deterioration he notices in his emotional and physical well-being. He cared for his mother who died of cancer, and is resolved not to be a burden on his own children. One evening, having carefully written letters of goodbye to his children, he takes an overdose of tablets and dies.

Shelly

Shelly is a 37-year-old accountant. Following a late night meeting at work four months previously, she was attacked by a stranger on her way home and raped. She has been devastated by this traumatic experience, has not returned to work and cannot envisage ever doing so. She feels vulnerable in her own home and can no longer trust even her closest friends and family. Friends are concerned when they cannot make contact with her, and on breaking into her flat they find her dead. She had taken an overdose and placed a plastic bag on her head to suffocate herself.

Rashid

Rashid is 21 years old and has a diagnosis of bipolar affective disorder (manic depression). He is cared for by his local mental health team, although he continues to experience the crashing lows of depression. He contacts his mental health team, feeling that he is reaching crisis point once again, and they make arrangements to see him later that day. On his way to the appointment he throws himself under a train and is killed outright.

Hannah

Hannah is 16 years old, and is a popular person at school. She has many friends, though she has been anxious and shy about engaging in more intimate relationships. She has known for several years that she is lesbian, and has recently told her family. While this was initially difficult, they appeared to be accepting. Her talking to her family was prompted by her first relationship with Susie, a person she met at school. The relationship with Susie was profoundly significant for Hannah, as not only was it her first 'proper' relationship, but it was also the first time she was open with others about her sexuality. Susie ended the relationship unexpectedly, without explanation. Hannah felt devastated by this, and interpreted it as a rejection of everything about her. She was found hanging in her room by her parents.

Each one of these people killed themselves because of the interpersonal and intrapersonal crisis they experienced. Responses to each scenario might range from one point, 'no one has the right to end their own life', through to another point, 'we all have the right to end our own life'. In between these two points, where the majority may fall, a range of factors, including gender, age, powerlessness, perspective, stereotypes and experience, for example, will inform our assessments and judgements. We may not like the initial judgements we make, but they belong to us and need to be acknowledged and considered.

The importance of reflection

I would suggest that judgements are not inherently 'bad' thoughts to have, but instead are important mechanisms by which we can understand a changing world. In the face of suicide, counsellors have the potential to experience their own distress and uncertainty in the face of another's. The challenge is to be open to the existence of these thoughts and feelings, to find ways of supporting ourselves with them, e.g. in supervision, consultation with colleagues, our own counselling, reading research, etc., and thus reduce the potential of them being acted out with our clients.

Our responses to suicidality will be influenced by several factors. Some of these are personal, others philosophical, others again professional. We will make sense of our own particular viewpoint on suicide based on how we have assimilated and integrated a variety of experiences, in addition to those that have been profoundly dissonant to our own view of the world. Such factors might include:

- Previous professional experiences of suicide potential, including client suicides that we might have experienced.
- The culture of the team or organization in which we work, or how supported we feel as an independent practitioner.
- Our interpretation of the ethical imperatives of our work, or of policies or procedures that guide or demand particular action with suicidal clients.
- Our own experience of feeling suicidal, or of previous suicide attempts.
- Our experience of suicidal risk or suicide amongst family or friends.
- Views about suicide informed by faith or religious conviction.
- Other influences, including films, books, music and television, and how suicide has been depicted in those.

There are other influences too. The diversity of these influences flags the changing and dynamic nature of our 'position' with regard to suicide. We are likely to think and feel different things in response to different situations. For example, the three following scenarios might provoke different responses.

Alan

Alan is a 36-year-old male. He has been diagnosed with MS, and his condition has worsened quickly and significantly. He is now confined to a wheelchair, has lost his eyesight and is losing fine motor control. His profession and passion as a publisher and typesetter is now no longer possible. He increasingly has to rely on his partner for his personal needs. His medical team have informed him that his prognosis is poor. He tells his counsellor that it is his intention to kill himself whilst he still has the physical wherewithal to do so. Alan is found dead having taken an overdose four weeks after talking about his intention.

Pete

Pete is a 17-year-old male. He has recently been diagnosed as having schizophrenia, and latterly has been experiencing distressing and traumatizing hallucinations. He hears voices telling him to kill himself because he is worthless. He has deteriorated physically and is no longer taking care of his personal needs, e.g. washing, changing clothes. He is terrified of the world and of life, and is admitted to hospital at his own request for his safety. With a week of his admission, he walks out of the hospital ward and jumps from a bridge on to a motorway and is killed.

Isobel

Isobel is a 54-year-old female. She is estranged from her family and is generally socially isolated. She has recently left a violent relationship. She has a long history of depression and has been admitted to hospital on numerous occasions, both at her request and compulsorily. She misuses alcohol and has taken drugs in the past. She feels 'flattened' by the psychiatric system and no longer wishes to go into hospital. She is now accessing counselling for the first time in her life and feels that she has choices that she has never experienced before. At the end of one counselling session, she tells her counsellor that she feels 'very, very good' as she leaves. A friend finds her dead in her bed later that day; she had taken a large overdose with a bottle of vodka.

Each of these scenarios, all drawn from practice, present us with different challenges and responses. These might include respecting the choice of the individual to end their own life, through to sadness that more should have been done to prevent their suicide. It is unlikely that we will feel neutral or untouched by these stories. Neither is there a 'right' or 'wrong' position to take: there is our own position that will be influenced by many of the factors highlighted above.

I will take Isobel more specifically, as it is useful for me to reflect on my own position with Isobel in more detail, given that it was her death that took me into suicide research. I had worked with her when a trainee counsellor, and we had been meeting together weekly for approximately six months prior to her death. In summary, I have two different and conflicting views about Isobel's death that I am still not in a position to resolve.

While Isobel had been involved in psychiatric services for many years, this had been in the context of social isolation, a difficult relationship, ongoing depression, alcohol misuse, and a cycle of self-harm and suicide attempts. Psychiatry had not offered her anything beyond containment at various points of crisis in her life. In this sense, psychiatry had kept her alive, although she was not thankful that this had been the case. However, things were now changing. She had escaped a violent relationship, had a growing friendship group, was beginning to undertake voluntary work, had stopped drinking, and was feeling much more hopeful. Her life to this point had been characterized by unrelenting despair and hopelessness. More specifically, Isobel was exploring the changes she was making in counselling and, by her own acknowledgement, felt affirmed in her life. Herein are my conflicting positions:

1. With hindsight, the risk factors signalling Isobel's imminent self-annihilation were evident: her mood was lifting (the depression that had perhaps kept her alive was no longer an inhibiting factor) and she had the availability of means, i.e. large quantities of medication prescribed over several years. Given that things were so different for Isobel interpersonally, intervention might have 'held' her through her crisis until she was able to fully access and engage with the real changes she was making for herself. At news of her death, I remember feeling furious with what seemed to be 'selfish' choices, in addition to my own feelings of incompetence and failure as a counsellor. If I was a 'good enough' counsellor, I could have kept her alive. However,
2. Isobel was indeed making positive interpersonal choices, but perhaps her death signalled that intrapersonally she remained hopeless and in turmoil. She felt that her internal robustness had disintegrated through many years of medication and psychiatry, and she felt sufficiently small and helpless in the face of the 'system' that she acquiesced to any demands it made of her, irrelevant to her own thoughts and desires, which had been too deeply hidden through years of abuse. The moment she placed the tablets into her mouth and washed them down with large quantities of vodka, perhaps she felt that she regained control. My position, albeit heavily informed by my own grief, could be supported in the knowledge of her retaking control of her life: arguably a good 'outcome' for any therapeutic encounter?

This dichotomous position is not replicated in my thoughts about Alan. For me that seems much clearer, in that Alan made a decision about taking control of his losses and inevitable death, while he was able to do it, and not 'making any demands of [his] partner' (Alan's comments). Pete's death, however, leaves me profoundly saddened. Pete did not make a clear choice about his life and death, but was instead driven to suicide by erroneous voices that taunted him until he jumped to end their noise. He did not have 'capacity' to make such choices, and should have been safely contained through his crisis.

By making transparent my thinking, my intention is not to make any claim that my thoughts are 'right'. Instead, I aim to illustrate how different my thinking is in response to different situations, people and contexts. The three scenarios outlined here are all drawn from my practice as a counsellor. Undoubtedly they continue to exercise their influence in my ongoing work as a counsellor with suicidal clients, together with other personal and professional experiences I hold. By denying them, I just move them from a conscious processing to an unconscious one: they remain as relevant and influential whether I acknowledge them or instead pretend they no longer exist.

The relationship we have with suicide potential, our own life and death, will be a key factor in how we are able to assess and explore suicidality with our clients. Being open to that position will play an important role in facilitating the counselling discourse. As Shea (2002) states,

> When a clinician begins to understand his or her own attitudes, biases, and responses to suicide, he or she can become more psychologically and emotionally available to a suicidal client. Clients seem to be able to sense when a clinician is comfortable with the topic of suicide. At that point, and with such a clinician, clients may feel safe enough to share the immediacy of their pull towards death. (p. 4)

Discussion questions

1 Consider the following two statements: 'I always retain the right to end my own life', and 'I should always intervene to prevent my clients from taking their life, if they indicate to me it is their intention to do so.'
2 Notice how you respond to each statement, the aspects of each statement you agree/disagree with, and any contradictions between the two statements for you professionally and personally.
3 Reflect on your work with a client who was suicidal, or consider potentially working with a suicidal client, and explore how your views and beliefs will help and hinder your counselling relationship with them.
4 What factors in your life shape and influence your views on suicide?

15 Potential Dangers and Difficulties

> **Chapter overview**
>
> Following on from the previous chapter, the discussion here highlights the real and perceived risks for the counsellor in working with suicidal clients, such as the emotional responses they might experience as a consequence of working with suicide, and how, because of such feelings, they might inadvertently 'avoid' suicidality in their therapeutic dialogue with clients.

Much that has been written about the skill and practice of assessing suicide risk has been centred on the client process. The understood scenario is quite clear: the 'client', during initial assessment or later on in the counselling process, alludes to or talks about their wish to die. The 'counsellor', hearing this intention (whether implicitly or explicitly articulated), works through a process of identifying risk 'factors' that might make the likelihood of the client acting out their intention more likely; balancing those factors that might make the risk of a suicide attempt less likely; and then making a judgement as to the best form of intervention. This process, as described, is pretty clear (and possibly leaves you wondering why someone should go to the bother of writing a book about it). However, anyone who has talked with someone contemplating suicide, or indeed has experienced their own suicidality, will know that things are invariably not that simple.

The intention of suicide risk assessment, as outlined above, is to balance possibility with probability in an attempt to predict future behaviour. As a crude comparison, this is something akin to predicting the outcome of a horse race. In this scenario, the person attempting to predict the winner is likely to make use of various pieces of information: the current fitness of the horse (client presentation); the horse's form (history of suicide risk or suicide attempts); the current conditions (the client's demographic and socioeconomic context); the other runners (availability or lack of significant others in the client's life); and 'gut feeling' (the 'hunch' that can justify our decisions in the absence of an ability to articulate a more coherent rationale). As I say, this is a crude comparison that does not sit comfortably alongside the painful process of suicidality, but one that does perhaps highlight the application of predictability and probability when applied to human processes.

It is a sobering fact that very few people make a sustainable living out of betting on horses. There are obvious ways in which this comparison falls down: a person's history in relation to suicide potential is much more complex than 'winning or losing'; the person's ability (or inability) to communicate with their support network is wholly different to the rest of the field in a horse race. However, the essential point is perhaps made: that predicting outcome, especially in relation to human dynamics and behaviour, is notoriously difficult and not an easy process.

An added complication is that when one is reflecting on the process of assessing suicide risk, the focus is almost exclusively on the client's process, for it is they who present with the risk. In research terms, very little attention has been given to the process of the counsellor. This is a surprising fact given that suicide risk assessment is invariably a relational process, where one individual makes an assessment of another. As has been highlighted in other chapters, the medicalizing of suicidality has, in turn, seen an attempt at objectifying an inevitably subjective process. The plethora of forms and risk assessment 'tools', all attempting to measure and quantify human distress, is perhaps symptomatic of a treatment culture which at times is more preoccupied with 'doing to' than 'doing with'. In the context of this positivist (and arguably reductionist) approach to suicide risk assessment, the process of the 'assessor' understandably becomes a redundant area for exploration or consideration.

It could be argued that by overlooking the process of the assessor (their thoughts, feelings and responses in relation to trying to understand another's suicidal pain), we view the whole endeavour of suicide risk assessment with one eye closed. That is, what is a multi-layered, three-dimensional process is reduced to the interpretation of a few tick boxes in a two-dimensional way. The greatest tragedy of this is that, as counsellors, we think in terms of suicide risk 'assessment' as opposed to suicide risk 'exploration'; we absent ourselves from the suicide discourse and take a position that removes ourselves from the other's pain and despair. Perhaps this is because pain and despair in self-annihilation is too overwhelming or frightening?

The 'disappeared' counsellor

I remember hiding behind the settee while watching frightening programmes on television when I was young. The principle was that if I could close my eyes, or make myself disappear from the terror (albeit only behind a settee), then the terror might go away, or not exist, or be less threatening, or I might avoid being caught up in it. A counsellor, while talking about her feelings when working with suicide risk, talked of her terror when she said,

> If I am honest I still carry a terror of losing a client ... a terror of suicide ... perhaps I was half asleep on some of these issues and I thought, oh yes, I am a person centred counsellor, therefore people have the right to take their own life if they want to. But then there was another aspect to it, which was, have I done my job enough with them before they go and do it. Have I explored every avenue with them and worked with all parts of them ... so yes, that terror is still there.

The temptation for any of us to find ways of disconnecting with difficult processes is very strong, even though we might delude ourselves into thinking that this is something we would never do. If the assertion that runs throughout the chapters of this book is true – that assessing suicide potential fundamentally lies in engaging with the suicidal client at a deeper relational level – then the need for counsellors to reflect on their degree of presence with suicidal clients is an imperative. So too is the need to reflect on the dangers of 'disappearing' themselves – hiding behind the settee – when things become terrifying. Returning to the point made earlier, that suicide risk assessment is more about suicide risk exploration, the importance of counsellor presence in that process is significant. Given that for many suicidal clients, their pull towards death can be overwhelming and persistent, the readiness of the counsellor to engage with that pull can be instrumental in facilitating change.

The metaphor I would offer here to illustrate this point is that of potholing. For me, counselling is a bit like potholing in pairs or groups. The task is to explore cave systems, caverns, passageways and pathways. These represent client experiences, memories, histories, fears and joys. Many will be familiar to the client, as they introduce them to you and describe them in some detail. As counsellor – as co-potholer – you bring a new perspective, and can reflect on the journey to these places and what you find on arrival in ways that might provide the client with new insights. In the course of that journey you might uncover new cave systems or passage ways that take you both into unexplored territory. The client may have known that these new areas exist, but felt too overwhelmed or frightened to explore them on their own. Your task is to accompany them on that journey. Of course, your task is also to pay careful attention to safety: to ensure that you have ropes and a means of exiting this place when you need to, and that you give due consideration to the capacity of you and the client to manage this journey safely.

The suicidal journey makes this cave system profoundly perilous and unpredictable. Again, this particular cave system may be familiar to the client – a place where they spend a great deal of their time, or perhaps one that is unknown and thunders out of the darkness in a newly menacing way. In this cave system the footing can feel precarious, the handholds limited, and we are exploring at the limits of the rope – the limits of our sense of safety. There is a strong temptation to retreat to safer ground, or perhaps to wander past the entrance to this particular cave system, knowing it is there but best avoided. We might feel aghast at the thought of asking our clients to go in and explore it on their own, but that is often what we do through our own fear and terror.

The dangers of unacknowledged countertransference

The assertion here is not of unethical behaviour, or of deliberately or knowingly leaving our clients to face their despair and pain alone. Instead, this chapter highlights the potential outcome of the counsellor process remaining invisible and unexplored. As was stated earlier, the suicide risk assessment 'industry' colludes with this by increasingly trying to objectify an essentially subjective process – to measure 'risk factors' without always listening to the subtleties of individuality. The dynamic of invisibility that occurs at an institutional level can easily become paralleled at an individual level. The structures of suicide risk assessment can facilitate our disappearance, driven by fear and anxiety.

Much research has highlighted the profound effect that working with suicidal clients and client suicide can have on the practitioner (e.g. Fox and Cooper, 1998; Pompili et al., 2002a; 2002b; Reeves and Mintz, 2001; B. Richards, 2000). Many of these studies identify a number of difficult responses, including fear, anxiety, feelings of impotence and incompetence, sleeplessness and nightmares, for example. These are profound feelings that are often associated with vicarious trauma (Fox and Cooper, 1998). In this context, behind the settee seems a much safer place to be.

My own research (Reeves and Mintz, 2001) into counsellors' experience of working with suicide risk highlighted a number of important considerations. In addition to the feelings identified above, counsellors talked about doubting their own professional competence and their ability to work safely and appropriately with suicide potential. This was regardless of how long the counsellor had been working, or their experience of suicide risk in their work. For example, one counsellor stated, 'My immediate response is that I'd think, "Oh God, I'm not getting it right. I haven't been able to be effective here – I haven't reached this person."' The importance of supervision was highlighted here, with counsellors talking of needing their supervisor to affirm their competency in the face of self-doubts.

Counsellors in the study talked of feeling that they were 'betraying' their client if they needed to consult or refer for a specialist mental health assessment. Post-session, counsellors talked of using strategies to distance themselves from the anxiety of suicide potential. As one described, 'I would write my notes first so then I would be doing it to try and put me in another place. Just to try and distance me from where I'd been.'

Counsellors, when reflecting on their practice, acknowledged the implications of strongly held views about suicide. They generally understood the importance of self-awareness so that such views were not acted out with suicidal clients. For example, one counsellor said that, 'It's to do with letting a person go out there and kill themselves – I suppose really I don't approve of it'; and, 'Who can say you've got the "right" to do it? I think it is a dreadful thing to do.' Alternatively, 'I think a person has a right to kill themselves if they wish. [You sound really clear.] Yes, very clear about that.'

The threat of litigation and the accusation of malpractice (real or perceived) played an important role in informing how counsellors reacted to suicide potential. 'I think it's the fear of being held ultimately responsible for someone taking their own life, I think; and I should have intervened to stop them.' While another counsellor said, 'Something about responsibility and duty and ... I don't think that I could keep quiet about it – it doesn't seem right. I suppose I could be accused of not trying to prevent it, or not doing as much as was reasonably possible to prevent it.'

Leenaars (2004) offers a useful, albeit brief, overview of the process of transference and countertransference in the counselling process with suicidal clients. He defines transference as, 'a process arising in any therapeutic situation and involving reactions of the patient's previous experience, recollections, and unconscious wishes regarding (often early) significant people (object relations)' (2004: 101). Countertransference is defined as, 'all the clinician's unconscious reactions to the patient and the patient's transference. These reactions originate in the evaluator's own conflicts and/or real objective relations (object relations)' (2004: 101). It is important here not to be too focused on the terminology used. *Transference* and *countertransference* are terms most commonly associated with psychoanalytic or psychodynamic approaches to counselling. As such, they may be viewed as irrelevant or counterproductive in other counselling modalities, such as person centred or cognitive behavioural counselling. However, if it is possible to temporarily put aside the semantic qualities of these terms, their meaning can be transferable to all therapeutic approaches: clients don't arrive at the counselling room door *tabula rasa*, and counsellors will respond to their clients, their story and how their story is told. Transference and countertransference are arguably present in all counselling interactions (indeed all interactions), but how they are described, understood, and therefore worked with will be different depending on the theoretical orientation of the counsellor.

The counsellor's countertransferential responses to the suicidal client, as indicated previously, can be immensely powerful and difficult to contain. The potential for counsellors to dissociate from such feelings is high, given their dissonance with the more 'acceptable' counsellor qualities of empathy, care, attentiveness and presence, for example. Additionally, the power to self-delude can match the power to dissociate with equal intensity. The effect is that we can believe that we are fully engaged, listening, connected and present with a suicidal client, whereas in reality we are stood outside the cave, peering in with one eye on our escape.

Elias

Elias is an experienced counsellor who works in a primary care setting. He takes to supervision the case of his client Gavin with whom he has been working for two months. He talks to his supervisor about his concerns for Gavin, particularly following the last session. He has been worried about Gavin all week, hoping that he was okay. The supervisor asks Elias what the concerns centre on. He describes his client's distress in the last session, and that he suspected Gavin perhaps was suicidal. The supervisor asks Elias how Gavin responded when asked about this. Elias says, 'Oh gosh, I didn't ask Gavin about being suicidal. He was far too vulnerable and wouldn't have coped with that sort of question. It would just have made matters worse.'

---

1 If you were Elias's supervisor, how might you respond to what Elias said?
2 Do you think Elias was right not to ask Gavin about his suspicions of increased suicide risk?
3 What other reasons might explain Elias's reluctance to talk to Gavin about his suspicions?

Leenaars suggests a number of ways in which negative countertransferential responses can be present in counselling relationships, and additionally suggests that if unacknowledged, these can 'not only be problematic but also suicidogenic' (2004: 101). He states that:

> The following reactions in the clinician may arise if confrontation with the suicidal patient provokes feelings of guilt, incompetence, anxiety, fear and anger, and when these feelings are not worked through:

Potential Dangers and Difficulties 139

- Underestimation of the seriousness of the suicidal action.
- Absence of a discussion of the suicidal thoughts or actions.
- Allowing oneself to be lulled into a false sense of security by the client's promise not to repeat a suicide attempt [*or to act on suicidal thoughts*], perhaps with the use of a simplistic written suicide contract.
- Disregard of the cry for help aspect of the suicide attempt [*or thoughts*] and exclusive concentration on its manipulative character.
- Exaggeration of the client's provocative, infantile, and aggressive sides.
- Denial of one's own importance to the client.
- Failure to persuade the client to undergo counselling [*or to continue with counselling*].
- Feeling of lacking the resources for the evaluation required by a particular client.
- Exaggerated sense of hopelessness in response to the client's troubled social situation and abuse of drugs or alcohol.
- Being pleased with the client's claims to have all problems solved after only a brief period of time.
- Feeling upset when the client shows resistance after a brief course of enquiry, despite the therapist's initial profound commitment. (pp. 101–102, my italics)

I can reflect on times, and with people, where some of these responses have, with hindsight, been present. What is poignant in these responses in how invisible they generally are in the literature that talks about suicide risk assessment. You won't find these outlined in policy documents, in risk assessment guidelines or in the notes accompanying risk assessment tools and questionnaires. However, that they might be present in the discourse with a suicidal person, or in how counselling is negotiated, contracted or ended, is as important as any knowledge of 'risk factors' or ticking the boxes. The above list identifies ways in which counsellors can disconnect from their clients; the reverse therefore is how, in knowing of these dangers, we can connect with our clients in a way that is likely to be much more facilitative of a suicide exploration.

Table 15.1 offers a short excerpt from a transcript taken from a counselling assessment session with a suicidal client. When we review the transcript as a whole, we can see that the counsellor is competent and experienced. I have no doubt that, where suicide risk was suspected, they believe they would be willing to explore fully and openly that risk with their client. However, as this transcript demonstrates, suicide became almost unspeakable. The client refers implicitly to their own suicidal thoughts through the metaphor of 'getting in people's way' – and the need therefore to 'get out of their way'. Getting out of their way

Table 15.1 The difficulty of naming suicide: an example from a transcript

Client	Comes and goes yeah … when it gets bad I want to get out of the way.
Counsellor	I'm sorry, I don't know what you mean?
Client	Get out of the way … get out of everyone's way … it's not … [pause]
Counsellor	You feel that it would be a way to … [tailing off, then pausing]
Client	[pausing] …Yeah … everybody would be better off.
Counsellor	[pausing] … It really sounds as if this business that you feel like you get in everyone's way is important for you?
Client	That's what's happening, isn't it.

would mean the client's death, where they would no longer be present and an inconvenience. The counsellor begins a tentative enquiry with a clarifying question, 'I'm sorry, I don't know what you mean?', inviting the client to explore further their thoughts and intent. However, something happened in the discourse that made the naming of suicide too difficult. It was almost as if the terrible cave entrance was pointed at, but suddenly, in the moment, neither were able to venture inside. The counsellor makes an attempt at making the implicit explicit when saying, 'You feel that it would be a way to …', but in their hesitation, they perhaps communicated that the word was too difficult, too terrible to say. The client jumped in, perhaps rescuing the counsellor from their difficulty by saying, 'Yeah … everybody would be better off …', before the counsellor flees in the opposite direction.

In 'assessment' terms, no more is known about the client's thoughts, plans or intentions at the end of this exchange (or indeed the full session) than was known at the beginning. The counsellor knows enough to know that this client 'wants to get out of everyone's way', but does not know what this means for the client. In professional terms, the counsellor is in a position of having to decide how best to respond to the risk, whilst evaluating it from behind the settee. Arguably, more importantly in terms of 'exploration', the client is left silenced by this exchange, perhaps thinking that his most terrible thoughts are too difficult for people to hear. He has no opportunity to explore this cave system, unless alone, only wondering what might lie inside; but he now certainly knows that it exists.

The purpose of this chapter has been to highlight the dangers of counsellors remaining disconnected from their own thoughts and responses, whilst also identifying the cultural and institutional dynamics that might allow this disconnection to take place. Potholing in unfamiliar and dangerous conditions is something that we should rightly be wary of, but not being prepared to go there, when required, does not mean that the danger no longer exists. The task is arguably about identifying the nature of the danger so that, if appropriate, clients can negotiate their own way through, in the context of their guide – counsellors – being aware of their own fears, and supporting themselves accordingly.

Discussion questions

1. Reflect on how you view the process of working with a suicidal client.
2. Are there any particular strategies or tools that you employ to ascertain suicide risk?
3. Which phrase best reflects your approach, *suicide risk assessment or suicide risk exploration*? Why?
4. With your supervisor or trusted colleague, reflect on your work with suicidal clients and identify times when unacknowledged countertransferential material was present.

Part VI

Key Aspects of Counselling with Suicidal Clients

16 Tightropes and Safety Nets: Supporting Practice

> **Chapter overview**
>
> We have now identified many of the 'tightropes' of working with suicide risk. This chapter considers some of the professional 'safety nets' that the counsellor can use to support their work and practice decisions. Drawing on the information contained in previous chapters, counsellors can use suicide risk factors to help inform decisions, and appropriate record keeping to ensure that decisions are fully accounted for, thus enabling them to remain client focused.

As has been discussed in previous chapters, the 'terror' of suicide – anxiety, fear, sleeplessness, nightmares, a sense of professional incompetence and impotence – can be present for most counsellors, some of the time, when working with suicidal clients (I would actually argue *all* counsellors as opposed to most, but some might not realize it). Those counsellors who say that they have never experienced such feelings in such work, to some degree or another, would do well to reflect on their own process in more detail, and consider the real possibility of dissociation. I would be concerned about any counsellor who claimed never to have felt anxiety or apprehension when working with suicidal potential, and would further wonder whether they are sufficiently present in their work to practise safely and ethically.

The assertion here is that such feelings, albeit difficult and sometimes painful, are an essential and understandable response to another's suicidality. When acknowledged, felt and self-supported, they provide a viscerally important psychological connection within the context of the therapeutic relationship. In other words, such feelings enable and facilitate real psychological contact between counsellor and client. They additionally enable a potential level of understanding of risk that questionnaires and other risk tools cannot even begin to achieve. Such tools, for all their generic value, are an example of risk assessment 'done to' another; the therapeutic discourse, lubricated by the emotional responses of one listening to another, is an example of risk assessment that is truly collaborative.

The important personal and professional consideration, however, is how the counsellor can support themselves with such difficult feelings so that they indeed can facilitate contact, rather than inhibit it: tightropes and safety nets. Without the safety net, the tightrope is dangerous and exposing and allows little room for error. With the safety net, the consequence of 'getting it wrong' need not be catastrophic. A quotation from a counsellor in an earlier chapter expressed their terror of suicide: 'Have I done my job enough with them before they go and do it? Have I explored every avenue with them and worked with all the parts of them?' The terror is fear of blame and failure, while the safety net is thoroughness, professional rigour and an appropriate use of knowledge and resources. Risk assessment does not require an ability to foresee the future, even though at times it appears that this is what is being demanded. Instead, risk assessment, or risk exploration, is about making an informed judgement wherever possible in collaboration with the client, about the *likelihood* of an event happening, given all the available information.

The best way to illustrate this is to consider a case scenario. Similar to Luke in Chapter 4, 'Suicide Risk Factors and Assessment', Josh is here described with the risk factors highlighted to the right.

Josh	Risk factors
Josh comes to see you as a counsellor in a service for young people. He self-refers and says that he is keen to start counselling 'to sort [his] problems out'.	
Josh is a 17-year-old male.	Age Gender
He has recently come out to family and friends that he is gay.	Sexuality
He left school when he was 16 with few qualifications, and since that time has been unemployed.	Unemployment
He lives alone in a flat. His family have disowned him because of his sexuality, saying they want nothing more to do with him 'until he grows out of it'.	Lives alone Family estrangement and relationship problems
He has recently split up with his first partner.	Relationship breakdown
Josh has some friends; some have been okay about his sexuality, whilst others have become a little 'distant'.	
Josh has self-harmed for some years (cuts his arms), and talks about 'eating problems' – vomits after eating. Went to see his GP (seven weeks ago) who prescribed anti-depressants.	Self-harm Eating disorder Availability of means (medication) Not responding to medication
Mood fluctuates: talks of anxiety and depression. Josh says that his mood changes quickly – sometimes low, angry – then elated and 'high'.	Anxiety Depression Lack of affective control
Josh talks of some drug use – smokes weed occasionally with friends. Drinks most evenings, either alone or with friends. Poor appetite and sleep.	Drug use Alcohol use Poor appetite Sleep problems

Talks about 'terrible thoughts', and has not told anyone else about them. Uncle works on a farm and has a gun. Josh thinks about 'putting the gun in [his] mouth and blowing [himself] away'. Feels ashamed by these thoughts.	Expressed suicidal ideation
On a scale of intent (0–10), Josh says at worst they are an 8, at best a 2, and currently a 6.	Some intent
Poor self-esteem and self-confidence. At the end of the session, says that he would like to continue with counselling. He presented as low risk, but engaged and interested in the process.	Low self-esteem

When a client says that they have no suicidal thoughts and no intention to self-harm, there is no further dilemma for the counsellor with respect to risk assessment at that point. The client is not suicidal and therefore the counsellor does not have to consider how best to respond to suicidal potential. Ironically, many counsellors report that the opposite of this situation is also relatively simple to manage: where a client talks of an immediate intention to kill themselves. Many counsellors in this situation feel that, in virtue of the contract of confidentiality agreed, it is their responsibility to seek additional help for that client and refer them to specialist services for assessment and intervention, preferably with the client's consent (but without consent if necessary and the threat of harm is immediate, bearing in mind the points made in Chapter 7, 'Confidentiality, Capacity and Consent').

Josh's situation, however, perhaps represents that which causes most anxiety: risk is clearly evident (with at least 18 risk factors identified), and yet he presents in counselling as engaging and willing to work with the process. He would prefer not to talk to anyone else about his 'dark thoughts', and is reluctant to give permission for the counsellor to do so. If the counsellor decides to respect Josh's wishes (as they are ethically obliged to do) and contract for further counselling, their assessment of risk has concluded that in this instance, and at this time, Josh is more likely to return to his next counselling session than not, and that by breaking his confidentiality at this stage would undermine and possibility eliminate any chance of a therapeutic relationship based on trust. The counsellor's (and the client's) position is of positive risk taking.

The principle of positive risk taking is one familiar to almost every counsellor. Without positive risk taking, the imperative would be to refer to a GP or specialist mental health service every client who attended counselling who indicated any level of risk. This premise returns to the comment made by the consultant psychiatrist psychotherapist highlighted early on in this book, that counsellors wouldn't work with suicidal clients because they are essentially not competent to do so, and would instead refer them elsewhere.

A list of risk factors was included in Chapter 4, 'Suicide Risk Factors and Assessment', and some might conclude in looking at that list that most of us would tick one or two of the boxes! The fact that counselling takes place with many thousands of distressed and vulnerable clients every day is testament to counsellors' and clients' willingness to take risks. However, the words of Shneidman take on more potent meaning when considering Josh: 'Most people who commit suicide talk about it; most people who talk about suicide do not commit it. Which to believe?' (1998: 57). Positive risk taking – the tightrope – demands that counsellors be clear in their thinking, and in their notes, as to the factors that have informed that decision – the safety net. Without the latter, counsellors make a decision to head off on the high wire without any means of self-support.

Some might argue that this 'back covering' has no place in the world of counselling. However, I would prefer to reframe 'back covering' as 'accountable professional practice', in which the counsellor is able to articulate to themselves, their client and their agency (if employed) a clear and informed rationale for the professional decisions made. This is particularly important because counsellors make decisions that draw on a full range of theories of counselling and personality to inform their thinking. Saying that a decision was based on 'gut feeling', or for some practitioners on their 'countertransference', does not do justice to the complex thinking that has almost certainly resulted in the outcome. Particularly in the unlikely event of having to account for decisions in a coroner's court, arguing that the practice decisions were based on 'gut feeling' is not likely to get you very far. However, a clearly thought through plan, based on the available information, drawing on theory and knowledge, is much more likely to be self-supporting.

This approach to counselling with suicidal clients is important. Not simply because it affords greater protection for the counsellor, but also because it facilitates therapeutic contact between counsellor and client. Given the assertion that most counsellors, some of the time, are likely to experience quite intense and difficult feelings in response to suicide potential, grounding themselves in the solidity of knowledge, theory and a clear process of thinking is arguably much more likely to focus on the client's process, rather than be distracted by their own. Likewise, if a counsellor has to make the difficult decision to go against a client's expressed wishes around confidentiality, because they believe them to be at immediate risk of suicide, it is important to be clear to the client (and then to any referring agency) why this is the case.

Table 16.1 represents sample case notes from the counsellor who met with Josh, detailing concerns and why a decision was made to break Josh's confidentiality. However, the counsellor might instead have decided to contract for counselling and work with Josh to manage the risks. Assuming the diary notes were the same as in Table 16.1, note how the counsellor articulates the decision in a different 'Outcome' section in Table 16.2.

What quickly becomes apparent when reading these two diary entries is that both outcomes are justifiable in the context of the same information. That is not to say that as a reader you are not likely to agree with one and disagree with another. You might have clear views as to which one you would follow in the same circumstances. However, risk assessment is not about predicting the future. No amount of information, whether obtained via questionnaires or dialogic assessment, will answer the 'what happens next' question. In the same way, it is impossible to guess your behaviour once you put this book down. It might be possible to predict a variety of behaviours given what we know, e.g. make yourself a drink, go to the toilet, watch the television, throw the book in the bin! However, it is impossible to accurately predict which of those behaviours is more likely.

As counsellors we are required to use current knowledge and research, and to be informed through the words and thoughts of the client, to consider which

Table 16.1 Breaking Josh's confidentiality

Meeting with Josh, date

Josh today attended a first session of counselling, self-referred.

Problems

- Josh is a 17-year-old male recently estranged from his family following his disclosure to them that he is gay.
- Recently experienced a breakdown in the relationship with his first partner, is quite distressed about this.
- Talked of low and fluctuating mood – anxiety and depression, but unpredictable 'highs' and 'lows'.

Social contact and support

- Josh currently has no contact with family. They have refused contact with him because of his sexuality – very distressed about this.
- Has some friends who have remained supportive. Josh is generally unwilling to talk to them about his problems, as he does not wish to burden them. Is generally quite secretive about how he feels.
- Recent breakdown of his first significant relationship. This, together with the family problems, is exacerbating an already low mood.

Coping strategies

- Josh does not feel that he is coping well at the moment; has little support and is reluctant to use the little he does have.
- Feels (and seems) isolated.
- In contact with his GP who has prescribed anti-depressants. Josh does not feel that these are working, but is reluctant to go back to his GP to discuss this. Did not wish me to talk to his GP about this (see 'Risk' below).

Daily coping

- Josh is not sleeping well – takes time to get to sleep, wakes early and has poor sleep generally. This has been the case for a couple of years, but is currently worse at the moment.
- Poor appetite. Josh described eating problems – has for some years vomited after food – continues to do this, though not eating regularly at present.
- Poor libido – Josh reports this as one of the reasons for the breakdown of the relationship. Did not feel confident about sex and therefore avoided it.

Subjective view

- Josh says that he has low self-confidence in most social situations. Feels too overwhelmed to apply for a job.
- Low self-esteem – does not think that he is a very nice person. Cannot understand why anyone would like him. Has felt this way for some time, but this has been exacerbated by family reaction to his sexuality.
- Poor body image – does not like the way he looks. Caused difficulties in his sexual relationship with his partner where he was reluctant to allow physical intimacy and withdrew.

Risk

Josh presents at high risk for the following reasons:

- Has self-injured for several years, cutting himself on his arms. This has become worse recently, though Josh is reluctant to seek medical help when required (advised him to go to A&E or see his GP regarding some cuts on his arm).
- Josh talked of 'dark thoughts'; of wanting to shoot himself in the head using his uncle's registered gun. Scored himself 8 at the worst, 2 at best and currently 6 on a scale of intent.
- Unwilling for me to discuss my concerns with his GP.

(Continued)

Table 16.1 (Continued)

Meeting with Josh, date

Outcome

We agreed that counselling was appropriate, and that Josh was keen to begin. However, I informed Josh that I would need to speak with his GP re my concerns about his suicide risk in the meantime. Josh was not willing to give permission for me to do this. However, I believed this was still necessary for the following reasons:

- Risk factors of gender and age place Josh in a higher risk group.
- Lack of affective control. By Josh's own acknowledgement he currently has little control over mood and affect, thus making an impulsive act of suicide more likely.
- Josh is currently drinking and using drugs: thus exacerbating the likelihood of an impulsive act.
- Clearly expressed suicidal thoughts, and plan. Additionally, a high level of intent with virtually no accessible support systems at a time of crisis.
- Recent crises (family disagreement and relationship breakdown with partner) increasing the likelihood of harm.
- Unwillingness to give permission for me to speak with GP – leaving counselling in potentially an isolated position and therefore less likely to help.

Table 16.2 Maintaining confidentiality with Josh

Outcome

We agreed that counselling was appropriate, and that Josh was keen to begin. I expressed my concerns to Josh about the risk he presented, but agreed to respect his decision for me not to speak to his GP currently (though we did agree to continue to review this situation), for the following reasons:

- Josh is clearly motivated to begin counselling, having referred himself initially.
- He acknowledges his difficulties and their severity. He was open and honest about his thoughts of suicide and was willing to proactively work with me to help himself be safe, and to reduce the immediacy and severity of these thoughts as an early priority.
- Josh has already discussed his anxiety and depression with his GP, who is aware of his fluctuating mood. I will continue to suggest to Josh that he revisits his GP to discuss medication, and will explore his reluctance to do so.
- Other than depression and anxiety, there was no evidence during the session that Josh was experiencing any additional psychopathology, e.g. disordered thinking, flight of ideas, pressure of speech. Throughout the session he remained responsive and psychologically connected and responded appropriately to me.
- Josh talked of suicidal ideation, some plans and some intent. However, he demonstrated insight into the factors that might influence the level of intent and was willing to access support should this change (gave him information on the local mental health crisis team and how to make contact).
- Josh is currently at risk, but did not appear to be at such immediate risk that would warrant me breaking his confidentiality.
- On that basis I believed him to have full capacity to make an informed decision about confidentiality. I therefore believe that breaking Josh's confidentiality at this stage would undermine any chance of us forming a trusting therapeutic relationship, thus exacerbating his low levels of support.
- Under my ethical framework, I therefore will respect Josh's wish to keep confidentiality to counselling, given it is his expressed wish. However, I will keep this under review with him.

intervention is most appropriate for our client at any given point. This is something we do with every client at every session. We may agree further sessions, end counselling, give information, refer to another counsellor or service, speak to a GP (with or without permission), and so on. Risk assessment is no different to that: with Josh the task of the counsellor was to consider what, in the light of the information available, was the next best course of action. One counsellor decided one course of action, while another followed a different course. However, each counsellor was able to clearly articulate their decision and the information that was used to reach it. In that sense, they ensured a safety net was in place prior to stepping out on to the wire.

Discussion questions

1 What information would be important to you, either about or from your suicidal client, in deciding against breaking confidentiality?
2 What 'safety nets' do you have in place to support your practice when working with suicide risk?
3 How do you record suicide risk in client notes? If you don't keep client notes, how do you ensure that your actions are accounted for?
4 How would you respond to Josh given the information you have?

17 Good Practice for Self-Support

Chapter overview

This chapter considers the ethical importance of self-care when counselling suicidal clients, and reflects on what support might be required in the event of client suicide. A 'chain of care' approach is suggested (Reeves and Nelson, 2006), with the development of a menu of support options that counsellors could consider. The different needs of independent practitioners are discussed, with various options for how self-care might be integrated into day-to-day practice decisions.

We have talked at various stages throughout the chapters of this book of the profound impact that working with suicidal clients, as well as client suicide, can have on the counsellor. Indeed, it is because of the profundity of this impact that counsellors might inadvertently absent themselves from therapeutic contact with their clients as a means of avoiding such painful feelings and responses. Of course, we will not always do that with knowledge or awareness, telling ourselves that we remain fully available to our clients at their time of crisis, but we can disconnect in a variety of ways as a means of self-protection.

The fear of a client dying as a consequence of suicide has been described as one of the most profound and disturbing events in a professional career (Hendin et al., 2000), with feelings including numbness, shock, denial, depression, disturbed sleep patterns and nightmares. As has been described in other chapters, it is easy to assume that trainee or newly qualified practitioners might be more susceptible to such responses, with experience providing some form of protection, but that does not appear to be true.

Chemtob et al. (1988) and Alexander et al. (2000) highlight that the fear of 'getting it wrong' is not exclusive to counsellors: other mental health professionals can share the same anxiety – consultant psychiatrists in the case of these papers. The fear of 'getting it wrong' can be persistent and pervasive for many counsellors; perhaps it is reinforced and contextually affirmed by the prediction-prevention culture already highlighted?

The fear of litigation can sometimes influence counsellors such that they behave in a contradictory way to what they would describe as good practice. For example, Kleepsies and Dettm (2000) note that some counsellors were reluctant to consult with colleagues in the aftermath of a patient's suicide because they feared how the conversation might be subsequently used.

The need for counsellors to pay careful attention to their wellbeing, for the sake of themselves and for their clients, is an ethical requirement. For BACP members, the *Ethical Framework for Good Practice in Counselling and Psychotherapy* (2007), under 'Care of Self as a Practitioner', states,

> Attending to the practitioner's well-being is essential to sustaining good practice.
>
> Practitioners have a responsibility to themselves to ensure that their work does not become detrimental to their health or well-being by ensuring that the way that they undertake their work is as safe as possible and that they seek appropriate professional support and services as the need arises.
>
> Practitioners are entitled to be treated with proper consideration and respect that is consistent with this Guidance. (p. 8)

A number of reasons then begin to emerge which signal the need for good self-care when working with suicidal clients. These include:

- The known detrimental effects on the mental health of counsellors both working with suicide risk, and following the suicide of one of their clients.
- The fear of 'getting it wrong' and the likelihood of counsellors not accessing their usual self-support strategies for fear of this being used as 'evidence' against them, e.g. consulting with colleagues.
- The need for counsellors to be open and in therapeutic contact with clients, particularly when clients are suicidal.
- The need for counsellors to remain self-aware to help limit the danger of acting out personally held views within sessions.
- The need for counsellors to make best use of all available information, to help support and sustain good quality assessments of suicide potential.

Chain of care in self-support

In 2006 I wrote a short article with Sue Nelson (Reeves and Nelson, 2006) which focused on some interesting work she was undertaking as part of her doctoral studies. She was developing what she called a 'chain of care' approach to self-support when working with suicide risk, and following completed suicide.

The chain of care approach to self-support, particularly when counselling is located within an organizational setting, is based on the premise that each 'link' of the chain relates to each aspect of the process in which the counsellor finds themselves. The aim of such a policy is to help safeguard the emotional and psychological wellbeing of all those affected by suicide potential, or actual client suicide. Its aim is to ensure that counsellors are not scapegoated, that they are supported through reflective practice processes, and that clients continuing to use the service are protected from the sometimes harmful organizational dynamics that can be present in a blame culture. The following areas of practice might be included in such a policy:

- initial and ongoing support needs
- supervision
- case contact
- case reviews
- continuing professional development.

Initial and ongoing support needs

Counsellors will have different needs at different stages of contact with a suicidal client. It is essential that counsellors are free to consult, where possible and within the confines of the confidentiality agreed, so that they are not making case management decisions in isolation. When working in a team this might be with a colleague, but certainly, when considering breaking confidentiality, with a senior counsellor or team manager. Any consultations should be appropriately recorded on the client's case file, in line with any organizational policy for record keeping. At this stage it is important to stress that any confidentiality agreements should not be so exclusive that they prohibit an appropriate and sensitive consultation with colleagues when the need arises.

Counsellors should have the availability of additional support to help them manage any 'actions' required to safeguard the wellbeing of a suicidal client, e.g. making contact with a relevant professional such as the client's GP, or liaising with relevant mental health services. It is often the simple, practical things that can be experienced as profoundly supportive in the actual event, e.g. getting hold of telephone numbers, supporting the client if they remain in the counselling service, that can easily be overlooked. Any support that leaves the counsellor feeling that they are not on their own with managing the situation will help ensure that it is managed efficiently, carefully and with as little distress for the client as possible.

In the event of client suicide, it is imperative that early responses should be about supporting those affected, rather than trying to apportion blame or seek answers at that stage. Any counsellor who finds themselves in this situation is likely to be feeling very vulnerable and shaky, and not in a position where they can offer clear insights into either the client's or their own process. There will be time for reflecting on practice and ensuring that paperwork is in order. As time progresses, it is useful for the counsellor to be able, through negotiation with a senior counsellor or line manager, to vary their support to best meet their changing needs. Support options might include time away from client work: a period with reduced client contact, additional supervision and the option of personal therapy, for example.

Supervision

In the UK, ongoing clinical supervision is an ethical requirement for all practising counsellors (BACP, 2007). Supervision offers normative, formative and restorative functions to counsellors in practice (Hawkins and Shohet, 2007). The restorative function, that is in supporting the counsellor and offering restorative space, is key in this context. As has been outlined in other chapters, counsellors will often look towards their supervisors to affirm professional competence and individual interventions, when anxious about their work with suicidal clients (Reeves and Mintz, 2001). In the event of client suicide, supervision is especially important in helping counsellors to safely reflect on their practice in a non-judging way, and to consider the rationale for any decisions made with respect to the client. It also provides an important audit (through the formative and normative functions) of how the counsellor had worked with the client and how/whether suicide risk had been identified and responded to. At a time of personal and professional crisis for the counsellor, additional supervision, wherever possible, is essential.

Case contact

By case contact I am referring to what involvement, if any, the counsellor may have in an ongoing way with the client's case. With a client who presents at ongoing risk of suicide, it may be that, through supervision and in discussion with colleagues, the counsellor feels the demands made are beyond their competency. This is an important insight for any counsellor to have; it is a question we should be continually asking of ourselves with respect to any client, and represents sound, ethical practice. While it can be difficult to acknowledge with a supervisor or manager that the client demands a level of knowledge and competency that we don't feel we possess, it is the cornerstone of ethical thinking to be reflecting on work in this way.

In the event of client suicide, 'what happens next' will be a thought that occurs to many counsellors. The worst fear might be of inquiry hearings and coroner's courts, and while this is a possibility (albeit a rare one), the immediate reality is usually more about managing contact with the deceased client's family or friends, who will want to know as much as possible to try and understand their loved one's actions. It has to be remembered that the counsellor and counselling agency offer the client the same degree of confidentiality in death as they did in life, and so the contact with family or friends needs to be managed carefully and sensitively, and probably not by the counsellor concerned.

The same is true for funeral arrangements. Sometimes it would be appropriate for the counsellor to attend the funeral, if invited, while other times this would not be the case. It is difficult to offer hard and fast rules given the complexities that might surround any particular situation. Wherever possible it is almost certainly better for someone other than the counsellor to make the final decision as to whether this is appropriate. The counsellors may 'need' to attend the funeral for themselves, but this might not necessarily be the right course of action, for example.

Case reviews

The fear is of scapegoating, and certainly when I have been witness to this process in various organizational settings over the years, the one consistent outcome is that little is learned and much damage is done. In the aftermath of a client suicide, the pull towards needing to apportion blame can be strong – either at an institutional level or within the individual counsellor concerned. Certainly, it is my assertion that in the prediction-prevention culture, where the subtext can often be that any suicide represents a 'failure' on the part of the treating clinician, the starting point for reflection can sadly too often be on any mistakes that can be uncovered.

However, where a reflective case review is managed carefully, chaired properly, and undertaken in a positive learning frame, the benefits can be great. Any client suicide represents a terrible human tragedy, regardless of your personal position on life and death. It is vital that the counsellor, supervisor, team manager, colleagues, other relevant members of the institution, for example, can spend time debriefing and talking through events that preceded the client's death. Much can be learnt and, equally importantly, counsellors can transfer that learning into their future client work.

Continuing professional development

Supportive and reflective case reviews can also provide the counsellor with opportunities to highlight future personal and professional development needs. Even if the case review identifies that all that could have been done was done (as is often the case), the experience of having worked with such a vulnerable client, or having experienced client suicide, will trigger the need for further training or reflective time.

My own experience of Isobel's death, which I described in the opening pages of this book, mean that I understand the importance of these support opportunities. It is important to say that generally speaking I was very well supported and, despite working within a statutory service at the time, was not subjected to the type of scapegoating that can take place. I was able to negotiate with a supportive team and wise manager all that I needed to help me though a terrible process. That said, I did not necessarily know what was best for me at the time, and mostly flew by the seat of my pants in getting through from one day to another.

Despite the *ad hoc* support that was available to me, the implications of Isobel's death on me personally and professionally were profound and long lasting. I blamed myself for a long time, felt that I had let Isobel down, felt incompetent as a practitioner, and was very 'risk averse' within my other client work. This latter point is one that is noteworthy. I likened Isobel's death to a physical pain – a burn or scald. Whenever exposed to a similar 'heat' thereafter, that is the risk of suicide, I would feel the pain again and try to turn from it. The 'turning from it' took several forms, including not wanting to hear, finding ways of neutralizing the risk of suicide in my mind, over-reacting to a client's need to explore their suicidality, struggling to maintain confidentiality in situations where it was appropriate to do so, always resisting the temptation to 'pass on the hot potato'.

It is for this reason that a 'menu of support', where possible, is perhaps the best way forward (Reeves and Nelson, 2006). That is, the sort of support options identified here should be negotiated and put in place *prior to* them being needed. In the event of them being required, the counsellor is able to select the most appropriate support at the time, in conjunction with advice from their supervisor and/or line manager. This provides for the counsellor the most responsive and comprehensive support option. It does however require time and financial commitment by the organization, though this need not be great. This 'menu of support' needs to be included in any organizational policy on suicide risk, as discussed in Chapter 9, 'Developing Procedures and Guidance'.

The independent practitioner

I am aware that many of the support options outlined here are particularly applicable to team-based working, usually within organizations. While the philosophy and ethos of all the support ideas outlined here are equally applicable to the independent counsellor, the implementation of them is not so straightforward.

Larcombe (2008) provides a useful overview of self-care strategies, including those for the independent practitioner. She identifies three distinct aspects of self-care:

- Care of the therapeutic self: that is, 'the unique way in which we use ourselves, "us", in what we do' (p. 286).
- Care of the managerial self: that is, the way in which we 'take responsibility for ourselves and our work in conjunction with fulfilling professional obligations' (p. 289).
- Care of the career self: that is, supporting our professional and personal development, 'acknowledg[ing] the fact that there is a developmental path that practitioners travel down' (p. 294).

Under each of these subheadings, Larcombe highlights a variety of ways in which both the independent counsellor, and the counsellor who works within an organizational setting, can take active steps to support themselves and their work.

It is always advisable to discuss self-care strategies with a colleague or supervisor to ensure that all aspects have been attended to. Too often self-care is something that is implicitly attended to – and as such can easily come under threat when other, competing demands are present. Working with suicidal clients, and the potential of client suicide, demand that self-care is instead explicitly attended to so that counsellors maintain focus on and awareness of their needs at any given stage of the process. This best protects counsellors, and clients in turn, from poor practice or burnout.

Discussion questions

1. What strategies do you use to reflect on how your work with suicidal clients affects you?
2. How do you manage the stresses of working with suicidal clients in your day-to-day work?
3. In the event of client suicide, how might you ensure that you receive the support you need from your organization?
4. If you are an independent practitioner, what steps have you taken to ensure that in the event of client suicide, you have support options in place in addition to existing supervision arrangements?

18 Training Implications for Counselling

Chapter overview

This chapter considers training implications for counsellors when working with suicide risk. Current counsellor training does not always seem to prepare counsellors for the challenges of working with suicide potential, including developing assessment skills, recognizing suicide risk factors, and understanding mental health systems or alternative intervention approaches. Primary competencies for counsellors in working with suicide are suggested.

The policy imperative surrounding mental health development and service delivery emphasizes the need for practitioners to be equipped to respond effectively to suicidal patients. The *Report of the National Confidential Inquiry into Suicide and Homicide by People with a Mental Illness*, a research project funded largely by the National Institute for Clinical Excellence (NICE: Appleby et al., 2001), states the importance of NHS and social care organizations implementing appropriate training for personnel. The need for appropriate, regular training in suicide assessment and intervention skills is also strongly embedded within the *Suicide Prevention Strategy for England* (Department of Health, 2002).

Training packages have previously been developed for health care professionals, particularly for those working within health care settings. The STORM Project (Skills Based Training on Risk Management) is a modular training programme for health care, social care, criminal justice staff and volunteers to raise awareness and skills in risk management strategies (Appleby et al., 2001; Morriss et al., 1999). Various other training packages have been developed internationally for mental health providers, such as the ASIST training programme (Applied Suicide Intervention Skills Training) developed by Livingworks Education in Canada (Livingworks, 2009), and The Training Institute for Suicide Assessment and Clinical Interviewing's development of the CASE approach (Chronological Assessment of Suicide Events) (Shea, 2002).

Within the UK, suicide risk assessment training tends either to be more generic in its target audience, or to have been developed for other professional groups, such as social workers, psychiatric nurses, etc. Whilst counsellors working within health care settings might benefit from generic programmes such as the STORM Project, no training tools have been specifically developed to reflect the particular dynamics of the counsellor–client relationship. The efficacy of existing programmes for counsellors is therefore dependent upon the transferability of knowledge from the general to the specific for each counsellor.

What perhaps is startling is how little attention suicide risk is given on counsellor training courses. In a study I undertook of BACP accredited training programmes for counselling, a large number of those who responded to a questionnaire acknowledged that risk was insufficiently addressed within their programme (Reeves et al., 2004a). Also, counsellors in an earlier study stated that they believed their counsellor training to have inadequately prepared them for working with suicide risk (Reeves and Mintz, 2001). As one counsellor said, 'I don't think my training equipped me to work with suicidal clients. It's something that I go on learning about all the time really, working with people and just doing it. I don't think we did enough on suicide and I don't think it prepared me for working with people who are more suicidal.'

It is true that, as in most professional training programmes, e.g. for social work, teaching and nursing, there is a relatively short amount of time to cover a large number of competency areas. However, given the implications for counsellor and client of the presence of suicide risk, greater attention needs to be given to preparing counsellors for that role. As one counsellor said, 'I just feel quite sad that it is an issue that does not come up more in training. It wasn't in ours but it is such an important thing that we should address … it was certainly true for me on my course. I don't remember anything in terms of risk and the only thing got was when I was in a voluntary agency.'

Given the diversity of counselling approaches practised, and the settings in which counsellors are located, a training programme that specifically attends to supporting counsellors in their work with suicidal clients needs to be sufficiently inclusive of orientation differences to allow for an integration of ideas and information into practice. The aim therefore should be not to provide a specific or rigid framework for counsellors to 'bolt on' to their practice, but instead to provide a set of ideas, research, information and questions through which counsellors can be prompted to evaluate their own practice and 'self' in relation to suicidality, and integrate new practice principles into their own style.

Such a training programme therefore needs to provide trainee and qualified counsellors with an opportunity to consider therapeutic work with suicidal clients at different levels – theoretical, political, philosophical, professional and experiential. Training needs to be accessible, in that elements of it can be usefully incorporated into existing core counselling training programmes, or could be delivered 'standalone' within the context of a counsellor's continuing professional development.

As stated previously, many of the existing risk assessment training programmes delivered within health-based settings, and then contracted out to other non-statutory agencies, tend to focus on factor-based approaches to assessing suicide risk. Much of the training highlights specific demographic, social or psychopathological risk factors which training participants can then incorporate into their work. As has been discussed in other chapters, this has two problems in my view. First, while risk factors are extremely useful in understanding trends, and in providing a context or structure for approaching an assessment of risk with an individual, they are insufficient in themselves in ultimately helping either the counsellor or the client to make an accurate assessment of suicidal potential. Second, a factor-based approach to understanding individual presentation is inconsistent with many of the mainstream counselling theories. Counsellors who work from a person centred approach, for example, are unlikely to comfortably understand their client's distress in terms of box ticking. Given the high numbers of person centred practitioners amongst the 30,000 plus BACP membership, this is an important consideration. As one counsellor said, 'There is a tension between ... categories that make people a higher risk and knowing what they are, and having them somewhere in the back of your mind; then also wanting to build a relationship with an individual and to listen to the bits of you in the relationship that are saying that there is something troubling me about this person that I need to explore a little more with them – to not treat them as a high risk factor, that gets in the way of the relationship.'

Instead, while many counsellors will find ways of using information that originates from a factor based approach, a majority will still prefer to talk to their clients about suicide and risk, and develop an understanding of suicide potential through the therapeutic relationship. It is at this point therefore that good quality training is required: to ensure that counsellors allow for the multi-layered dynamics of such a discourse, and therefore feel equipped to fully engage with their clients around suicidality.

Risk assessment competency

I believe that it is possible to 'map' the competencies required by counsellors for working with suicide potential. The concept of competencies for training in the psychological therapies has been around for many years (Wheeler, 1996). During preparations for regulation in the UK of the psychological therapies, competencies were mapped to help develop a consistent, high quality overview of the training needs of counsellors and psychotherapists. These were generic competencies that addressed all aspects of practice, including working with risk. From my own view, Table 18.1 presents a more detailed breakdown of the competencies I believe are required for working with clients around suicide potential.

These competency areas are relevant for all client work, given the importance for counsellors to check with all clients whether suicide is, or has been, a potential. This perhaps is the greatest difficulty for counsellors. When a client discloses suicide thoughts in a session, this is perceived by counsellors to give 'permission' for suicide to be discussed. If the client has mentioned suicide, then it must be okay to talk about it further. The anxiety or fear experienced by many counsellors when faced with suicide potential abates in the event of the client taking the lead. Indeed, some counsellors would argue that to ask about suicide when a client has not mentioned it already would go against their theoretical principles of a client-led agenda. For example, some counsellors might argue that person centred theory prohibits the use of questions in their work.

Cooper (2009) however states that 'There are no "mustn'ts", "musts", "don'ts" or "shoulds" about person centred practice, because person centred therapy is not about behaving in a particular way with clients, but about being a particular type of person with another human being.' I would additionally (and perhaps controversially) suggest that any argument proposed about not being 'allowed' to ask questions is instead a theoretical smokescreen to mask unacknowledged counsellor anxiety. As one counsellor described, 'I don't think that I don't ask but I am aware

Table 18.1   Counsellor competencies for working with suicide risk

1   *Policy and law*

1a   Demonstrate a working knowledge and understanding of relevant UK and international policy related to suicide and suicide prevention.
1b   Demonstrate an ability to critically appraise and reflect on relevant UK and international policy related to suicide and suicide prevention.
1c   Demonstrate a working knowledge and understanding of relevant UK and international ethical requirements when working with clients at risk of suicide.
1d   Demonstrate an ability to critically appraise and reflect on relevant UK and international ethical requirements when working with clients at risk of suicide.
1e   Demonstrate a working knowledge and understanding of legislation and legal parameters when working with clients at risk of suicide, e.g. mental health legislation, confidentiality, etc.
1f   Demonstrate an understanding of how policy and legal parameters influence and inform the practice of counselling when working with clients at risk of suicide.

2   *Counselling in context*

2a   Demonstrate an understanding of role and function of the organization in which counselling is practised.
2b   Demonstrate an understanding of how the counselling contract and relationship are informed by the context in which they are being offered.
2c   Demonstrate an understanding of the particular needs and requirements of clients accessing counselling within the organization.
2d   Demonstrate a knowledge and understanding of organizational policy and procedure with respect to suicidal clients.
2e   Demonstrate a knowledge and understanding of organizational policy and procedure with respect to clients in immediate danger of suicide.

3   *Self-awareness and support*

3a   Demonstrate a willingness to explore personally held views about suicide, e.g. in relation to spirituality, personal experience, etc., as an ongoing professional and personal development activity.
3b   Demonstrate a willingness to discuss personally held views about suicide in supervision.
3c   Demonstrate a willingness to arrange personal therapy, as required, when working with clients at risk of suicide.
3d   Demonstrate a willingness to establish appropriate self-support strategies when working with clients at risk of suicide, e.g. peer supervision, reading, time away from client work.
3e   Demonstrate a willingness and ability to use clinical supervision appropriately to explore the therapeutic relationship with suicidal clients fully and openly, and to reflect on the impact of such work on self.
3f   Demonstrate an understanding of the psychological implications for counsellors in working with suicide risk, e.g. vicarious trauma, heightened anxiety, etc.

4   *Assessing suicide potential*

4a   Demonstrate a knowledge and understanding of mental health diagnostic structures and how a diagnosis of mental illness is made, and by whom.
4b   Demonstrate an awareness of how psychopathology might be evident in client presentation.
4c   Demonstrate an understanding of the awareness of the link between psychopathology and higher suicide risk.
4d   Demonstrate a knowledge and understanding of the principles behind risk assessment questionnaires, tools and forms, and their use within counselling practice.
4e   Demonstrate an ability to explore suicide potential with a client congruent to the model of therapy implemented.
4f   Demonstrate a knowledge and understanding of how to use information obtained through the therapeutic dialogue to inform an assessment of suicide risk.

(Continued)

160 Counselling Suicidal Clients

Table 18.1 (Continued)

4g	Demonstrate an ability to engage a suicidal client in a discussion about their potential risk, and risk management.
5	*Working with other professional groups*
5a	Demonstrate a knowledge and understanding of the role and function of key professionals available for the care of suicidal clients, e.g. general practitioner, psychiatrist, social worker.
5b	Demonstrate an understanding of multi-disciplinary working and show an ability to work with other professionals, as required, within the context of the demands of the role of counsellor.
5c	Demonstrate an ability to negotiate an appropriate contract of confidentiality to enable appropriate and effective communication for the wellbeing of the client, as and when required.
5d	Demonstrate knowledge of key services and support in the locality for suicidal clients, and know how to access them when required.
6	*Professional considerations*
6a	Demonstrate an understanding of the importance of maintaining appropriate professional records, particularly in accordance with organizational requirements, as appropriate.
6b	Demonstrate an ability to identify and record key information, detailing the nature and degree of suicide risk assessed, and subsequent interventions and their rationale.

that if sometimes I am thinking that I need to ask there is a kind of dread that I feel and I delay. I just have to give myself a bit of space to get around to asking so I could then make the leap, but that you might then not ask the question at all.'

I cannot think of any act more client focused than to take the lead in naming something that might otherwise be too shameful for the client to talk about; but to name it in a sensitive and appropriate way so that the client can choose not to engage with the dialogue if they are not ready to. However, once suicide is named (even if then left), the door will have been opened, and 'permission' will be on the table. It is therefore with clients who do not talk about suicide that the greatest therapeutic challenge is set: how to ensure that the client knows they can talk about their suicidal thoughts (if they have them). As one counsellor described, 'when you have more longer-term clients it doesn't necessarily come up on such a regular basis; it's not in the forefront of your mind necessarily. I have found that that can be quite different when it has come up with clients I have worked with for a while, and it's not been present in the initial stage. It's almost like re-engaging with that bit.'

It is at this point that counsellors can readily cite many reasons why not talking about suicide is important, such as: it will be perceived as insensitive; it is not appropriate within my therapeutic approach; the client seems fine, so it would be clumsy to talk about suicide; it might put the thought in their mind when it didn't exist before. It's a bit like trying to tell someone they have spinach on their tooth midway through a conversation: best avoided. However, many clients report feeling a sense of relief when their counsellor names suicide. In my own experience of counselling, there have been numerous occasions when I have thought it best not to ask a client about suicide during early counselling, as it did not seem appropriate. Yet, when I have taken the 'risk' and posed the question ('I wonder how difficult this gets for you? Do you ever think about harming yourself or killing yourself?'), I am surprised at the number of people I have assumed would not be suicidal who have responded with, 'Yes, sometimes I do feel that way.' One counsellor, during an interview, said, 'I have often been quite surprised because I might have not assumed at all that someone was in any way suicidal – that might be quite far from my thoughts but sometimes when I am asking, they say, well, yes, actually – I am planning or made an attempt last week or something.'

I have demonstrated through my own research (Reeves, 2005) that training tools aimed specifically at the needs of counsellors can have long-term, positive benefits in practice. Reviewing the outcomes of my training workshop, six months post-training, strongly suggested that participants were still able to recall key areas, and believed they had been able to integrate their learning into their work supporting suicidal clients. I believe this was as a consequence of ensuring that the particular needs of counsellors were addressed, and that key aspects of their professional orientation were the foundation for the structure of the sessions. The fundamentals of this training programme have been transferred into a training DVD (Reeves et al., 2009), and it will be interesting to see whether the same outcomes are possible when delivered in this format.

Counselling is now sufficiently embedded as a viable treatment choice for suicidal clients that there is a strong argument for ensuring that appropriate training resources are developed to meet their specific needs. While it is important for counsellors to continue to have the opportunity to receive training around suicide risk factors, I believe that training that instead focuses on how suicide risk factors can be integrated into a discourse-based approach is much more pertinent for a large majority of counsellors in practice.

Discussion questions

1. How did your counsellor training prepare you for your work with suicidal clients? What was helpful, and what less so?
2. What training have you undertaken since qualifying as a counsellor around suicide risk that has been particularly helpful? Why?
3. When considering the competencies for working with suicide risk as suggested in this chapter, how many do you feel confident in?
4. How might you identify further training requirements around suicide risk, and how you will ensure these needs are met?

Part VII

Conclusions

19 Concluding Thoughts

> **Chapter overview**
>
> This chapter provides concluding thoughts for counsellors to consider in their work with suicidal clients. It summarizes the main areas covered in this book, and asks questions about future development that might support counsellors in working with suicide risk.

As I have been writing this book, I have been reflecting more on the moment-by-moment process in a counselling session with a suicidal client. It some ways it is like taking apart a watch, or looking inside the world of the human body. In its entirety, the experience is of something that just happens: you look at the watch and can tell the time, or eat some food when you notice the physical sensation of hunger. Yet, behind the apparent simplicity of the 'outcome' lies a process so sophisticated it is almost unimaginable.

Counselling is like that for me in many ways. We know the theories, have a sense of our 'self' in the work, can conceptualize client presentation or narrative, frame it all within the context of an orientation or perhaps an integration of modalities, and yet in the moment-by-moment process with another person, the complexities and shades of grey are almost unimaginable. Perhaps in any relationship we only ever experience some particular aspect or aspects of it, the rest remaining out of sight, or processed at an unconscious level? Perhaps any human encounter is only ever with a part of the picture, and never with the whole? Yet, as Mearns and Cooper (2005) write, there are moments of relational depth where we can perhaps transcend that 'part' view and engage with something deeper and more complete.

As I have stated on numerous occasions throughout the chapters, working with suicidal clients can be profoundly rewarding, and profoundly challenging for even the most experienced counsellor. It is too easy a presumption to make that suicide risk would challenge only trainee or newly qualified counsellors, with those who have more experience drawing more easily on previously gained knowledge, grounding themselves in 'knowing'. However, this is clearly not the case. That is not to say that every client we meet who expresses suicidal thoughts will be equally as difficult as any other. As in all human encounters, different aspects of each person – who they are, how they are, the quality and depth of relationship we experience with them, for example – will all influence our experience of the moment; but there is sufficient research evidence that points to the implications for counsellors of working with suicide risk. We must pay attention to this evidence, and our own experience, in helping to ensure that how we respond to suicidal clients remains appropriate and ethical.

I have met quite a few counsellors along the way who say, 'Oh, suicide isn't something that affects me; it's really not something that I worry about. I feel entirely confident in working with suicide risk.' I have to confess to being very suspicious of such grand claims. I do believe that it is possible to meet suicide potential with calmness and confidence, and that we do not inevitably have to slide into incompetence, fear and anxiety. However, not only do I think that it is understandable that another's suicidality might leave us feeling anxious, wary or momentarily out of our depth; to some extent I believe it to be essential. It is too easy to depersonalize clients in the day-to-day process of our professional lives, particularly when working in a busy environment of five, six or perhaps seven appointments a day. People can become 'appointments', blocks of time in a diary, separated by the theoretical construct of the 'therapeutic hour', their narrative just another story to empathically hear before we head off home at the end of the day.

By experiencing our own process in response to a suicidal discourse, are we not beginning a process of engagement – true engagement – with our client? Are we not beginning to move from a professional dissociation to a more connected place? Of course, this has to be achieved by degrees, and nothing is gained in losing ourselves in an anxious place where we are too preoccupied with our own safety to hear the client. Self-care is an imperative here that we must retain as central to our personal and professional actions.

In this book I have tried to highlight what I believe to be the essential aspects of working with suicide risks in counselling. Let me summarize them here:

- Counsellors regularly see clients who present with some degree of suicide potential.
- The typical contract of confidentiality that is agreed with a client prior to the commencement of counselling places a duty of care on counsellors to act in a particular way. That is, by limiting confidentiality in the context of risk of suicide, and stating that if the counsellor believes the client to be in imminent danger they would break confidentiality if consent was not possible, the counsellor has a duty of care to ensure that they are competent to act in the way that they say they would act. They need to be competent to make a judgement about the potential risk to inform any decisions they might subsequently make, and then to be able to articulate why they responded (or didn't respond) in the way they did.
- Counsellors need to be aware of the policy imperative that might inform the context of their work. This is particularly true if counsellors are working in statutory organizations, such as health trusts or social services. However, this is also true for all counsellors where policy directives might be viewed as a benchmark for good practice, and by which professional actions might be judged. In the UK and internationally, policy is clearly focused on the reduction of suicide through an efficacious use of current knowledge, e.g. suicide risk factors. This I have called the 'prediction-prevention culture': we have sufficient knowledge to inform prediction, and thus prevention becomes more possible. Suicide reduction targets would be meaningless without this premise.
- Good practice is not only defined by policy. Many counsellors, who are members of professional organizations, will subscribe to a code of ethics or ethical framework to inform their work. Counsellors need to pay careful attention to how such ethical requirements can facilitate and inhibit their actions, ensuring that all interventions with clients remain both ethically sound and defensible.
- Counsellors need a basic awareness of legislation that is pertinent to their work. Practice issues, which might include confidentiality, consent, and the capacity of the

client to make informed decisions about their life and death, for example, are often considered within a legislative context. Counsellors do not need to be legal 'experts', but must be able to access resources or consultation when situations arise that might have a legislative imperative. In considering the legislative context, counsellors need also to understand their particular client in that context: their age, presentation and capacity to engage with counsellor, and their own lives.

- For counsellors who work within the context of organizations, any existing policy or guidance needs to be accounted for when making intervention decisions with clients. Organizations will often have stated expectations of counsellors when working with suicidal potential. Policies might contradict personally held views about suicide; however, as an employee, a counsellor must manage this appropriately and meet the employer's expectations. Where formal or written policies do not exist, counsellors must still ensure they clearly understand how their organization expects them to respond to suicide risk.

- Risk factors that indicate the potential for higher suicide risk have been subject to extensive research for many years. Risk assessment tools, questionnaires and suicide risk inventories essentially all draw on this same information to help guide an assessor through the process of identifying risk potential. Information is generally drawn from demographic variants, such as gender, age, culture, relationship status and social support, but also includes psychopathological factors such as depression, bipolar affective disorder or PTSD, for example, to indicate higher risk potential. Counsellors need to be aware of and understand the implication of these factors in assessing their clients for suicide risk. Additionally, such information can positively inform how decisions are reached and can structure a rationale in written notes, etc.

- Counsellors must engage with a process whereby they raise self-awareness with respect to their personally held views on suicide. There is a no 'right' or 'wrong' position to hold, but we must be aware of our position at any given point. The dangers of not adopting this self-reflective style can be significant for both the counsellor and the client. Ultimately, counsellors are in danger of acting out a position with suicidal clients if they do not take steps to acknowledge and 'hold' their own views. Examples include making a decision to break confidentiality unnecessarily where they do not 'approve' of the act of suicide, or perhaps not allowing themselves to hear the client's level of risk, or calls for help, while holding the position that everyone has the right to end their own life.

- Counsellors need to understand that suicidal ideation will be experienced differently by different people. The stereotype of the suicide person – the person who plans their own death, writing suicide notes and putting their affairs in order – is true for some people, but not all. Equally important are those situations where the thought of suicide is a long-term one: knowing that the person retains the choice to end life is sufficient to sustain it. So too are those situations where no plans are made or previously suicidal thoughts held, and the act of suicide is an impulsive, spontaneous one that occurs in the light of a life crisis.

- Suicide potential is not always clearly articulated in counselling sessions. Some clients may talk openly and freely about their suicidal ideation; however, many will find this too difficult and may only hint at it or refer to it through other mechanisms. Counsellors need to be very aware of the reluctance of many people to freely talk about their suicidal thoughts, perhaps because of shame, embarrassment or fear of the consequences, and adapt their approach accordingly. For example, using reflective responses predominantly might not help open a dialogue about suicide and might, as has been discussed in detail elsewhere, inadvertently silence the counsellor also. That is not to say that reflective responses are not helpful, because they evidently are; but a variety

of skills must be employed in helping clients to explore their distress, and thus the counsellor making decisions with clients as to the best way forward.
- Other aspects of professional practice can help inform and support counsellors in their work with suicidal clients. For example, appropriate record keeping can provide counsellors not only with a clear record of client risk and subsequent responses – informed by an appropriate discourse and with reference to risk factors and policy – but also with an important mechanism for reflective practice and to support a full discussion in supervision.
- Counsellors need to ensure that they have appropriate and sufficient support for their work. Ongoing clinical supervision is a requirement of ethical practice for counsellors in the UK. Counsellors need to be able to discuss openly their anxieties about working with suicidal potential, as do supervisors. Both need to be clear about mutual expectations when working with risk, and how they can work collaboratively in supporting the counsellor who is supporting the client. Additional consultative support needs to be readily available outside supervision, through peer supervision opportunities, or discussions with line managers.
- In line with ethical requirements, counsellors need to pay careful attention to self-care, in all client work, and particularly when working with suicide risk. Good self-care strategies will not only support the counsellor in working safely and ethically, but in turn help them feel sufficiently grounded to maintain therapeutic contact with their client at a time of crisis, and potentially model good self-care strategies for the client.

It is staggering to think that all of these factors will be present, in some form, during the counselling discourse with a suicidal client. The counsellor is indeed spinning many plates, while at the same time trying to ensure that they remain client focused. The reality is that counsellors achieve this seemingly impossible feat on a regular basis. I am firmly of the opinion that suicidal clients are offered a hugely important opportunity to explore their own self-destructive process through counselling, and that consequently counselling has become a relevant and respected choice for clients who previously would have been only offered psychiatric intervention – at either primary or secondary care level – as a treatment option. Additionally, whereas previously suicidality might have been 'treated' through the use of psychopharmacological routes, talking therapies are increasingly seen as viable and effective in supporting high risk clients.

Of course, the 'cost' of this is for counsellors to continue to work in such a way that this option continues to be viable. As the profession continues to develop, and as in the UK it moves towards statutory regulation, counsellors will need to embrace additional ways of working. Evidence-based practice is here to stay, and counsellors need to consider how they might use existing research evidence to support their work, or integrate research methods into their practice to help demonstrate efficacy. Cooper (2008) provides an eloquent demonstration of how research awareness can inform thinking in counselling.

During my own research journey, an interesting thing happened to me. Following on from the death of Isobel, I think I embarked on a search for certainty. My research proposal talked of developing a risk assessment tool that all counsellors, regardless of theoretical orientation, could use to help them determine the future risk of a client. I didn't quite imagine what this tool would look like, but I guessed that it would have a few tick boxes and a few simple questions, and at the end the counsellor would *know* whether or not their client was going to act on their suicidal thoughts. It seems strangely naive now to imagine that any such tool would ever exist. It spoke more of my own distress and my need to avoid the pain of the reality of suicide.

As my research progressed, I increasingly realized that the skill in working with suicide potential is not about searching for the certain and concrete, but instead about being able to sit alongside the not knowing and uncertainty without being lost in it. In evaluating the training programme I had developed, a participant said something of real insight:

> I was wondering, is this a personal journey, are you Sir Galahad on his horse riding out to save the nation because you felt such a failure in yourself. And I wondered about that. I didn't in any way feel judgemental, I just felt, oh, what's that about. This poor man has to tell the nation, to protect the nation … What I was left with was the fact that it was something that you were passionate about … which is a strange use of words … but from your experience you had been through with your client, you didn't want any of us … you were quite protective … you didn't want any of us going through what you had been through.

This perceptive insight captured a process within me that had been present in the research journey, but that had ended during the development of the workshops. It was in the development of the workshops that I had realized that 'saving the nation' was missing the point when working with suicidality. However, it is a sentiment that appears to remain prevalent in a UK policy discourse – the culture of suicide prevention and suicide reduction targets – that perpetuates the idea that suicide risk may be predicted, and perhaps should always be predicted, through the application of knowledge drawn from suicidology, thus leading to the prevention of client suicide. The actual suicide of a client therefore represents a 'failure' on behalf of the individual counsellor or organization in their duty to 'save the nation'.

This paragraph marks the end of a chapter – and yes, the end of the book. More importantly, it marks the culmination of many years of research and enquiry in trying to make sense of Isobel's death. Of course, I do not have any more answers about Isobel's death than I did after putting the telephone down having been told of her suicide; and that is the point. For those bereaved by suicide, the spectre of unanswered questions can sit heavily. The immobilizing anxiety and impotency that can be present when working with suicide potential surely acknowledges that spectre to some degree. We can only do our best, in good faith, to meet with and support those facing the precarious edge of their existence. I hope there are things in this book that help in that process, and anchor in difficult times.

References

Aldridge, D. (1998). *Suicide: The Tragedy of Hopelessness.* London: Jessica Kingsley.

Alexander, D. A., Klein, S., Gray, N. M., Dewar, I. G. and Eagles, J. M. (2000). Suicide by patients: questionnaire study of its effect on consultant psychiatrists. *British Medical Journal* 320, 1571–1574.

Allison, S., Roeger, L., Martin, G. and Keeves, J. (2001). Gender differences in the relationship between depression and suicidal ideation in young adolescents. *Australian and New Zealand Journal of Psychiatry* 35, 498–503.

American Psychiatric Association (1994). *Diagnostic and Statistical Manual of Mental Disorders: IV-T-R.* Arlington, VA: American Psychiatric Publishing.

Amir, M., Kaplan, Z., Efroni, R. and Kotler, M. (1999). Suicide risk and coping styles in post-traumatic stress disorder patients. *Psychotherapy and Psychosomatics* 68, 76–81.

Angst, J., Angst, F. and Stassen, H. H. (1999). Suicide risk in patients with major depressive disorder. *Journal of Clinical Psychiatry* 60, 57–62.

Appleby, L., Shaw, J., Sherratt, J., Amos, T., Robinson, J. and McDonnell, R. (2001). *Safety First: Five Year Report of the National Confidential Inquiry into Suicide and Homicide by People with a Mental Illness.* London: HMSO.

Babiker, G. and Arnold, L. (1997). *The Language of Injury: Understanding Self-Mutilation.* Leicester: British Psychological Society.

Baby, S., Haridas, M. P. and Yesudas, K. F. (2006). Psychiatric diagnosis in attempted suicide. *Calicut Medical Journal* 4(3), 1–5.

BACP (2007). *Ethical Framework for Good Practice in Counselling and Psychotherapy.* Lutterworth: British Association for Counselling and Psychotherapy.

Baerger, D. R. (2001). Risk management with the suicidal patient: lessons from case law. *Professional Psychology: Research and Practice* 32, 359–366.

Barraclough, B. M. (1990). The Bible suicides. *Acta Psychiatrica Scandinavia* 86, 64–69.

Battle, A. O. (1991). Factors in assessing suicidal lethality. Paper presented at Crisis Center Preservice Volunteer Training, University of Tennessee College of Medicine, Department of Psychiatry, Memphis.

Battle, A. O., Battle, M. V. and Tolley, E. A. (1993). Potential for suicide and aggression in delinquents at juvenile court in a southern city. *Suicide and Life Threatening Behavior* 23(3), 230–243.

Baxter, D. and Appleby, L. (1999). Case register study of suicide risk in mental disorders. *British Journal of Psychiatry* 175, 322–326.

Beck, A. T., Kovacs, M. and Weissman, A. (1979). Assessment of suicidal intention: the scale of suicidal intention. *Journal of Consulting and Clinical Psychology* 47, 343–352.

Beck, A. T., Resnick, H. and Lettieri, D. (1974). *The Prediction of Suicide.* Bowie, MA: Charles Press.

Bell, D. (2008). Who is killing what or whom? Some notes on the internal phenomenology of suicide. In S. Briggs, A. Lemma and W. Crouch (eds) *Relating to Self-Harm and Suicide: Psychoanalytic Perspectives on Practice, Theory and Prevention.* London: Routledge, pp. 45–60.

Bernard, J. L. and Bernard, M. L. (1985). Suicide on campus: response to the problem. In E. S. Zinner (ed.) *Coping with Death on Campus.* San Francisco: Jossey-Bass, pp. 69–83.

Bertolote, J. M. and Fleischmann, A. (2002). Suicide and psychiatric diagnosis: a worldwide perspective. *World Psychiatry* 1(3), 181–185.

Billig, M. (1997). Rhetorical and discursive analysis: how families talk about the royal family. In N. Hayes (ed.) *Doing Qualitative Analysis in Psychology*. Hove: Psychology Press.

Billig, M. (2001). Discursive, rhetorical and ideological measures. In M. Wetherell, S. Taylor and S. J. Yates (eds) *Discursive Theory and Practice: A Reader*. London: Sage, pp. 210–221.

Blair-West, G. W. and Mellsop, G. W. (2001). Major depression: does a gender- based down-rating of suicide risk challenge its diagnostic validity? *Australian and New Zealand Journal of Psychiatry* 35, 322–328.

Bond, T. (2009). *Standards and Ethics for Counselling in Action*, 3rd edn. London: Sage.

Bond, T. and Mitchels, B. (2008). *Confidentiality and Record Keeping in Counselling and Psychotherapy: Legal Resources for Counsellors and Psychotherapists 2*. London: Sage/British Association for Counselling and Psychotherapy.

Brent, D. A., Baugher, M., Bridge, J., Chen, T. H. and Chiappetta, L. (1999). Age- and sex-related risk factors for adolescent suicide. *Journal of the American Academy of Child and Adolescent Psychiatry* 38, 1497–1505.

Brown, G. and Yule, G. (1993). *Discourse Analysis*. Cambridge: Cambridge University Press.

Brunner, J. and Bronisch, T. (1999). Neurobiological correlates of suicidal behaviour. *Fortschritte Der Neurologie Psychiatrie* 67, 391–412.

Buelow, G. and Range, L. M. (2001). No-suicide contracts among college students. *Death Studies* 25, 583–592.

Burton, R. (1883). *The Anatomy of Melancholy* (1621). New York: New York Review of Books (classic edition 2001).

Caplan, G. (1964). *Principles of Preventive Psychiatry*. New York: Basic.

Cautin, R. L., Overholser, J. C. and Goetz, P. (2001). Assessment of mode of anger expression in adolescent psychiatric inpatients. *Adolescence* 36, 163–170.

Centre for Suicide Research in Oxford (2009). http://cebmh.warne.ox.ac.uk/csr/index.html. Accessed 19 January 2009.

Chemtob, C. M., Hamada, R. S., Bauer, G., Kinney, B. and Torigoe, R. Y. (1988). Patients' suicides: frequency and impact on psychiatrists. *The American Journal of Psychiatry* 145, 224–228.

Cooper, M. (2008). *Essential Research Findings in Counselling and Psychotherapy: The Facts Are Friendly*. London: Sage.

Cooper, M. (2009). Person-centred therapy: myths and reality. www.strath.ac.uk/Departments/counsunit/features/article_pct.html. Accessed 19 January 2009.

CORE Systems Group (1998). *Clinical Outcome in Routine Evaluation Outcome Measure*. Leeds: The Psychological Therapies Research Centre.

Cristofoli, G. (2002). Legal pitfalls in counselling and psychotherapy practice, and how to avoid them. In P. Jenkins (ed.) *Legal Issues in Counselling and Psychotherapy*. London: Sage, pp. 24–33.

De Hert, M., McKenzie, K. and Peuskens, J. (2001). Risk factors for suicide in young people suffering from schizophrenia: a long-term follow-up study. *Schizophrenia Research* 47, 127–134.

Department of Health (1999a). *Saving Lives: Our Healthier Nation*. London: The Stationery Office.

Department of Health (1999b). *National Service Framework for Mental Health: Modern Standards and Service Models*. London: The Stationery Office.

Department of Health (2001). *Treatment Choice in Psychological Therapies and Counselling: Evidence-Based Clinical Practice Guideline*. London: The Stationery Office.

Department of Health (2002). *National Suicide Prevention Strategy for England*. London: The Stationery Office.

Department of Health (2007). *National Suicide Prevention Strategy for England: Annual Report 2007*. London: The Stationery Office.

Department of Health, Social Services and Public Safety (2006). *Protect Life – A Shared Vision: The Northern Ireland Suicide Prevention and Action Plan*. Belfast: DHSSPS.

Dryden, W. and Thorne, B. (1991). *Training and Supervision for Counselling in Action*. London: Sage.

Durkheim, E. (1951). *Suicide: A Study in Sociology* (1897). London: Routledge (classic edition 2002).

Evans, W. P., Marte, R. M., Betts, S. and Silliman, B. (2001). Adolescent suicide risk and peer-related violent behaviors and victimization. *Journal of Interpersonal Violence* 16, 1330–1348.

Fawcett, J. (2001). Treating impulsivity and anxiety in the suicidal patient. *Clinical Science of Suicide Prevention*. New York: New York Academic Sciences.

Ferrada-Noli, M., Asberg, M., Ormstad, K., Lundin, T. and Sundbom, E. (1998). Suicidal behavior after severe trauma. Part 1: PTSD diagnoses, psychiatric co-morbidity, and assessments of suicidal behavior. *Journal of Traumatic Stress* 11, 103–112.

Firestone, R. W. (1997). *Suicide and the Inner Voice: Risk Assessment, Treatment and Case Management*. London: Sage.

Flannery, D. J., Singer, M. I. and Wester, K. (2001). Violence exposure, psychological trauma, and suicide risk in a community sample of dangerously violent adolescents. *Journal of the American Academy of Child and Adolescent Psychiatry* 40, 435–442.

Fox, R. and Cooper, M. (1998). The effects of suicide on the private practitioner: a professional and personal perspective. *Clinical Social Work Journal* 26, 143–157.

Freud, S. (1974a). Mourning and melancholia. In J. Strachey (ed.) *The Standard Edition of the Complete Psychological Works of Sigmund Freud. Vol. XIV*. London: Hogarth Press. (Original work published 1917.)

Freud, S. (1974b). A case of homosexuality in a woman. In J. Strachey (ed.) *The Standard Edition of the Complete Psychological Works of Sigmund Freud. Vol. XVIII*. London: Hogarth Press. (Original work published 1920.)

Freud, S. (1974c). Group psychology and the analysis of the ego. In J. Strachey (ed.) *The Standard Edition of the Complete Psychological Works of Sigmund Freud. Vol. XVIII*. London: Hogarth Press. (Original work published 1921.)

Friedman, T., Newton, C., Coggan, C., Hooley, S., Patel, R., Pickard, M. and Mitchell, A. (2006). Predictors of A&E staff attitudes to self-harm patients who use self-laceration: influence of previous training and experience. *Journal of Psychosomatic Research* 60(3), 273–277.

Frottier, P., Fruhwald, S., Ritter, K., Eher, R., Schwarzler, J. and Bauer, P. (2002). Jailhouse blues revisited. *Social Psychiatry and Psychiatric Epidemiology* 37, 68–73.

Gilliland, B. E. (1985). Surviving college: teaching college students to cope. Paper and presentation at the Symposium on Suicide in Teenagers and Young Adults, University of Tennessee College of Medicine, Department of Psychiatry, Memphis.

Goffman, E. (1974). *Frame Analysis*. New York: Harper and Row.

Green, H., McGinnity, A., Meltzer, H., Ford, T. and Goodman, R. (2005). *Mental Health of Children and Young People in Great Britain 2004*. London: Office for National Statistics.

Grilo, C. M., Sanislow, C. A., Fehon, D. C., Lipschitz, D. S., Martino, S. and McGlashan, T. H. (1999). Correlates of suicide risk in adolescent inpatients who report a history of childhood abuse. *Comprehensive Psychiatry* 40, 422–428.

Hallam, A. (2002). Media influences on mental health policy: long-term effects of the Clunis and Silcock cases. *International Review of Psychiatry* 14, 26–33.

Harkavy-Friedman, J. M., Nelson, E. A. and Venarde, D. F. (2001). Suicidal behavior in schizophrenia and schizo-affective disorder. *Clinical Neuroscience Research* 1, 345–350.

Harriss, L. and Hawton, K. (2005). Suicidal intent in deliberate self-harm and the risk of suicide: the predictive power of the Suicide Intent Scale. *Journal of Affective Disorder* 86, 225–233.

Hawkins, P. and Shohet, R. (2007). *Supervision in the Helping Professions*. Buckingham: Open University Press.

Hawton, K., Rodham, K., Evans, E. and Weatherall, R. (2002). Deliberate self-harm in adolescents: self report survey in schools in England. *British Medical Journal* 325, 1207–1211.
Hawton, K. and van Heeringen, K. (2002). *The International Handbook of Suicide and Attempted Suicide*. Chichester: Wiley.
Hazell, P. and Lewin, T. (1993). An evaluation of postvention following adolescent suicide. *Suicide and Life Threatening Behavior* 23(2), 101–109.
Heard, H. L. (2002). *Psychotherapeutic Approaches to Suicidal Ideation and Behaviour*. In K. Hawton and K. van Heeringen (eds) *The International Handbook of Suicide and Attempted Suicide*. Chichester: Wiley.
Hendin, H., Lipschitz, A., Maltsberger, J. T., Pollinger Haas, A. and Wynecoop, S. (2000). Therapists' reactions to patients' suicides. *American Journal of Psychiatry* 157(12), 2022–2027.
Hersh, J. B. (1985). Interviewing college students in crisis. *Journal of Counselling and Development* 63, 286–289.
Hirschfeld, R. M. A. (2001). When to hospitalize patients at risk for suicide. In H. Hendin and J. J. Mann (eds) *Clinical Science of Suicide Prevention*. New York: New York Academy of Sciences.
Hodapp, V., Sicker, G., Wick, A. D. and Winkelstrater, R. (1997). Anger and suicide risk: a study with older psychiatric patients. *Nervenarzt* 68, 55–61.
Horesh, N., Rolnick, T., Iancu, I., Dannon, P., Lepkifker, E., Apter, A. and Kotler, M. (1997). Anger, impulsivity and suicide risk. *Psychotherapy and Psychosomatics* 66, 92–96.
Jenkins, P. (2007). *Counselling, Psychotherapy and the Law*. London: Sage.
Jenkins, R., Griffiths, S., Wylie, I., Hawton, K., Morgan, G. and Tylee, A. (1994). *The Prevention of Suicide*. London: Department of Health.
Jenkins, R. and Singh, B. (2000). Policy and practice in suicidal prevention. *British Journal of Forensic Practice* 2, 3–11.
Johansson, S. E. and Sundquist, J. (1997). Unemployment is an important risk factor for suicide in contemporary Sweden: an 11 year follow up study of a cross-sectional sample of 37,789 people. *Public Health* 111, 41–45.
Kaplan, S. J., Pelcovitz, D., Salzinger, S., Mandel, F., Weiner, M. and Labruna, V. (1999). Adolescent physical abuse and risk for suicidal behaviors. *Journal of Interpersonal Violence* 14, 976–988.
Kelly, T. M., Soloff, P. H., Lynch, K. G., Haas, G. L. and Mann, J. J. (2000). Recent life events, social adjustment, and suicide attempts in patients with major depression and borderline personality disorder. *Journal of Personality Disorders* 14, 316–326.
Kinder, A. (2005). Workplace counselling: a poor relation? *Counselling at Work* Spring, 22–24.
Kleepsies, M. and Dettm, E. L. (2000). Clinicians stressed by client emergencies. *Journal of Clinical Psychology* 56(10), 1353–1369.
Kleepsies, P. M., Deleppo, J. D., Gallagher, P. L. and Niles, B. L. (1999). Managing suicidal emergencies: recommendations for the practitioner. *Professional Psychology: Research and Practice* 30, 454–463.
Koivumaa-Honkanen, H., Honkanen, R., Viinamaki, H., Heikkila, K., Kaprio, J. and Koskenvuo, M. (2001). Life satisfaction and suicide: a 20-year follow-up study. *American Journal of Psychiatry* 158, 433–439.
Kotler, M., Iancu, I., Efroni, R. and Amir, M. (2001). Anger, impulsivity, social support, and suicide risk in patients with posttraumatic stress disorder. *Journal of Nervous and Mental Disease* 189, 162–167.
Kposowa, A. J. (2001). Unemployment and suicide: a cohort analysis of social factors predicting suicide in the US Longitudinal Mortality Study. *Psychological Medicine* 31, pp. 127–138.
Lambert, M. T. and Fowler, R. D. (1997). Suicide risk factors among veterans: risk management in the changing culture of the Department of Veterans' Affairs. *Journal of Mental Health Administration* 24, 350–358.

Larcombe, A. (2008). Self-care in counselling. In W. Dryden and A. Reeves (eds) *Key Issues for Counselling in Action*, 2nd edn. London: Sage, pp. 283–297.

Leenaars, A. A. (1994). Crisis intervention with highly suicidal people. In A. A. Leenaars, J. T. Maltsberger and R. A. Neimeyer (eds) *Treatment of Suicidal People*. London: Taylor and Francis, pp. 45–49.

Leenaars, A. A. (2004). *Psychotherapy with Suicidal People: A Person Centred Approach*. Chichester: Wiley.

Lejoyeux, M. and Rouillon, F. (1996). Suicide and psychotropic agents. *Encephale – Revue de Psychiatrie Clinique Biologique et Therapeutique* 22, 40–45.

Lemma, A. (1996). *Introduction to Psychopathology*. London: Sage.

Lewinshohn, P., Garrison, C., Langhinrichsen, J. and Marsteller, F. (1989). *The Assessment of Suicidal Behavior in Adolescents: A Review of Scales Suitable for Epidemiological Clinical Research*. Rockville, MD: National Institute of Mental Health.

Litman, M. M. (1994). The dilemma of suicide in psychoanalytic practice. *Journal of the American Academy of Psychoanalysis* 22, 273–281.

Livingworks (2009). *Applied Suicide Intervention Skills Training*. Calgary, Alberta: Livingworks. www.livingworks.net

Lukas, C. and Seiden, H. M. (2007). *Silent Grief: Living in the Wake of Suicide*, rev. edn. London: Jessica Kingsley.

Maltsberger, J. T. (1997). Ecstatic suicide. *Archives of Suicide Research* 3, 283–301.

Marris, R., Berman, A., Maltsberger, J. T. and Yufit, R. (1992). *Assessment and Prediction of Suicide*. New York: Guilford.

Marttunen, M. and Pelkonen, M. (2000). Psychiatric risk factors for adolescent suicide: a review. *Psychiatria Fennica* 31, 110–125.

McCarthy, P. and Walsh, D. (1975). Suicide in Dublin: under-reporting of suicide and the consequences for national statistics. *British Journal of Psychiatry* 126, 301–8.

McKee, G. R. (1998). Lethal vs. nonlethal suicide attempts in jail. *Psychological Reports* 82, 611–4.

McLeod, J. (2003). *Introduction to Counselling*, 3rd edn. Buckingham: Open University Press.

McLeod, J. (2008). *Counselling in the Workplace: A Comprehensive Review of the Research Evidence*, 2nd edn. Lutterworth: BACP.

Mearns, D. and Cooper, M. (2005). *Working at Relational Depth in Counselling and Psychotherapy*. London: Sage.

Meltzer, H., Harrington, R., Goodman, R. and Jenkins, R. (2001). *Children and Adolescents Who Try to Harm, Hurt or Kill Themselves*. London: Office for National Statistics.

Mental Health Foundation (1997). Suicide and deliberate self harm: the fundamental facts. Mental Health Briefing no. 1. London: The Mental Health Foundation.

Mental Health Foundation (2006). *Truth Hurts: Report of the National Inquiry on Self Harm in Young People*. London: Mental Health Foundation.

Merkel, L. (2003). The history of psychiatry. www.healthsystem.virginia.edu/internet/psych-training/seminars/history-of-psychiatry-8-04.pdf. Accessed 24 January 2009.

Merry, T. (2002). *Learning and Being in Person Centred Counselling*. Ross-on-Wye: PCCS.

Miller, M. C., Jacobs, D. G. and Gutheil, T. G. (1998). Talisman or taboo: the controversy of the suicide-prevention contract. *Harvard Review of Psychiatry* 6, 78–87.

Minois, G. (1999). *History of Suicide: Voluntary Death in Western Culture*. London: Johns Hopkins University Press.

Morriss, R., Gask, L., Battersby, L., Francheschini, A. and Robson, M. (1999). Teaching front-line health and voluntary workers to assess and manage suicidal patients. *Journal of Affective Disorders* 52, 77–83.

National Institute for Clinical Excellence (2004). *Self-Harm: The Short-Term Physical and Psychological Management and Secondary Prevention of Self-Harm in Primary and Secondary Care*. London: NICE.

Neimeyer, R. A., Fortner, B. and Melby, D. (2001). Personal and professional factors and suicide intervention skills. *Suicide and Life-Threatening Behavior* 31, 71–82.

Nemeroff, C. B., Compton, M. T. and Berger, J. (2001). The depressed suicidal patient: assessment and treatment. In H. Hendin and J. J. Mann (eds) *Clinical Science of Suicide Prevention*. New York: New York Academy of Sciences.

Newnes, C., Holmes, G. and Dunn, C. (eds) (1999). *This is Madness: A Critical Look at Psychiatry and the Future of Mental Health Services*. Ross-on-Wye: PCCS.

O'Connor, R. and Sheehy, N. (2000). *Understanding Suicidal Behaviour*. Oxford: Blackwell.

Office for National Statistics (2009). National statistics online. www.statistics.gov.uk/default.asp. Accessed 19 January 2009.

Oquendo, M. A. and Mann, J. J. (2001). Identifying and managing suicide risk in bipolar patients. *Journal of Clinical Psychiatry* 62, 31–34.

Oquendo, M. A., Waternaux, C., Brodsky, B., Parsons, B., Haas, G. L., Malone, K. M. and Mann, J. J. (2000). Suicide behaviour in bipolar mood disorder: clinical characteristics of attempters and non-attempters. *Journal of Affective Disorders* 59, 107–117.

Orbach, I. (1997). A taxonomy of factors related to suicidal behavior. *Clinical Psychology – Science and Practice* 4, 208–224.

Panove, E. (1994). *Treating Suicidal Patients: What Therapists Feel When Their Patients Make Suicidal Threats*. PhD thesis, Columbia University, New York.

Paris, J. (2002). Chronic suicidality among patients with borderline personality disorder. *Psychiatric Services* 53, 738–742.

Parker, I. (1992). *Discourse Dynamics: Critical Analysis for Social and Individual Psychology*. London: Routledge.

Plunkett, A., O'Toole, B., Swanston, H., Oates, R. K., Shrimpton, S. and Parkinson, P. (2001). Suicide risk following child sexual abuse. *Ambulatory Pediatrics* 1, 262–6.

Pompili, M., Manchinelli, I. and Tatarelli, R. (2002a). Dealing with patient suicide. *Minerva Psichiatrica* 43, 181–186.

Pompili, M., Manchinelli, I. and Tatarelli, R. (2002b). Beyond the therapeutic challenge: on countertransference problems with the patient at risk of committing suicide. *Psichiatria a Psicoterapia Analitica* 21, 217–228.

Potter, J. and Wetherell, M. (1987). *Discourse and Social Psychology: Beyond Attitudes and Behaviour*. London: Sage.

Pritchard, C. (1995). *Suicide: The Ultimate Rejection? A Psycho-Social Study*. Buckingham: Open University Press.

Qin, P., Agerbo, E., Westergard-Nielsen, N., Eriksson, T. and Mortensen, P. B. (2000). Gender differences in risk factors for suicide in Denmark. *British Journal of Psychiatry* 177, 546–50.

Range, L. M., MacIntyre, D. I., Rutherford, D., Billie, S., Payne, B., Knott, E., Brown, M. and Foster, C. L. (1997). Suicide in special populations and circumstances: a review. *Aggression and Violent Behavior* 2, 53–63.

Reeves, A. (2005). *Assessing Suicide Risk in Counselling: Training Counsellors to Integrate Suicide Risk Assessment into the Therapeutic Discourse*. PhD thesis, University of Birmingham.

Reeves, A. (2008). Client assessment. In W. Dryden and A. Reeves (eds) *Key Issues for Counselling in Action*, 2nd edn. London: Sage, pp. 61–75.

Reeves, A., Bowl, R., Wheeler, S. and Guthrie, E. (2004b). The hardest words: exploring the dialogue of suicide in the counselling process – a discourse analysis. *Counselling and Psychotherapy Research* 4(1), 62–71.

Reeves, A. and Coldridge, E. (2007). A question of balance: using CORE-OM when assessing suicide risk. *Association for University and College Counsellors Journal* March, 10–12.

Reeves, A. and Howdin, J. (2008). *Considerations for Working with Clients Who Self-Harm*. Lutterworth: BACP Information Sheet.

Reeves, A. and Mintz, R. (2001). The experiences of counsellors who work with suicidal clients: an explorative study. *Counselling and Psychotherapy Research* 2, 37–42.

Reeves, A. and Nelson, S. (2006). Tight ropes and safety nets. *Therapy Today* 17(1), 14–17.

Reeves, A., Wheeler, S. and Bowl, R. (2004a). Confrontation or avoidance: what is taught on counsellor training courses. *British Journal of Guidance and Counselling* 32(2), 235–247.

Reeves, A., Wheeler, S. and Shears, J. (2009) *Tight Ropes and Safety Nets: Counselling Suicidal Clients.* Training DVD, University of Leicester.

Remafedi, G., French, S., Story, M., Resnick, M. D. and Blum, R. (1998). The relationship between suicide risk and sexual orientation: results of a population-based study. *American Journal of Public Health* 88, 57–60.

Richards, B. M. (2000). Impact upon therapy and the therapist when working with suicidal patients: some transference and countertransference aspects. *British Journal of Guidance and Counselling* 28, 325–337.

Richards, K. A. (2000). Training and the assessment and management of suicidal patients. U Southern Mississippi.

Rogers, C. (1997). *On Becoming a Person: A Therapist's View of Psychotherapy.* London: Constable.

Roy, A. (2001). Genetic influences on suicide risk. *Clinical Neuroscience Research* 1, 324–330.

Rubenstein, H. J. (2003). *Psychotherapists' Experiences of Patient Suicide.* Thesis, City University of New York.

Ruddell, P. and Curwen, B. (2008). Understanding suicidal ideation and assessing for risk. In S. Palmer (ed.) *Suicide: Strategies and Interventions for Reduction and Prevention.* London: Routledge, pp. 84–99.

Russell, S. T. and Joyner, K. (2001). Adolescent sexual orientation and suicide risk: evidence from a national study. *American Journal of Public Health* 91, 1276–1281.

Saarinen, P. I., Lehtonen, J. and Lonnqvist, J. (1999). Suicide risk in schizophrenia: an analysis of 17 consecutive suicides. *Schizophrenia Bulletin* 25, 533–542.

Samaritans and the Centre for Suicide Research, University of Oxford (2002). *Youth and Self-Harm: Perspectives.* London: Samaritans.

Schiffrin, D. (1994). *Approaches to Discourse.* Oxford: Blackwell.

Schneider, B., Maurer, K. and Frolich, L. (2001a). Dementia and suicide. *Fortschritte Der Neurologie Psychiatrie* 69, 164.

Schneider, B., Philipp, M. and Muller, M. J. (2001b). Psychopathological predictors of suicide in patients with major depression during a 5-year follow-up. *European Psychiatry* 16, 283–288.

Schwartz, R. C. (2000). Suicidality in schizophrenia: implications for the counseling profession. *Journal of Counseling and Development* 78, 496–499.

Schwartz, R. C. and Cohen, B. N. (2001). Risk factors for suicidality among clients with schizophrenia. *Journal of Counseling and Development* 79, 314–319.

Scottish Executive (2002). *Choose Life: A National Strategy and Action Plan to Prevent Suicide in Scotland.* Edinburgh: The Stationery Office.

Seber, P. (2000). *The Factors that Influence General Practitioners and Practice Nurses When Referring Clients for Counselling.* MA dissertation, John Moore's University.

Shah, A. and Ganesvaran, T. (1999). Suicide among psychiatric in-patients with schizophrenia in an Australian mental hospital. *Medicine, Science and the Law* 39, 251–259.

Sharma, V., Persad, E. and Kueneman, K. (1998). A closer look at inpatient suicide. *Journal of Affective Disorders* 47, 123–129.

Shea, S. C. (2002). *The Practical Art of Suicide Assessment: A Guide for Mental Health Professionals and Substance Abuse Counsellors.* Chichester: Wiley.

Sher, L., Oquendo, M. A. and Mann, J. J. (2001). Risk of suicide in mood disorders. *Clinical Neuroscience Research* 1, 337–344.

Shneidman, E. S. (1998). *The Suicidal Mind.* Oxford: Oxford University Press.

Smith, K., Conroy, M. and Ehler, P. (1984). Lethality of suicide attempt rating scale. *Suicide and Life Threatening Behavior* 16, 67–69.

Snyder, L., Sulmasy, D. P. and Golden, W. E. (2001). Physician-assisted suicide. *Annals of Internal Medicine* 137(3), 216–217.

Sommerbeck, L. (2003). *The Client-Centred Therapist in Psychiatric Contexts: A Therapists' Guide to the Psychiatric Landscape and its Inhabitants*. Ross-on-Wye: PCCS.

Stanistreet, D., Taylor, S., Jeffrey, V. and Gabbay, M. (2001). Accident or suicide? Predictors of coroners' decisions in suicide and accident verdicts. *Medicine Science and the Law* 41, 111–115.

Stepakoff, S. (1998). Effects of sexual victimization on suicidal ideation and behavior in US college women. *Suicide and Life-Threatening Behavior* 28, 107–126.

Szanto, K., Gildengers, A., Mulsant, B. H., Brown, G., Alexopoulos, G. S. and Reynolds, C. F. (2002). Identification of suicidal ideation and prevention of suicidal behaviour in the elderly. *Drugs & Aging* 19, 11–24.

Szanto, K., Reynolds, C. F., Conwell, Y., Begley, A. E. and Houck, P. (1998). High levels of hopelessness persist in geriatric patients with remitted depression and a history of attempted suicide. *Journal of the American Geriatrics Society* 46, 1401–1406.

Szasz, T. (1971). The ethics of suicide. *The Antioch Review* 31, 7–17.

Szasz, T. (1986). The case against suicide prevention. *American Psychologist* 41, 806–812.

Tanaka, H., Tsukuma, H., Masaoka, T., Ajiki, W., Koyama, Y., Kinoshita, N., Hasuo, S. and Oshima, A. (1999). Suicide risk among cancer patients: experience at one medical center in Japan, 1978–1994. *Japanese Journal of Cancer Research* 90, 812–817.

Teasdale, T. W. and Engberg, A. W. (2001). Suicide after a stroke: a population study. *Journal of Epidemiology and Community Health* 55, 863–866.

Thakkar, R. R., Gutierrez, P. M., Kuczen, C. L. and McCanne, T. R. (2000). History of physical and/or sexual abuse and current suicidality in college women. *Child Abuse & Neglect* 24, 1345–1354.

The Priory (2005). *Adolescent Angst*. London: The Priory Group.

Thorne, B. (2004). Review of *Person Centred Therapy in Focus* by P. Wilkins (2003). *British Journal of Guidance and Counselling* 32(1), 123.

Thornicroft, G. (2000). Developments in UK services: a UK perspective. *International Review of Psychiatry* 12, 233–239.

Torre, E., Guaiana, G., Marangon, D., Migliaretti, G., Rudoni, M., Torre, E. and Usai, C. (2001). Suicide among young people: an epidemiological analysis in three Italian provinces. *European Journal of Psychiatry* 15, 180–188.

Tsai, S. Y. M., Kuo, C. J., Chen, C. C. and Lee, H. C. (2002). Risk factors for completed suicide in bipolar disorder. *Journal of Clinical Psychiatry* 63, 469.

University of Manchester (2002). *Working with People Who Are Suicidal or Who Self-Harm: Training Resource*. Manchester: University of Manchester.

Van Dijk, T. A. (2003). Critical discourse analysis. In D. Schiffrin, D. Tannen and H. E. Hamilton (eds) *The Handbook of Discourse Analysis*. Oxford: Blackwell.

Warwick, I., Aggleton, P. and Douglas, N. (2001). Playing it safe: addressing the emotional and physical health of lesbian and gay pupils in the UK. *Journal of Adolescence* 24, 129–140.

Watt, T. T. and Sharp, S. F. (2001). Gender differences in strains associated with suicidal behavior among adolescents. *Journal of Youth and Adolescence* 30, 333–348.

Weiss, M. G., Isaac, M., Parkar, S. R., Chowdhury, A. N. and Raguram, R. (2001). Global, national, and local approaches to mental health: examples from India. *Tropical Medicine and International Health* 6, 4–23.

Welsh Assembly (2008). *Talk to Me: A National Action Plan to Reduce Suicide and Self Harm in Wales 2008–2013*. Cardiff: The Stationery Office.

Werth, J. L. (2002). Incorporating end-of-life issues into psychology courses. *Teaching of Psychology* 29, 106–111.

Wheeler, S. (1996). *Training Counsellors: The Assessment of Competence (Counsellor, Trainer and Supervisor)*. London: Sage.

Williams, R. and Morgan, H. G. (eds) (1994). *Suicide Prevention: The Challenge Confronted*. London: HMSO.

Woods, E. R., Lin, Y. G., Middleman, A., Beckford, P., Chase, L. and DuRant, R. H. (1997). The associations of suicide attempts in adolescents. *Pediatrics* 99, 791–796.

World Health Organization (1982). *Changing Patterns in Suicidal Behaviour*. European Reports and Studies no. 74. Copenhagen: WHO.

World Health Organization (1992). *ICD-10. The ICD-10 Classification of Mental and Behavioural Disorders: Clinical Descriptions and Diagnostic Guidelines*. Geneva: WHO.

World Health Organization (2003). *SUPRE. WHO Suicide Prevention: Saving Your Life*. Geneva: WHO.

World Health Organization (2009). Suicide prevention. www.who.int/mental_health/prevention/en/. Accessed 19 January 2009.

Wymer, R. (1986). *Suicide and Despair in the Jacobean Drama*. Brighton: Harvester.

Zahl, D. L. and Hawton, K. (2004). Repetition of deliberate self-harm and subsequent suicide risk: long-term follow-up study of 11,583 patients. *British Journal of Psychiatry* 185, 70–75.

Zilboorg, G. (1936). Suicide among civilized and primitive races. *American Journal of Psychiatry* 92, 1347–1369.

Index

abetting of suicide, 65, 69
accident and emergency departments, 117
accountability of counsellors, 54–5, 64, 146
accreditation of counsellors, 7
'acting out' of feelings, 117, 128, 137, 167
action plans for clients, 110–11
administrative aspects of counselling, 81
affective disorders, 33, 36
age-specific suicide rates, 23–8
alcohol abuse, 38
Aldridge, D., 50
Alexander, D.A., 150
American Psychiatric Association, 19
anxiety disorders, 36
Aristotle, 17–18
Arnold, L., 115
ASIST training programme, 156
assessment
    at start of counselling, 39–41
    questionnaire-based, 41
    see also risk assessment
asylums, 18
autonomy of clients, 55, 69, 111, 113
availability of methods for committing suicide, 38

Babiker, G., 115
Baby, S., 27
'back covering', 146
Barraclough, B.M., 16
Battie, A.O., 18
Bedlam Hospital, 16
Bell, D., 92
benchmarks, clinical, 76–7, 166
benefits of counselling for suicidal clients, 12, 168
bereavement, 127–8
Bertolote, J.M., 22, 27
biblical descriptions of suicide, 16
blame culture, 151–3
Bolem case, 69
Bond, T., 56, 61, 64, 66, 69–70
Bragga, Council of (AD 566), 16
breathing techniques, 109
British Association for Counselling and Psychotherapy (BACP), 4–9
    Ethical Framework, 53–8, 61, 64, 127, 150–1
    membership, 5, 158
    training programmes, 157

Buber, Martin, 121
burnout, 58, 155
Burton, Robert, 16

capacity, mental, 62–6, 70, 132
case contact, 153
case reviews, 153–4
caseload management, 79
'chain of care' approach to counsellors' self-support, 151–2
Chemtob, C.M., 150
children, definition of, 66
Chronological Assessment of Suicide Events (CASE), 156
Church teachings, 16, 18
Clinical Outcome of Routine Evaluation outcome measure (CORE-OM), 41
cognitive behavioural counselling, 8, 112, 138
Coldridge, E., 41
competency
    of counsellors, 153, 158–60
    of supervisors, 6
concerns about suicide, reporting of, 65, 69, 145
confidentiality, 54–7, 60–70, 77–8, 82, 84, 100, 108, 119, 145–8, 152–3, 166–7
    definition of, 61
confidentiality agreements, 68–9, 152
consent to treatment, 62–70, 145
constricted thinking, 91–2, 108, 110, 113
continuing professional development, 154
contracts, therapeutic, 65–6, 69, 111, 118–19, 166
Cooper, M., 9, 158, 165, 168
coping strategies of clients, 115–16
'core conditions', 5–6, 8, 113
coroners' hearings, 22, 146, 153
costs
    of counselling, 77
    of supervision, 78–9
counsellors
    'invisibility' or 'disappearance' of, 135–6
    own feelings about particular cases, 143, 166
    own views on suicide, 65, 83–4, 120–1, 127–33, 137, 167
    see also self-care for counsellors
countertransference, 136–8, 146
'cries for help', 116

crisis intervention, 109–12; *see also* existential crises
Cristofoli, G., 69

Dante Alighieri, 16
Data Protection Act (1998), 69
death, attitudes to, 127–8
decriminalization of suicide, 65, 128
depression, 12, 19, 33, 35, 66, 112
Descartes, René, 18
Dettm, E.L., 150
diagnosis, psychiatric, 8–9, 27, 100, 112
Diagnostic and Statistical Manual of Mental Disorders (DSM), 8
discourse analysis, 93
Donne, John, 16
Durkheim, Emile, 16–17, 44
duty of care, 55, 69, 77, 83–4, 166

emotional language, 112
emotional stress, 19
ending of counselling sessions, 110–11
envy of practitioner colleagues, 80
ethical requirements, 166, 168; *see also* British Association for Counselling and Psychotherapy: *Ethical Framework*
euthanasia, 51–2, 65
evidence-based practice, 9, 168
existential crises, 93–4
explicit references to suicide, 101–2, 110, 139–40
exploratory discourse, 106–7, 112

factor-based suicidology, 33–4, 39, 99, 157–8
failures in counselling, perceptions of, 79–80, 153, 169
families of deceased clients, contacts with, 153
family histories of suicide, 37
Firestone, R.W., 106
Fleischmann, A., 22, 27
frame analysis, 105–6
Freud, Sigmund, 93
funeral arrangements, 153

Galen, 18
gender-specific suicide rates, 23–8
genetic factors in suicide, 38
'Gillick competence', 66
Goffman, E., 105
Greece, ancient society of, 16
'grounding' of clients, 109
guidance documents for counsellors, 85–7

Hawton, K., 22
Heard, H.L., 111–12
Hinduism, 17
Hippocrates, 17–19
humanist movement, 19

independent practitioners, self-care for, 154–5
integrative counselling, 5
interpersonal relationships and suicide, 92–3
intrapsychic elements in suicide, 91–2
Islamic culture, 18
isolation
 of counsellors, 78
 see also social isolation

Janet, Pierre, 19
Jenkins, R., 31
judgements, making of, 128–30

Kinder, A., 75
Kleepsies, M., 150
The Koran, 17–18
Kraepelin, Emil, 19

Larcombe, A., 154–5
Leenaars, A.A., 22, 32, 51, 91–3, 96, 100, 109, 112–13, 137–9
legal implications of working with suicidal clients, 65–7, 70, 166–7
litigation, fear of, 84, 137, 150
Litman, M.M., 112
Lukas, C., 128

McLeod, J., 39, 76
manuals, diagnostic, 19
meanings of suicide, 101–6
Mearns, D., 165
medicalization of suicidality, 19–20, 135
Mental Capacity Act (2005), 62–3, 65–6
Mental Health Foundation, 21
mental illness, 14, 55, 65–6, 70
 categorization of, 19
 causation of, 17–18
 relationship to suicide, 20, 22
 treatment of, 17–19
'menu of support' for counsellors, 154
Merkel, L., 18–19
Merry, T., 5
Minois, G., 15
Mitchels, B., 56, 61, 64, 66, 69–70
Mohammed the Prophet, 17
Morgan, H.G., 99
multi-professional teams, 56–7, 75

National Institute for Clinical Excellence (NICE), 115, 156
National Service Framework (NSF) for Mental Health, 21, 44
National Suicide Prevention Strategy for England, 22–3, 44–7, 156
negligence claims, 69
Neimeyer, R.A., 6
Nelson, Sue, 151

'no-harm' contracts, 111
Northern Ireland, 46, 48
note-taking in counselling, 56, 137, 167

O'Connor, E., 15–17
occupational factors in suicide, 32–3
Office for National Statistics, 24, 28
options for suicidal clients, 112–13
organizational working, constraints of, 75–85, 119, 166–7

pain, psychological, 91, 116, 119–20, 135
paranoia, 33, 35
parental responsibility, 66
peer support from fellow practitioners, 78
person centred counselling, 5, 8–9, 138, 157–8
physical illness and suicide risk, 38
Plato, 18
pointlessness, sense of, 93–4
polarized thinking, 113
policy
    counsellors' knowledge of, 10–11
    development of, 85
post-traumatic stress disorder, 33, 36–7
'potholing' metaphor, 136, 140
prediction of suicide, 33, 39, 51, 99–100, 134–5, 166, 169
'prescriptive' instructions to counsellors, 84–5
prevention of suicide, 31–2, 44–6, 50–2, 169
principles of counselling, 53–4
prisoners and suicide, 37–8
Pritchard, C., 16–17
probity in professional practice, 57–8
procedures in counselling, 84
psychiatry, development of, 16–19
psychoanalytic theory, 19, 96, 137–8
psychodynamic theory, 5, 8, 137–8
public interest, 66

questionnaire-based assessment, 41

Range, L.M., 31
rape victims, 16
rapport, 109
record-keeping, 55–6, 62, 69, 77, 152, 168
Reeves, A., 41
reflective practice, 130, 136, 151, 168
rejection-aggression hypothesis on suicide, 92–3
research awareness, 9
'results' of counselling, 76–7
risk assessment, 4–9, 31–3, 39–43, 50–1, 57–8, 97, 99–100, 107–8, 114–15, 134–6, 139, 143–9, 167–9
    positivist approach to, 135
    training and competency in, 158–61
risk policy, 83–5
risk-taking, positive, 108, 145–6

risks faced by counsellors, 134
Rogers, Carl, 5, 19, 113
Roman Empire, view of suicide in, 16

Safety First report (2001), 45–6
'safety nets', 143–4, 146, 149
scapegoating, 153
schizophrenia, 33, 36
Scotland, 46–8
Seber, P., 4
Seiden, H.M., 128
self-care by counsellors, 58, 143, 150–5, 166–8
self-injury, 35, 115–24
    definitions of, 115
    explanations of, 119
    prevalence of, 117
sexuality, 37
Shakespeare, William, 16
Shea, S.C., 133
Sheehy, N., 15–17
Shneidman, E.S., 32, 97, 145–6
Skills Based Training on Risk Management (STORM), 156
social isolation, 37, 132
social policy, 10
Sommerbeck, L., 8
Stanistreet, D., 22
statistics of suicide, 21–8
statutory regulation of counselling and psychotherapy, 61, 158, 168
'stuckness', sense of, 94–5
substance abuse, 38
suicide
    author's personal position on, 14
    changing views on, 15–17
    first use of term, 15–16
    trends in, 23–7
    types of, 16–17
Suicide Act (1961), 65, 69
suicide rates, 23–7
suicidology, definition of, 31
supervision, clinical, 7, 68, 70, 77–9, 82, 137, 152, 168
    training and competency in, 6, 54
Sydenham, Thomas, 18
Szasz, T., 20, 50, 52

talking to clients
    about self-injury, 121–2
    about suicide, 101–6, 140, 158–61, 167–8
talking therapies, 168
target-setting, 44, 51, 166
terrorism, 61, 66
therapeutic relationship, 113, 128, 143, 145, 158
training
    of counsellors, 4–10, 156–61
    of supervisors, 6, 54

transference, 136–8
transient nature of suicide, 113
Truth Hurts report (2006), 116–17

unemployment, 32
university settings for counselling, 79

van Heeringen, K., 22

Wales, 46, 49–50
Williams, R., 99
witchcraft trials, 18
workplace counselling, 75
World Health Organization (WHO), 21–2, 26, 28
Wymer, R., 16

Zilboorg, G., 93

Research Methods Books from SAGE

Read sample chapters online now!

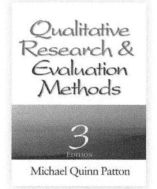
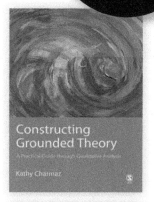

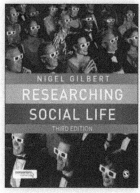

www.sagepub.co.uk

The Qualitative Research Kit
Edited by Uwe Flick

www.sagepub.co.uk

Research Methods Books from SAGE

Read sample chapters online now!

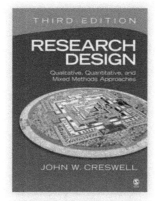

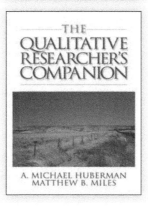
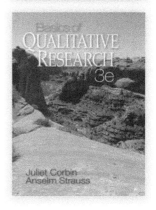

www.sagepub.co.uk

Supporting researchers for more than forty years

Research methods have always been at the core of SAGE's publishing. Sara Miller McCune founded SAGE in 1965 and soon after she published SAGE's first methods book, *Public Policy Evaluation*. A few years later, she launched the Quantitative Applications in the Social Sciences series – affectionately known as the 'little green books'.

Always at the forefront of developing and supporting new approaches in methods, SAGE published early groundbreaking texts and journals in the fields of qualitative methods and evaluation.

Today, more than forty years and two million little green books later, SAGE continues to push the boundaries with a growing list of more than 1,200 research methods books, journals, and reference works across the social, behavioural, and health sciences.

From qualitative, quantitative and mixed methods to evaluation, SAGE is the essential resource for academics and practitioners looking for the latest in methods by leading scholars.

www.sagepublications.com